What people are saying about

Home of t⁺⁻ ͏

Despair in rural communities a
veterans are two of the biggest chall͏   ͏ ͏untry. Donna
Bryson gives a detailed and honest accounting of how residents
of a struggling Colorado town revitalized their community by
helping veterans desperately looking for a place to call home.
From the Girl Scout who urges customers to donate cookies to the
veteran's center, to the veteran's support meetings and the city
council meetings, Bryson's unsentimental reporting and eye for
detail takes the reader through the small victories and frequent
setbacks faced by the well-intentioned people of Montrose as they
grasped the enormity of their challenge. This book reminds us that
compassion, kindness and service can transform lives and inspire
entire communities and is a blueprint for others who want to make
a difference.
Chris Tomlinson, author of the New York Times Bestseller
*Tomlinson Hill: The Remarkable Story of Two Families Who Share the
Tomlinson Name - One White, One Black.*

The story of one woman touched by the pain of veterans to build
them a community and in the process define her town. The writing
is powerful and the book is amazing in that it shows how far one
person can change her own life and the lives of others.
Toula Vlahou, co-author with Brian Murphy of *81 Days Below
Zero: The Incredible Survival Story of a World War II Pilot in Alaska's
Frozen Wilderness*

A tragic consequence of America's commitment to war is its
veterans who commit suicide or suffer PTSD. Sadly, few Americans
offer help to our wounded. Donna Bryson's fine book describes

a small town, Montrose, Colorado where people and programs come together and offer a place where healing occurs. This book is a must read for community leaders in our towns and cities. It's time to understand the consequences of our wars, time to care for those our wars have crippled.

Edward W. Wood Jr., author of *On Being Wounded, Beyond the Weapons of Our Fathers and Worshipping the Myths of World War II: Reflections on America's Dedication to War.*

Deanna Brysa

Home of the Brave

A small town, its veterans and the
community they build together

Home of the Brave

A small town, its veterans and the
community they build together

Donna Bryson

Winchester, UK
Washington, USA

First published by Chronos Books, 2018
Chronos Books is an imprint of John Hunt Publishing Ltd., Laurel House, Station Approach,
Alresford, Hants, SO24 9JH, UK
office1@jhpbooks.net
www.johnhuntpublishing.com

For distributor details and how to order please visit the 'Ordering' section on our website.

Text copyright: Donna Bryson 2017

ISBN: 978 1 78535 636 0
978 1 78535 637 7 (ebook)
Library of Congress Control Number: 2017932672

A CIP catalogue record for this book is available from the British Library.

Design: Stuart Davies

Printed and bound by CPI Group (UK) Ltd, Croydon, CR0 4YY, UK

We operate a distinctive and ethical publishing philosophy in
all areas of our business, from our global network of authors to
production and worldwide distribution.

Contents

To my family

Essayons
Motto of the U.S. Army Corps of Engineers

It's a Black-White Thing (Tafelberg, 2014)

Acknowledgments

My thanks to Chronos Books for taking on this book, flaws and all.

The flaws are entirely my own. As to the rest, I am grateful to scores of people who gave generously of time, experience and expertise. First and foremost among my benefactors are veterans and non-veterans in Montrose, Colorado, many of whom put up with repeated interviews over four years. I also was able to consult in person or through their writings with others who have devoted themselves to the well-being of veterans across Colorado and the United States and national experts in mental health, the economy, military history and the science and politics of marijuana. Many of those I tapped are proud veterans. Most are named in the narrative; those who are not nonetheless helped shape my thinking and writing and added authority to those who are. All are credited in a bibliography and a list of those interviewed at the end of this work.

Judi Buehrer welcomed me into the Colorado Press Women writers' group. She and the other members strengthened this book month by month, chapter by chapter, line by line, extraneous comma by extraneous comma.

I hope other writers benefit from as varied and talented a safety net. And I hope communities like Montrose find inspiration in these pages.

Introduction

I call Denver home. These days, flocks of construction cranes roost in the heart of Colorado's capital. Chitchat over dinner at yet another new restaurant is often about rising rents.

The contrast is stark when reporting assignments take me across the Rocky Mountains to the Western Slope, a region of small towns, farms, ranches, hunting grounds and rugged tourist attractions.

On the Western Slope, I might find one Main Street storefront touting a "grand opening," only to see a "for rent" sign in a dusty window a few doors down. Other American small towns have similar complaints. Perhaps it's the very lack of wealth as defined by building projects and rosy employment statistics that has encouraged rich inventiveness and innovation in this other America.

I first visited western Colorado's Montrose while writing an article about an intriguing grassroots program to support war veterans. I initially found in Montrose a nostalgia for more secure times; a sense of isolation; a worry that the future is rushing away along with all the young people seeking opportunity elsewhere. The mood would be familiar in many communities.

But Montrose had the audacity to look for solutions by taking on yet another conundrum: Can those on the sidelines of an enormous conflict find a way beyond saying "thank you for your service" to support America's warriors? In this part of the country, the phrase "freedom isn't free" trips easily off lips. Montrose showed it takes the responsibilities of democracy seriously when it set out to remake itself as a place where former fighters could be nurtured. And the mood in Montrose began to shift.

The non-profit project, christened Welcome Home Montrose when it got started, hosts a biannual outdoors festival that brings vets from across the country to hunt and fish. Welcome Home

Montrose helped the town of 20,000 people and county of 40,000 develop a white water river park they hope will boost local tourism. The project also organized internships that offered young wounded vets a chance to consider what they would do with the rest of their lives now that they were no longer fit to fight.

A volunteer-run drop-in center is the engine of the project. There, vets can get a cup of coffee along with counseling and advice on jobs and training. Men and women who made the choice to volunteer to fight in strange lands can start to feel at home again at the drop-in center, and encounter people who stepped up to welcome them.

Montrose exemplifies a very American determination. Our nation also has been defined, for better or worse, by a war for each generation. For this generation, it is not everyone's war. While, as one vet put it to me, the rest of America "was at the mall," the same volunteers, often from hometowns that resemble Montrose, have been asked to serve longer and longer and more and more often. Less than one percent of Americans have fought in the wars that followed 9/11.

As President Obama was moving toward ending the war in Iraq and winding down the war in Afghanistan, his White House said more than a million servicemen and women were projected to leave the military between 2011 and 2016. Bringing them truly home is a national challenge, one with which small towns in particular must grapple.

Vets are more likely than the general population to live in rural areas. They could simply be returning to their small hometowns, where the high rates of signing up for military service may be traced to a combination of patriotic tradition and economic necessity. Some vets have told me that returning warriors deliberately seek solace and calm in isolated, sparsely populated areas.

According to the Veterans Administration, more than 20 million veterans are living in the United States, and just under a third of those are Gulf War era vets. We can recognize our nation in the vets. The men and women who served are ethnically, racially and socio-economically diverse and come from across the country.

We can see ourselves. Or, we could look away, allowing a widening of a troubling gulf. Civilians on one side of the divide are unsure of how to reach out to those returning and perhaps even fearful of how war has changed the warriors. Veterans feel misunderstood and alone. What I saw in Montrose was not simply a desire to close the gap, but a recognition that connecting is crucial.

As former Veterans Administration Secretary Eric K. Shinseki told The Washington Post, this generation of soldiers has been asked "to do a lot more, in a smaller serving force, in some of the longest wars in our history." The toll is evident in soaring rates of post-traumatic stress disorder, divorce and unemployment. One poll found that half the Americans who made it back from Iraq and Afghanistan say they know a fellow service member who attempted or committed suicide.

Since al-Qaida terrorists brought down the Twin Towers on September 11, 2001, the war on terror has spread beyond Iraq and Afghanistan to include some three dozen countries, places like Djibouti, Syria and Pakistan. Halfway through 2015, the toll was more than 6,000 Americans dead and more than 50,000 wounded. The end is hard to predict.

"In an earlier time," former U.S. Defense Secretary Gates wrote in his memoirs, "people would speak of winning or losing wars." But this is the time of "the forever war," as veteran journalist Dexter Filkins titled his book on the conflicts in Iraq, Afghanistan and so many elsewheres. Victory seems impossibly distant. Instead, Americans must confront an ambivalent series of personal post-wars.

As I explored Montrose's history, I saw scars of the earliest conflicts that made America and considered our reluctance as a nation to acknowledge that bitter disappointment is part of our story. I've met Vietnam vets in Montrose who tell me they see parallels to their own long conflict in the war on terror, and not

3

only in the political and social divisiveness of both eras. These vets have volunteered to help out at Welcome Home Montrose. In counseling and supporting younger returning fighters, the older vets have found their own healing. I also met vets of Korea and World War II who came to Welcome Home Montrose in a show of solidarity with men and women young enough to be their grandsons and granddaughters. Some older men and women surely found in the drop-in center a safe place to confront their own pain.

Failure is possible for Welcome Home Montrose. Newcomers who respond to the invitation that the project has extended and vets who are already in Montrose could have grievous physical and mental war wounds that need treatment and monitoring that are beyond the ability of people in a small town, no matter how well-meaning they are. The nearest Veterans Affairs hospital is an hour's drive away. The vets may need jobs that economically struggling Montrose can't provide.

The consequences of losing the battle that this small town took on could be dire. But that is no reason not to try.

The people of Montrose are bringing everything they have to the fight. Because they are open to the ideas of others, the nondescript shopping center where Welcome Home Montrose established the drop-in center became a broad tent. Taciturn Westerners raised to be suspicious of big government developed a new respect for, for example, federal legislation that ensures Americans with disabilities, including young wounded veterans, can work, play and shop where they choose. One vet who has embraced a New Age dream of a world without war has become a mentor to a fellow Vietnam-era warrior who is at the opposite end of the spectrum, over where the urge is strong to stock up the storm shelter for some civil conflagration. Welcome Home Montrose showed me what can happen when we are able to share more than one story about what it means to be an American. Conversation is possible. And measured, sober talk is a necessary precursor to action that can transform lives and communities.

Welcome Home Montrose is an extraordinary idea that came from an ordinary place. The initiative is as much for as by the community where it was born. It offers lessons in creating jobs based on a community's strengths and history; finding strength in binding diverse elements; and building platforms from which to demand fixes for the net of mental, physical and social services few realized was in such a dire state.

In the coming chapters, I will welcome readers to Montrose. It is a place to contemplate resiliency, to take stock of the past, to find hope for the future. A place to explore the possibilities of creativity, commitment and cooperation.

Chapter 1

Identities

Sticky notes in a rainbow of colors and pens were passed around at a town hall-style meeting. Montrose residents used the humble office supplies to jot down comments on plans that business leaders hoped would bring new energy to a small community that, like so many across America, had been exhausted by the Great Recession. Its Main Street was in such tatters that Montrose residents grumbled they had to go to the next town to find a shoe repair shop.

It was 2011. Leading entrepreneurs were convened as the board of directors of the Montrose Downtown Development Authority. They were searching for something that could enliven the kinds of brochures you find on the racks at tourism centers, go viral on social media or catch the eye of a potential angel scanning a prospectus.

They invited their neighbors to brainstorm about links to the romantic Wild West that might appeal to the nostalgic. Maybe foodies would be drawn by a campaign around the fresh produce featured at the weekly farmers market.

Montrose was too far from the interstate to present itself as a potential manufacturing hub, though it does have a candy factory attached to a supersized store that is a sweet tooth's dream. Maybe the key was to portray the town as a gateway to escaping urban crowds and seizing outdoor adventure.

One Downtown Development Authority board member, Melanie Kline, had scoured the Internet for background on famous people who haled from Montrose. She found information on such luminaries as Dalton Trumbo, the Oscar-winning screenwriter who a few years after Kline was researching him became the subject of a movie starring Bryan Cranston about the blacklisted

Hollywood 10.

Trumbo's link to Montrose illustrates an aspect of this rugged, rancher, Republican country I would come to understand more deeply with each visit: it is a rich resource of sometimes unexpected talents, skills and points of view.

Still, while Trumbo may have been born in Montrose, he left with his family in 1908, when he was only three years old. He had been a southern Californian for decades by the time he was making a name for himself as a writer.

Kline's neighbors were unimpressed with the ideas they were hearing at the meeting. Those no-nonsense citizens weren't looking for Hollywood glitz. They prided themselves on a rough, pioneering authenticity.

Their town's original 320-acre site was laid out by D.D. Loutsenhizer and Joseph Selig in 1882. The former had been a member of the infamous Alfred Packer expedition that passed through the region in 1873. Loutsenhizer had the sense to question Packer's guiding ability and split off before the party found itself snowbound in the high mountains during winter. Packer dined on the men he had been leading in an episode of cannibalism that has fascinated chroniclers and even inspired a movie musical.

Loutsenhizer and Selig originally called their town Pomona, a Spanish name for a Roman goddess of orchards. The reference was aspirational for a region that would not become known for its agricultural bounty until the early 20th century brought a major irrigation project. Town lore credits Selig for the name change to something that, while sounding more prosaic, actually had literary pretensions. The new name came from a character in Sir Walter Scott's novel *A Legend of Montrose*, a stirring tale of love and war set in 17th century Scotland. Selig, who died in 1886 at the age of 36 from stomach cancer before he could see what Montrose would become, was evidently a Scott fan.

In the early days, mules would winter in Montrose after spending the bulk of the year helping men work the silver and gold mines in the surrounding hills. Ranchers headed to the train depot drove cattle through the main streets, kicking up dust, noise and the pungent-sweet aroma of manure. At the depot, the beasts were loaded into cars to be taken to market. It is an image, like the profile of a Native American in a feather headdress gracing a wall to greet visitors at Montrose High School that brings to mind the cherished, gritty icons that have shaped the idea we have of ourselves as Americans.

For centuries, the region where Montrose would develop into a town "was a land known only to the Ute Indians and a handful of white men who ventured within its borders," local historian Elaine Hale Jones wrote in *Many Faces, Many Visions: The Story of Montrose, Colorado*.

Jones recounts that "following much publicity about the removal of the Utes from the Uncompahgre Valley in 1881, this isolated area now open for settlement held a type of mystique for people seeking new opportunities and adventure 'Out West.'"

"Removal of the Utes" is a sterile phrase for a bloody and protracted chapter of American history. The tendency to gloss over the subjugation is reinforced in articles like one I saw in the local newspaper. *The Montrose Daily Press* told readers in the summer of 2015 about the upcoming family reunion of the descendants of a town pioneer. The story quoted so engagingly from his unpublished autobiography that I sought out the manuscript in the main library, an example of sleek modern architecture that contrasted with that of the traditional courthouse nearby.

In the library I found a photocopy of a closely typed pamphlet bound with tape and cardboard and, according to a hand-scrawled note, written in 1940. The publication date was given only as 19 followed by two question marks. It was grandly titled: *Passing of the Two-Gun Era: Memoirs of the late Alva W. Galloway, Cowboy, Rancher, County Official and Businessman*.

Galloway wrote that he had been working for a newspaper in the southern Colorado town of Pueblo when an uncle persuaded him he could find his fortune farther west. He arrived six weeks after Montrose's incorporation papers were filed. He wasn't the only dream-chaser.

There were young men "seeking work in the mines, little co-ed graduates of the East just landing in the big open West seeking a job as school teachers and eventually landing a good-looking cow puncher in marriage and growing up with the country," Galloway wrote.

"Montrose wasn't much for looks," he added. "But, boy, there were things doing that you had no idea of. One could at anytime of day or night strike a $5.00-ante poker game or over at the hotel meet all kinds of mine promoters just returning from the east with pockets of money gleaned from the poor suckers who wanted to own a gold mine and suddenly become rich."

He concluded his reminiscences with a description of a 1924 U.S. Senate election. I was startled to find an almost casual reference to the Ku Klux Klan. I should not have been surprised. The Klan, by exploiting prejudices and appealing to a narrow vision of what it meant to be American, had spread into America's southwest from the south following the Civil War. The KKK dominated Colorado politics in the 1920s, stoking resentment and fear of Hispanics, Catholics and Jews as well as blacks. Galloway wrote that during that 1924 political race, Klansmen swept around town in a silent, menacing campaign against the local favorite for Senate. They even went into churches.

"When these boys, sheathed in long white shrouds with slitted holes in the hood for eyesight, long white gloves covering the hands, entered the place of worship, everything folded up in the beat of an eyelash, the atmosphere took on a ghostified eery feeling, a sensation often felt in the presence of the dead."

Galloway linked the Klansmen to one death and to threats against a resident known only as "colored Bob," but gave no details.

In 1862, the passage of the national Homestead Act had helped speed settlement of areas that would become the states of Colorado, Kansas, Montana, Nebraska, Wyoming and other states. The act offered land to adult heads of household who had never taken up arms against the United States and could pay a small filing fee, build a home and farm and endure for five years. Freed slaves and women were as entitled to land as white men. War was liberating African-Americans. And creating widows.

The rise of the Klan showed that that offer of opportunity to black Americans enshrined in the Homestead Act had not set well with all their fellow countrymen. There's little evidence many blacks ever joined "colored Bob" in inhospitable territory. According to the U.S. Census estimate for 2013, most people in Montrose are, as Galloway was, white. White's make up 86 percent of the population. I've seen a visit by a national veterans' group exponentially increase, for a day or two at least, the number of African-Americans in town.

By some time in the 2040s, demographers say, Latinos, blacks and other minorities will together comprise the majority of Americans. In Montrose, where Hispanics comprise about 20 percent of the population now, any shift could be influenced by those who answer the call that townspeople have put out to veterans. Demographics are changing in America's armed forces, which were segregated until 1948 and in which advancement has often been denied to minorities. Between 1990 and 2011, according to Pew researchers, the percentage of racial minorities among officers and enlisted personnel increased from about a quarter to about a third. Whites are just over 70 percent of the military, less than their 77 percent of the general population. Blacks are 17 percent of all servicemen and women, while they are only 13.5 percent of all Americans.

America's experience of race relations gives little reason to hope the coming change will be smooth. The past can be instructive. But not if we only take note of the exceptional chapters. If we accept that in places like Montrose the current racial profile was the result of considered action in the past, perhaps we can be more considered about our own reactions as our world changes.

The *Daily Press* had left out the KKK in its article about a family gathering that had prompted me to seek out Galloways's memoirs. My own initial response when I read of the hooded racists rampaging through the region was to recoil from something that did not fit my stereotype of the West. I had to return to the library a day later to take proper notes on Galloway's final passages.

Galloway was an old newspaperman who knew it was crucial to give a fair and balanced accounting, to record the dark along with the romantic. He documented that America has been multicultural since its earliest days, and that the struggle for equal treatment and true democracy is a work in progress. No wonder we so often backslide into bitter conflict over narrow interests. We're still perfecting our union, even as we venture into the world to build the nations of others.

In the 19th century victory in the Mexican War vastly and with seeming suddenness enlarged the United States and sharpened the internal struggle for dominance between northern and southern states. The North refused to extend slavery to the new national holdings, the swaths of desert and mountains that would become Texas, Arizona, New Mexico, Nevada, Utah, California and parts of Colorado. The calls for secession made during that debate over slavery were calmed by compromise, but not for long. Southerners stalled efforts to settle the west and thereby increase the number and influence of free states.

During the Civil War southern lawmakers abandoned their seats in Washington to don grey uniforms at home, taking with them opposition to legislation designed to develop the West. In 1862, the passage of the Homestead Act helped speed settlement of the West. When Civil War at last came to an end in 1865, development accelerated. "Utes must go" was a political rallying cry the year Colorado became the 38th state, 1876.

The river that runs through Montrose is the Uncompahgre,

the name of a Ute clan. The Utes, who pride themselves on being the oldest residents of Colorado, remember the earliest whites to arrive, the Spanish in the 16th century, for bringing new tools and livestock, including horses that allowed them to hunt buffalo; for bringing small pox and cholera; for bringing a fierce and violent competition for land. As the 19th century drew to a close, more and more clashes erupted between whites and Utes.

In 2015, legislators in Denver considered requiring schools in the state with Native American mascots to seek permission from tribes if they wanted to continue using images like the black-and-white-on-red face of an Indian in a feathered headdress that adorns the Montrose High School building. Tribespeople, some tearfully, testified before lawmakers in Colorado's Capitol about the pain of seeing such stereotypes. But the proposal failed, which made sense to people in the Montrose area like a broadcaster who opined online that even if some might call him insensitive, "I would have to argue that Redskins, Braves, Chiefs, or any other Indian moniker is not any more disrespectful to native Americans than Cowboys, Vikings, Titans, Patriots, or Packers are to the respective groups of people their name represents."

It's strong, this temptation to discount the power of the past to shape the present and the future. To discount history. Or drive right by it.

Most cars roar past a cornfield, farmhouse, RV and trailer repair shop and a billboard-sized placard on the outskirts of Montrose on the main road heading into the mountains. I stopped once for a closer look and found the sign is not advertising. It was a page from history in white letters on fading brick-red paint erected by the State Historical Society. It identifies the roadside spot as the site of Fort Crawford, built in the 1880s. Later, I run across a photograph in a book by a local historian showing Fort Crawford in the 19th century. The sharp black-and-white image is dominated by what looks like a farm house with a comfortable front porch and several other buildings on a dirt field that is, perhaps, a parade ground. I learn from the caption that the farm house is a guard house, and that the fort also had a hospital and a bakery. The cantonment was, I read, established to "keep the Indians from going on the warpath."

Until the global war on terror reached its first decade and kept going, the Vietnam War was often referred to as America's longest war. But according to Veterans Affairs our Indian Wars lasted eight decades. The fighting may have been sporadic from 1817 to 1898, and many Americans may have claimed ignorance of what was happening to the continent's indigenous people. But that does not make the story less brutal.

Americans don't like to think of ourselves as warlike, a term usually reserved for our enemies. Who wants to read history as some multi-count indictment? But what if never accounting for the crimes means never truly assessing the limits of power? We don't like to contemplate the costs others bear for our successes, let alone the way violence can haunt even the winner. But leaving out that part of the story also leaves out the lessons that survival, renewal and resilience can offer. The history we forget leaves its marks.

A small town, any town, has a secret history you have to dig to see and work to understand. Violence and broken promises are part of the American story and of the Montrose story. We don't have to gloss over hard truths to draw something from a story. We're on shaky ground when we see the past as cliché. We need to build the future on a firm foundation.

The novelist Chimamanda Ngozi Adichie grew up in Nigeria, was educated in the United States and has written about both countries. She once said in an oft-shared TED talk: "Stories matter. Many stories matter. Stories have been used to dispossess and to malign, but stories can also be used to empower and to humanize. Stories can break the dignity of a people, but stories can also repair that broken dignity."

Adichie lamented that the single story often told of her own country and continent is a negative one. I propose that the single story of America we're used to reading makes the work of creating peace and prosperity, community and common purpose seem simple, a matter of a determined people, destiny and a few other details. Focusing only on the winners leaves us without the language or the resources to cope with change. Forgetting hobbles us.

Sally Johnson, who presides over Montrose's municipal museum, doesn't lock history up in her glass cases. She leads walking tours to the cemetery where pioneer families once gathered for Memorial Day picnics, or through the streets of the old brothel district. Of the latter, she said: "We had a fort outside town. Those soldiers had to have something."

Johnson's bifocals and long, graying hair are a teacherly cover for her impish humor. She does, as it turned out, occasionally fill in as a substitute teacher in Montrose schools. She prefers engaging with younger children over taking on a high school classroom, where she says there's often little to do but sit up front watching teens do their homework or play with their cell phones. She takes the same hands-on attitude to her work at the museum. When a longtime Montrose resident dies and his or her papers end up at the museum, Johnson has to back off and let her volunteers go through the letters, diaries and property deeds. If the director were to start reading, she might not stop for hours.

Johnson also has been a cop. Her degree, from the university in nearby Grand Junction, is in law enforcement and criminal justice. She's also been a probation officer, a victims' advocate for the district attorney and a family therapist. She joked that it was only when she reached her 50s and started working at the museum that she found her calling, one that has rooted her in the town she has called home for 20 years.

"I can go down to the post office or downtown and see someone I know every time," said Johnson, who grew up in Salida, a small, rural town in Colorado's central mountains. "I like being able to sit on a bench on a street corner and say hi to people passing by.

It's nice to go to Horse Fly or Two Sisters and know I'll run into somebody I know to talk to," she told me, naming a Main Street microbrewery and a gastropub. Don't let anyone say the latest trends are passing by this town.

In its heyday, the railroad allowed the flow of commerce and communications in and out of Montrose.

"You bring the railroad, you bring the mining. You get the bankers, then the suppliers, the mercantiles," Johnson told me. "If we didn't have the railroad come through here, we wouldn't be here."

Trains aren't stopping like they once did. One pauses weekly to load lumber. Because passenger trains no longer call at this town made by the railroad, the century-old main station is free to house the museum, where Johnson's displays include two vintage cars out back that draw trainspotters.

At the turn of the last century came an ambitious infrastructure project that ensured the flow of a crucial element: water.

Johnson again: "If we didn't have the water, we wouldn't have the sugar beets, the potatoes, the sweet corn."

The pioneers diverted water through a system of ditches from the Uncompahgre River, and the area's soil proved fertile. Once that system's capacity reached its limits, farmers eyed the Gunnison River, some six miles west.

The Gunnison carved the Black Canyon, so-called because its walls are so deep and sheer that little light reaches its floor. The U.S. National Park Service, which stewards the gorge, quotes legendary U.S. Geological Survey geologist Wally Hansen as saying of the canyon: "Some are longer, some are deeper, some are narrower and a few have walls as steep. But no other canyon in North America combines the depth, narrowness, sheerness and somber countenance of the Black Canyon of the Gunnison."

This was the terrain into which men ventured to bring water to Montrose. In the 19th century, railroad survey crews said the canyon was inaccessible. As that century ended, a party set out to

15

determine whether an irrigation project was feasible. The explorers gave up after a month of floating. Another group persevered, traveling 33 miles on a rubber craft over nine days in 1901. It was determined a tunnel could work and construction started that year.

The project that made the region a larder is commemorated on a sidewalk plaque near the corner of Montrose's two key streets, Main and Townsend. A stroller can pause to read about "the tunnel that made the desert bloom."

Over eight years, which included a hiatus when funding temporarily ran out, some 500 men worked on the project. "None lasted long," the sidewalk plaque notes. Some men gave up in exhaustion. Some were hurt or killed, including six who died when drillers encountered a pressurized stream that threw jets of water into the cavern where they were working.

The effort was so ambitious a private company was unable to complete it. Enter the federal government, in the form of the Bureau of Reclamation, the agency that gave Arizona and Nevada the Hoover Dam.

On July 6, 1909 crews drilling from the east met counterparts who had started from the west. President William Howard Taft came to Montrose for the Gunnison Tunnel's dedication a few months later. Day-long celebrations drew 10,000 people to the Montrose fairgrounds. Taft noted the beauty of the "incomparable valley with the unpronounceable name," referring to the Uncompahgre.

When Taft visited, he could have seen people from Spain, France, Mexico, China, Japan, Sweden, Russia, Germany, Croatia, Ireland, Italy. They came for jobs on the tunnel. Many stayed to farm or ranch.

People in Montrose today might have grandparents who were farmers. Agricultural sectors now account for only 6 percent of jobs, according to state statistics. Government is the biggest employer these days, at 16 percent of work. Most of the ranches have, along with the passenger trains, disappeared. The spreads have been divided into housing lots or are little more than playgrounds for the wealthy who have bought land on which to build vacation retreats. But not far from downtown you can still find cornfields, and the crops, county fairs and farmers markets attest that today's Montrose has not lost touch with its past. Pomona, goddess of orchards, smiled on the region even if the town did reject her name. Along with the sugar beets, potatoes and sweet corn, museum director Johnson mentioned, the area is known for onions, alfalfa, apples, peaches, grapes and strawberries

I'm a connoisseur of small-town museums, and Montrose's has a quirkiness that enlivens its archives of conquest and industry. Johnson's exhibits include a log cabin out back. Inside is a mock-up of a country store with a shelf of empty bottles that once held the promise of miraculous cures.

"Every once in a while I find a kid reading the labels on the medicines and they're just amazed," Johnson said.

Johnson loans crisply folded uniforms, including one her mother wore as a World War II Army nurse, to adorn floats that parade through town on the Fourth of July.

Vietnam-era uniforms, though, have escaped her collector's grasp. Does the Vietnam generation lack the hoarding instincts that the Depression instilled in World War II veterans, making clothing from the '60s scarce? Maybe it's something more troubling, Johnson mused, thinking of a 2008 trip to Washington, D.C. with her daughter, who was then starting high school. Her teen did not recognize the Vietnam War memorial, leaving Johnson to wonder whether a generation was failing to tell its story.

"I think we skip over those parts in the history we teach our kids."

When Johnson was a kid in high school in south-central Colorado in the 1960s, she wore a bracelet etched with the name of a prisoner of war and heard the daily death toll on the evening news.

Recalling World War II, bloody as it was, is somehow more romantic. Montrose old-timers know that a prominent wall on a Main Street shop was once inscribed with the names of every hometown soldier who died in World War II. The wall has long since been painted over, but a nostalgic idea of World War II lingers.

One of Johnson's museum cases holds a March, 1946 article from *Our Navy* magazine that recounts the tradition of naming attack transport ships after U.S. counties. Kathy Ellis, whose grandparents owned bakeries on Main Street, told me Montrose was granted a ship because the townspeople donated an impressive amount of scrap metal to the war effort.

"The Navy looked at that and said: "Wow, we need to do something to honor what these people did,"' Ellis said. And so, a link was forged between a landlocked Colorado county and the nation's maritime force.

The ship named for Montrose served in World War II, Korea and Vietnam before it was decommissioned in 1969. Those wars have shaped and reshaped modern America's idea of its place in the world. Savior of democracy in World War II. The nation's confidence in its strength and purpose starting to diminish in Korea and Vietnam. Now, we struggle to define victory in the war on terror and await history's judgment on how it will shape us.

In 2000, veterans who had sailed on the USS Montrose held their reunion in the ship's namesake county. For the event, the American Legion hosted a barbecue, at which a city official offered what could be the local motto: "Veterans are recognized and appreciated here."

Our Navy magazine described the USS Montrose as having "slung no record amount of lead at the enemy. Her skipper wears no slew of Navy Crosses on his chest.

"The USS Montrose is just another attack transport, one of those hard-working, little-talked about babies who did their jobs faithfully.

"She's neither beautiful nor inspiring. She's top heavy, she's bulky and she rides the heavy swells like a wooden duck decoy."

There's something of the town's character in that hard-bitten description.

Across the United States, in the big cities, employment is rising to levels not seen since the Great Recession started in 2007. In Montrose and other rural areas, numbers can't seem to catch up. The policy and advocacy organization Economic Innovation Group found that three-quarters of America's distressed zip codes are in rural areas. An Associated Press analysis of the group's data found central cities were, in economic terms, doing less poorly in 2016 than in 2000, while the areas with most of the country's rural populations had grown worse over that decade and a half.

According to the U.S. census, an average of 19 percent of Montrose residents were living below the poverty line between 2009 and 2013, compared with the statewide average of 13 percent during that period. The town's median household income averaged $42,925 for that five-year period; it was $58,433 statewide. Per capita income was slightly above $21,000 in the town and the county, compared with the statewide average of $31,109.

As employment levels in Colorado's economic hubs like Denver were regaining and even surpassing pre-recession levels, Montrose's county, which shares the town's name, had many fewer jobs than it once had.

The Montrose area's population dipped between 2010 and 2013. Montrose is not alone. Declining populations only increase the challenge for communities struggling to attract teachers to train the next generation, managers to guide development, doctors and nurses to treat the sick. National trends show cities enjoying a concentration of the most highly educated workers.

A look at national census figures led William H. Frey of the Brookings Institute to say in 2014 that the "prognosis does not look good for much of small town America." The think tank expert noted that from 2010-2013, some six out of 10 rural counties lost population, up from less than half in the mid-2000s.

"As job and housing markets gradually pick up, it appears that large economically vibrant metropolitan areas will begin to grow. The situation for smaller places seems less certain. Still, small town America has been counted out before, but has, in many parts of the country, found ways to reinvent itself. This may well occur again," Frey wrote.

The U.S. Department of Agriculture's research arm tracked dropping unemployment rates in both urban and rural areas since the end of the 2007-09 recession, but found that, particularly in rural areas, that was because so many people had given up looking for work or were no longer around to do so. Nationally, since the great recession, urban employment rose by 5 percent between the second quarters of 2010 and 2014, while rural employment rose by 1 percent over the same period.

In light of those grim statistics, no wonder Montrose's Downtown Development Authority leaders saw their community as an equation to be solved. If they could crack it, they could subtract all those boarded up Main Street storefronts and add new families.

You can define and dissect, measure and rank a town. You can know where the bodies are buried, trace the family trees of political feuds, map the streets that lead to the banks and those that lead to the brothels. What the Downtown Development Authority wanted was a tougher calculation: How to sum up possibilities?

Montrose and environs are almost pretty enough to distract from the grim economic realities. At the town's heart is a red-and-blond brick confection of a City Hall, erected in 1926. Around the corner, multi-colored tiles fight one another for attention in the lobby of the Fox Theater, an art deco gem that still shows first-run movies.

Outside town are dramatic canyons carved by ancient rivers and bare hills called adobes whose undulating forms are hypnotizing. In this landscape of few trees and long grasses, loners who are happy to stake a claim to a trailer park plot share spectacular vistas with millionaires who have winter homes in the region. During the not-too-hot summers, retirees retreat from city life for months at a time at RV campgrounds. Anglers stalk rainbow, brown, cutthroat and brook trout. From autumn into early winter, which isn't too cold, the hunt is on for everything from rabbit to mountain lion through archery, rifle and black powder season. Local guides hire out their expertise, some gleaned from the savvy placement of cameras that act as electronic scouts. Birders come for a glimpse of the great horned owl or peregrine falcons. Once winter has set in, skiers stop at the Montrose airport and perhaps grab a meal or groceries in town before heading on to the Telluride resort. Come spring and the snowmelt, adventurous kayakers take to the area's rivers.

Across 2,240-square-mile Montrose County, population density is 18 people per square mile, compared to the statewide average of 48.5. And if you live outside the town that is home to half its namesake county's population, you'd have more than the average share of elbow room.

At the town hall meeting, Kline wasn't alone in thinking that she and her neighbors weren't coming up with a way to explain all that this ruggedly beautiful setting promised.

"We just can't nail it," Kline thought that day. Her neighbors saw something foreign about the whole exercise and the ideas it had produced struck them as gimmicky or stale. The chronicler of the USS Montrose or Galloway, that blunt newspaperman of Montrose's early days, might have thought the same.

Kline perused the jottings on the sticky notes.

"What I kept seeing, over and over again, was, 'Why can't we just be us?'" she said. "I asked people, 'Well, what does that mean to you? What is 'us'?

"They said: 'Friendly. Patriotic. Independent. Embracing. Welcoming.'"

Kline, a transplant, admitted she did not know Montrose well enough at the time to understand the meaning behind those words. But the scrawls on the bright squares of paper stayed in her mind. They prepared the ground for the seed of an idea that would change her and change her town.

Chapter 2

Getting to Home

Kline was watching television on a Sunday morning not long after that less-than-conclusive brainstorming session called by Montrose's Downtown Development Authority. As she watched, what her neighbors had had to say about her town was at the back of her mind.

The diminutive, 60-something brunette had been thinking not only of how to define Montrose, but how to redefine her life. She was contemplating retiring. That would mean giving her two sons complete control of their shared jewelry businesses, one in Montrose and one in the nearby mountain town of Ouray, each called Ouray Silversmiths.

As a child, Kline had been taught to translate the Hebrew phrase tikkun olam as "lifting the sparks." The words, which other Jews might choose to translate as "repairing the world," became central to her personal philosophy. The concept is linked to rabbinical teachings about the power of the divine in the world. For that reason, it has fueled campaigns against slavery and inspired efforts in aid of the politically or socially marginalized. In her day-to-day life, the concept of tikkun olam pushes Kline to keep trying new things as she pursues a goal of "elevating everything to its best."

It can look like restlessness.

"I can never leave things alone. I always see potential for making things better. If I can see a way to improve something, I have to go do it. Sometimes I'm jealous of people who can just be. I'm a do, not a be. I strive to be."

Kline, with her mystical take on religion, may be a bit of an exotic in a remote area of a state that overall has a Jewish population of less than two percent. But faith of some kind is a common touchstone for Kline and for others I've met in Montrose, though her neighbors are more likely to speak of God in a way as familiar to me as the lessons I learned at Vacation Bible School. Townspeople who felt the development board's branding effort was lacking pointed out one other thing to Kline: that Montrose has some three score churches.

From my time in Montrose, I'd say that large number of churches is testament to the residents' independent outlook. I can't see many in Montrose herding into any one mega church.

Kline can sometimes feel like an outsider because of her faith. She responds by being open. Her sons might even say she is too eager to inform neighbors who are curious about Judaism. She believes she can counter any anti-Semitism by helping those who have never known a Jew understand her religion. She has found the concept of tikkun olam is often a good way to engage.

"It means finding the good in everyone. That might be a Jewish thing. But it's not only a Jewish thing," she said. "My tendency is and always has been to see the potential in things. Is that an artist thing? I don't know. But I realize that I've done it all my life."

Home can be the place where your family has attended the same church for generations. But you don't have to have a history to make a future in a place, to create your own family after circumstances and choices wash you ashore. Kline, who had lived in Denver and out East before settling in Montrose, knows something about making a new place home.

She adheres to the unassuming dress code that defines style in a part of the country where high heels and designer dresses can easily come off as pretentious. Still, outdoorsy women in the West can spend hundreds of dollars on footwear that strikes the right note of clunky chic. In cooler weather, Kline is unassuming in a pale fleece vest and dark pants.

There are touches that say, "I'm from elsewhere." Kline's dark curls are long, while many other women in Montrose sport short, no-nonsense styles.

Kline wears jewelry of silver and semi-precious stones that she designs herself. Her work is delicately detailed and drawn from nature and Jewish tradition. The motifs include bunches of grapes and sheaves of wheat. Her pieces have an art deco charm with an eastern European or Middle Eastern flair, not the Santa Fe aesthetic you might expect when you think about a jeweler in the Southwest who works in silver and stone. Kline gathered the stones strung on one of her silver chains at Masada, the fortress where Jewish rebels committed suicide rather than fall to the Romans in the first century. Other stones she has turned into jewelry came from Yad Vashem, Israel's center for Holocaust research and remembrance.

Kline apprenticed as a jewelry maker and designer in Denver, where she grew up. She opened her first jewelry shop in the resort town of Aspen in 1968.

In 1980, recently divorced and with two boys under the age of 5, Kline left Colorado to follow a boyfriend to Cape Cod. He had three children of his own, creating a Brady Bunch of a family when he and Kline married. The marriage lasted only a few years, but Kline stayed in Massachusetts. She did what many of us do when trying to remake a life: she threw herself into her work.

As a small-scale jewelry maker, Kline used affordable materials like silver out of necessity. She had a close relationship with a colleague whose business was bigger. When she joined him as a partner, she had a chance to explore what she could do with gold and precious jewels. She traveled up and down the East Coast to sell her creations at craft and jewelry shows and to consult with wealthy clients.

In 1991, she was able to buy a vacation house in Ouray, a Victorian resort town near Montrose that is known for its hot springs. It's as quaint as Cape Cod but without the ocean. Kline began to spend winters there. She built a small workshop where she could teach jewelry-making to give troubled teens in Ouray a creative outlet and where she began to explore a different side of her own creativity.

A Cape Cod synagogue had put out word it was looking for an

art installation to mark its 150th anniversary. Kline was reading a book about the Kabbalah. She found herself visualizing a mobile in which the letters of the Hebrew alphabet would move with the wind, their shadows as ethereal and agile as breath or thought.

"That was the first piece of Judaica for me."

Kline won the Cape Cod commission. That led to other projects, including designing medals and trophies for the Israel government to bestow on dignitaries. One of her pieces is buried in a time capsule at the King David Hotel in Jerusalem. She also spent two years creating 40 seder plates, candlesticks, finials and other pieces for a congregation in the nation's capital that wanted art for an anniversary.

In Cape Cod, she had been making tiny sculptures to be worn by customers she was increasingly beginning to see as superficial and self-absorbed. In Colorado, she was making beautiful things with a spiritual purpose, and working toward something greater than herself.

Kline was looking for meaning in her life, a yearning she would find she shared with many military veterans.

"I poured my heart into that work," she said. "Until I didn't have one drop of Judaica left."

One of her sons felt so at home in Ouray he decided to stay there without his mother to finish high school. That was part of her motivation when, in 2001, a decade after first buying a vacation home in Ouray and two decades after moving to Cape Cod, Kline told her business partner she was going to make Colorado home.

"The whole time I was in Cape Cod I felt like I was about 80 percent present. In Colorado, I felt I was 100 percent present. Whenever I would come here and get in the mountains, I felt I was breathing deeper."

Her other son joined her full-time in Colorado. Both sons expressed interest in making jewelry a family enterprise. Her sister came to help out with the business. They opened a shop they called Cowgirl at Heart. The name might seem ironic for a city girl. Perhaps it shows how at home all Americans are in the West of our myths.

For one jewelry line, Kline fashioned pendants out of antique tokens that silver miners had used as payment at brothels in the days of a grittier Ouray.

Ouray was a place of imagination and creativity for Kline. It also was a place of politics and community building. Kline served for a time on the Ouray city council.

"I was just so happy to be back in Colorado and Ouray was just such a beautiful community that I wanted to get involved," she said.

She added with a laugh that doing so while running a Main Street business wasn't necessarily smart. It was too easy for constituents who wanted to complain about trash pickup to find her at her jeweler's bench.

Throwing herself into work had not made Cape Cod home. In Colorado, getting home meant getting involved.

After leaving the Cape Cod partnership, Kline needed more than a small shop open only during Ouray's May-to-October high season. She added a store on Main Street in nearby Montrose that is open year-round. She later moved to a home in Montrose, and a town Kline finds to be the right size.

"People aren't in your business," she said. "But you're not invisible."

In Denver and on the East Coast, unabashed talk of patriotism and defending freedom are rarer than in southwestern Colorado. I've seen rows of tiny Stars and Stripes decorating the strip of lawn between the parking lot and the highway at a motel near the Montrose airport. The flags looked like red-white-and-blue dandelions. On the drive from Denver at holiday time I know I've almost reached Montrose when the vista is brightened by a Christmas tree draped in red, white and blue tinsel outside an otherwise nondescript farmhouse.

Kline said Montrose "really, really appreciates anyone who's served. We know they're out there defending our freedoms."

Kline's own sons did not serve. One tried to enlist after the 9/11 terror attacks and was rejected.

"I just have two sons," said the mother who wanted to keep them safe. "Thank God they were color blind."

Her family, her community, her own future. All of that was on her mind as Kline settled in her living room to watch the CBS News show *Sunday Morning*. It was November 1, 2011. The segments that day included one on a Rockville, Maryland-based group called Team River Runner. The organization, founded in 2004 near Walter Reed National Military Medical Center, introduces wounded active duty and veteran service members to white water kayaking and other river sports. It is a way of helping those torn apart by war put their lives back together.

The *Sunday Morning* clip took no more than three minutes. As Kline watched, she realized she had never before confronted "how young and beautiful these fighters were, and how traumatic their injuries were."

She saw a man named Gary Love hoist his twenty-something son onto his back.

"You could see he was going to carry his kid wherever he needed to," Kline said.

He carried him to a river bank and placed him as gently as you would a baby into the arms of another young vet.

Todd Love, a Marine when he lost both legs and his left arm in a bomb blast in Afghanistan, was then settled into a kayak on the Potomac River outside Washington, D.C. The vet who had taken Todd Love from the arms of his father was named Jared Bolhuis. Bolhuis, who had suffered a debilitating brain injury in Afghanistan, got into the kayak as well. The two wounded young men sat one behind the other in a small, orange craft that looked like it could be so easily smashed against the boulders by the roaring waters. But boat and its whooping, grinning, fragile passengers were up to the ride.

"When I am in the kayak, it definitely makes me feel free," Todd Love told CBS reporter Chip Reid. "It's something about being on the water."

"Team River Runner is what gave me my life back," Bolhuis told Reid. "When I am with the other wounded veterans, when I am teaching, I am alive. There is nothing better in the world than to take someone who thinks they have had everything stripped from them, that they are never going to lead a functional life again and to teach them a whole new skill."

Kline teared up in front of her television screen.

"There's something about watching that and seeing Jared's face and seeing Todd's face that just got me thinking about how young these guys are, and how many more were going to be coming back," she said. "I thought: What if my kid came home like that? What would be his future?"

When she was young and Vietnam was raging, Kline used to imagine what she would do if she were a mother of sons. Years later, when she did have sons and America was again at war, she was sure she would have taken them to Canada if they faced a draft, and would have felt no remorse. But she also felt a connection to parents like Gary Love. Kline is always ready to conjure in her mind a replay of the older Love carrying the younger, seeing a fellow parent "living my worst nightmares."

Kline was not alone in seeing the war on terror from a distance. In a survey of the public mood as the nation neared the 10th anniversary of 9/11, Pew Research Center interviewers spoke to 1,853 veterans, among them 712 who served after the September 11, 2001, terror attacks, and to 2,003 adult non-vets. The researchers found that 84 percent of the veterans of the war on terror believe the general public "has little or no understanding of the problems that those in the military face." Among the non-vets, 71 percent agreed.

Some 4 million Americans served in the active-duty military during the first decade after 9/11. Pew researchers offered some telling comparisons: 8.7 million Americans were in the armed forces during the 1963-1973 Vietnam conflict; during the four years of U.S. involvement in World War II, 16.1 million Americans served.

The Pew researchers went on to say:

"Since 1973, there has been no military draft. So unlike other U.S. wars waged in the past century, the post-9/11 conflicts have been fought exclusively by a professional military and enlisted volunteers. During this decade of sustained warfare, only about 0.5 percent of the American public has been on active duty at any given time. (At the height of World War II, the comparable figure was nearly 9 percent.) As a result of the relatively small size of the modern military, most of those who served during the past decade were deployed more than once, and 60 percent were deployed to a combat zone.

"The American public is well aware that the sacrifices the nation was called upon to make following the terrorist attacks of September 11, 2001, have not been borne evenly across the military-civilian divide. More than eight-in-ten Americans (83 percent) say that members of the military and their families have had to make "a lot of sacrifices," while 43 percent say the same about the public as a whole.

"But even among those who say the military's sacrifices have been greater than the public's, seven-in-ten say they see nothing unfair in this disparity. Rather, they say, it's "just part of being in the military."

Kline's sons are in their 30s, but she calls them kids. She uses the same word and with the same warmth for those young men she saw on TV that Sunday morning.

"These kids really had their lives shaped by 9/11 in a way I can't relate to."

Many of her small-town neighbors, though, can relate. Scott Rizzo, a retired Navy officer, heads a Navy Junior Reserve Officer Training Corps program at Montrose High School. The ocean is far away so his cadets build small boats in a campus warehouse and travel to lakes to sail them. After 9/11, Rizzo's principal postponed homecoming out of respect for the dead. Montrose residents lined up at the city hospital to give blood. No one knew if the blood donations would help, but they wanted to do something, said Rizzo, a Pennsylvania native who writes a column for the daily newspaper and calls his adopted hometown the heart of "rugged, rancher, Republican country." In 2008, two-thirds of Montrose County voters chose John McCain and Sarah Palin over Barack Obama and Joe Biden. Support for the Republican presidential ticket was even stronger in 2012, when the candidates were Mitt Romney and Paul Ryan. In both years, the state as a whole went for Obama.

The Montrose High School yearbook published shortly after 9/11 included a page of photos showing the anguish of that day. It also featured a quote from President Bush: "We will rally the world to this cause by our efforts, by our courage. We will not tire, we will not falter and we will not fail."

A few years later, the album devoted a page under the headline "honor" to teens who had joined the National Guard or army or were on their way to military colleges. Patriotism isn't the only inspiration. In this as in other economically ailing parts of the United States, military service is a path to education, career and upward mobility.

The local American Legion post once arranged for a Montrose stop for a traveling display to commemorate all those from across America killed in Iraq. Hundreds of tiny white crosses spilled from the front of the Montrose courthouse onto the lawn of the nearby library. Montrose's Post 73 was founded in 1920, a year after the American Legion came into existence. It was named for the first local men to die in World War I: Adelbert Armitage, John Paul Baranowski and John Brewer.

Watching Sunday morning television, Kline's mind turned to the images the development board had played with. They no longer seemed cliché. Washington had the Potomac. Montrose had the Uncompahgre running through a setting with a beauty that offered peace and a ruggedness that ensured solitude. Kline surmised that the hunger for adventure that had led some vets to the military could be assuaged, at least a little, in rock and ice-climbing, backcountry skiing and other adventure sports. And who better to bring new energy and ideas to her town than men and women like those she was seeing on television, old soldiers but still kids, so eager to keep serving even after sacrificing so much?

An audacious idea came to Kline as she sat on her couch. The words "Welcome Home Montrose" expressed the direction in which she was thinking. Why not bring vets to Montrose?

Kline relies on her computer engineer husband Craig Hollabaugh to rein her in when her imagination carries her away. After watching the TV report, she tried to get him to play devil's advocate. What risks were posed by making Montrose a welcoming place for vets?

"Because he's analytical, he's going to look for the weak points."

Hollabaugh could find none.

Meeting Hollabaugh had been another outcome of Kline's move from Cape Cod back to Colorado in 2001. Hollabaugh had preceded her in shifting from the East Coast to the Rocky Mountains. He had been working as a computer consultant and living in Massachusetts. He felt hemmed in. He decided he could work anywhere. He began scouting with three criteria in mind: for play a place with easy access to the slopes because he loved to ski; and for work access to high-speed Internet; and an airport nearby with national connections

Ouray had all three. Hollabaugh was surprised when someone at its Chamber of Commerce assured him there was broadband. He was directed to a restaurant owner who had paid for expensive Internet infrastructure because he wanted to use it himself and hoped to recoup the investment by selling subscriptions. Hollabaugh moved to Ouray in 2000 and met Kline's sons who were buddies of the restaurant owner. Hollabaugh was introduced to Kline when she settled in Ouray the next year.

"When I got to Ouray, I started making Shabbat dinners every week, because my family was there, and because I had the time and I loved doing it," Kline said.

Hollabaugh became a fixture at those intimate weekly Jewish rituals of food and connection with community and history. He started asking to come early to set up and staying late to clean up.

"He started arriving earlier and earlier and staying later and later. And pretty soon, he wasn't leaving," Kline said.

Making a family can also be a way of making a place home.

Hollabaugh jokes that he's glad Kline became so busy with Welcome Home Montrose that she soon had no time to watch Sunday morning television and get any more bright ideas. Joking aside, his pride in her is evident.

When it came to the military and veterans, Kline knew she had a lot to learn. Years later, she would look back ruefully at what she did not even realize that she did not know at the start.

"I was pretty naïve," she said. "At the beginning, I called everybody a soldier. Until somebody finally said: 'Melanie, soldiers are only in the Army. There are Marines who don't like to be called soldier.' And I have no idea of ranks. I don't come from a military background. Maybe I was lucky and people thought it was cute."

What we don't know can hold us back. But so can knowing what others think is impossible.

When a couple would come into one of her jewelry shops looking for a wedding ring, Kline would first listen, trying to understand what held meaning for the potential customers and what she could bring in experience and skill to realize their dreams. She has a way of giving her own opinion in a relaxed tone, then asking, "Well, what do you think?" with a smile that says she really wants to know the answer.

She brought humility, a sense of how to engage with other

people and leadership to the journey that began on a Sunday morning in front of the TV.

It's not a path for anyone who gives up easily.

Picture Kline late one evening, at a keyboard. Particularly in the early days of Welcome Home Montrose, Kline was given to spending long days on her laptop or cell phone, as connected in her way at 63 as a teenager on Snapchat.

That night, her mission was keeping the person at the other end online even though their messages started out testy and got increasingly so.

"She's really pissed off," Kline thought.

The correspondent, a vet herself, felt strongly that her fellow Americans had paid no attention to far-away conflicts written off as failures when they were underway, and wanted them quickly forgotten now that they were winding down. Her complaints, unspooling on Kline's computer screen, could be summed up thus: Local businesses weren't doing enough to help men and women who had served in Iraq and Afghanistan.

Kline responded with names of businesses that, through Welcome Home Montrose, were offering vets discounts and special deals. The woman countered that the list of 27 was too short, and that none of the shops on it sold anything she wanted to buy.

At that point, Kline, digitally speaking, could have walked away. But "there's clearly passion there," she thought. She gamely tapped out another few lines, describing the dozens of shop owners who hadn't been approached yet. Did the disgruntled vet want to take over the canvassing?

She did.

"Now, that woman is setting the street on fire," Kline said later of a new friend and supporter.

Kline has a knack for turning negativity into action and doubters into dedicated volunteers. She doesn't lead by commanding.

"I don't have ownership of the idea. I don't have fear of outcome, because I don't need to control it," she said. "It isn't me.

I'm not qualified to do this alone. My background is in sales and in jewelry making: making something from nothing and making a living at it."

From the beginning, Kline knew she would need collaborators. She started by downloading a digital version of the Team River Runner segment that had inspired a great notion in her mind. Then she set out to see who else could be moved to action.

Chapter 3

Building on an Idea

Small towns are full of stories everybody knows. If you're from Montrose, surely you'll remember the time a county manager quit, leaving behind a three-page letter of resignation that quoted Franklin Roosevelt and Oliver Cromwell and in which he joined former New Jersey Gov. Jim McGreevey in lamenting that citizens seemed to be "losing sight of civility."

Local political junkies also will recall a city manager's email, quoted by local media, stating he couldn't work anymore with the head of the Montrose Economic Development Corporation after a city council meeting in which he felt he was subjected to "spiteful, misleading and hurtful" comments. That outburst was followed by what amounts to a divorce between the city and the corporation. The latter is a nonprofit that works county-wide to try to attract new businesses.

Even if you're not from Montrose, you'll be familiar with issues such as whether the mayor is overstepping authority, operational matters at the airport, the pace and direction of development, the hiring and firing of civil servants. And because bickering in public is as all-American as River City, Iowa you might not be baffled at the way small-town politics can seem packed with drama simply because the players are all too familiar with each other. In Montrose, they can seem like squabbling family members who know which buttons to push. Positions are more dearly held because the stakes are close to home.

Add a dose of "Out West" individualism, and you get a sense of why that departing county manager claimed the region "has the reputation of being the most contentious county in the state of Colorado." And you glimpse what Kline was wading into with that video of wounded, spirited young vets.

Kline acknowledged that getting two Main Street businesses to keep the same hours, as convenient as that might be for shoppers, can be like herding cats. Even knowing that, she told me she did not realize until after the fact that she brought people together on the Welcome Home Montrose board who weren't on speaking terms elsewhere. She didn't pick and choose among factions.

When the idea of Welcome Home Montrose "knocked me off the couch, I knew who to take it to."

By "who," Kline meant anyone who would take time to crouch over her laptop screen and watch her video.

Among those she initially approached was Melanie Hall, who headed the private, philanthropic Montrose Community Foundation. Hall, who would join the founding board of Welcome Home Montrose, said Kline's project brought "positive energy that creates more opportunity for all in the community."

"It's a tremendous point of engagement. And I think our community needs it," Hall said.

While Montrose is no model town, that departing county manager wasn't engaging in hollow boosterism when he added in his letter of resignation that he also found it a wonderful place in which to live. If Montrose were a person, she might be a veteran with a tough exterior and a helping heart. If townspeople are ornery, perhaps it's because they care so deeply.

"I got to see that we have a really big heart," Kline said of what happened when she started showing her video around town. With each screening she wept, as she had done the first time she watched the segment alone in her living room.

"I don't know when that will ever stop," she said of her emotional reaction.

That empathy may be why she is, as Montrose City Manager Bill Bell told me, easy to follow. Kline once asked Bell whether he thought she was crazy to keep showing the news segment around town. Bell's answer can be gleaned from the list of members of the founding board of directors of Welcome Home Montrose: his name leads the alphabetical pack. The board also included the head of the Montrose Economic Development Corporation, the very body with whom Bell had so publicly clashed over hurtful language.

By March of 2012, the city and the corporation were sharing language, at least when it came to Welcome Home Montrose. Each body passed a similarly worded resolution that month that backed Kline's project. The city pledged, among other things, to support Welcome Home Montrose fundraising and "to ensure that any future planning of public facilities or community resources, such as parks and recreational facilities, considers the needs of physically and psychologically disabled vets." The corporation's resolution said Kline's program "could support job creation and job retention." Similar statements were made by the county commissioners and the boards of the Montrose Association of Commerce and Tourism, the Downtown Development Authority, a U.S. congressman, the Veterans Administration and other health and mental healthcare providers.

Kline's approach was not just top-down.

"If it's supposed to be a grassroots effort, then we have to engage them all," she said.

In December of 2011 Kline organized two days of community forums that were similar to the Downtown Development Authority's session on branding, complete with those brightly colored sticky notes. Kline canvassed for ideas, volunteers and assessments of the possible impact of making Montrose a vet-friendly hub. She divided participants into focus groups around specific issues, such as mental health or education, with no overlaps in the schedules because many people wanted to weigh in on more than one issue. Government offices and nonprofits sent representatives during the day on paid time, a measure of how seriously Montrose was taking Kline's crazy idea. In some of the sessions, Kline said, community members were telling one another things they had not had time to have a conversation about before.

"You're supposed to be doing that," was heard. As was: "You're doing something we're doing!"

The most heated session, Kline said, was on services for vets. The region's Veterans Administration officials sat with their arms folded as accusations flew.

"Everybody was defensive. No one wants to be told that they're not doing all they should or all they could be doing," Kline said. "We had a pretty explosive meeting. But it was good."

At that VA encounter and others, important gaps and overlaps were discovered. The mood moved from accusatory to a sense of determination to change.

The talks were held at an event center known as the Pavilion located halfway between downtown and a newer business district on the south side of Montrose that is anchored by the local outposts of several high volume retail chains. The vast Pavilion is so nondescript it could have been a big box store itself. We have all been in such generic spaces, perhaps being bored by a keynote speaker at a professional conference or trapped in conversation at a college reunion with a classmate you can't quite remember knowing while at school. Imagine instead the conference rooms of particle board and acoustic tile transformed into marketplaces of ideas, enlivened by the kind of big-hearted, engaged and engaging folks I have come to associate with Welcome Home Montrose.

Rich Parr had read in the local paper about the focus groups days before they were held in April of 2012. He was intrigued enough to give up his days off from his job as a pharmacy manager to attend Kline's gathering. Looking back a few years later, Parr remembered speaking to others of the 200 or so townspeople who attended about how the faith community could support former warriors and about finding jobs for those veterans.

What he remembered most was not what he heard, but how he felt. He belonged.

"I was very impressed by the number of people who wanted to help make this organization into something very special. Montrose is a very patriotic community and I am privileged to live here,"

Parr, a clean-shaven man with a soft voice and button-downed air, told me. "That's not to say that the appreciation of the military veteran doesn't exist in other areas of the U.S. I just believe that Montrose is exceptional in that regard."

Speaking as a lifelong civilian, Parr added: "I've thought for a long time that veterans do not get the recognition, the appreciation they deserve."

Parr's brother was a military police officer in Vietnam. Parr remembered his sibling coming home to a cold welcome and never sharing much about his war experiences.

"He's more or less had to deal with it the rest of his life without any support."

Parr's own son joined the Navy. Parr contemplated his son's life after service.

"If he ever decided he wanted to live in Montrose, he's already got an organization that is ready to help him settle into the community," the father said.

Parr began volunteering for Welcome Home Montrose immediately after leaving the second day of the Pavilion event. In the beginning, he organized bake sales and other fundraisers for vets in his pharmacy's parking lot. He would go on to join the board of Welcome Home Montrose.

From the first event at the Pavilion, "I recall Melanie's talk about how she became inspired to form the organization and later on how she always told me that people such as myself could help drive it forward just because of our passion and desire to assist veterans."

Parr came away a volunteer.

Kline left the meetings convinced that "the first thing you need to do is engage your community. All the rest will follow."

As she talked and listened at that community meeting, Kline's idea moved toward realization. An early document she and her team wrote pledged that Welcome Home Montrose, or WHM, would be driven by the "strength created when others are empowered to drive their own futures." The document went on to outline six points that townspeople, either in talks with her or jotted on those sticky notes, had agreed should be the priorities.

The first area was the need to build on support services. The document, which might be called a manifesto, went on to say that Montrose was supportive of the military and had strong institutions including charities, many of them faith-based.

"A coordinated, publicized local initiative to reintegrate wounded veterans to useful, significant lives would bring broad community support. WHM would organize in-home services, personal assistance and family services for the veterans. By collecting many veterans in a single community, WHM would facilitate peer-to-peer support. Veterans would have other veterans who understand their challenges and can provide encouragement, advice, accountability, and role modeling to help them make successful transitions."

The manifesto's second point involved ensuring veterans would find purpose in Montrose. Kline had realized while watching her Sunday news program that vets very much needed to feel useful and productive.

"Montrose is a center for skiing, fishing, off-roading and other recreation. Montrose could become a leader in developing adaptive equipment and training for disabled participants.

"In developing solutions for their problems, they (vets) could create rewarding career paths by disseminating these solutions to others in need of them."

Flowing from that second point was a third on morale:

"Opening avenues for skiing, mountaineering, snowmobiling, off-roading, fishing, hunting, horseback riding, biking, kayaking, climbing for these veterans could renew their zest for life's possibilities. Montrose could not only service its resident population of veterans but also become a destination for veterans all over the U.S. who wanted to experience adventure tourism geared to their capabilities."

Montrose knew it wasn't ready to do all it could for disabled veterans. Point No. 4 showed citizens were trying to see their deficits as opportunities: "WHM would intend to develop adapted housing for individual, family and group settings. In the present economy, there is a substantial inventory of foreclosed real estate that could be acquired reasonably and modified for this purpose. Perhaps the lenders who hold these properties would provide favorable financial terms for putting these properties to use for this cause."

Points 5 and 6 looked to the physical and mental health of veterans. Welcome Home Montrose would reach out to the Veterans Administration and others to ramp up services.

"WHM believes that such a grassroots effort would have a substantial benefit for Montrose," according to the manifesto. "It would be a classic case of 'doing well while doing good.' The community would receive the blessing of service, of saying thank you to those who have served us at such a high cost. Communities prosper from a sense of common purpose as much as individuals do. Focusing on serving the needy provides satisfaction and motivation to the whole community. But also, developing expertise in meeting these special needs will create jobs in construction, health, adaptive tourism and retailing ...."

It summed up: "The virtuous spiral of organizing to serve can create exponential growth in economic and social benefit."

September 11, 2012, was the 11th anniversary of 9/11 and about a year after Kline first watched that compelling news story. It was opening day of what was dubbed the Welcome Home Montrose Warrior Resource Center. A somber date became a day of possibility.

The Montrose Daily Press called the drop-in center "a place where local and visiting veterans can learn about the growing number of local benefits available to them, and serve as a bridge for state and national veterans agencies to reach for their constituency." It reported that dozens of people had gathered in the center's parking lot on a Main Street corner for the ribbon cutting.

The center's 4,000-square-foot space was a few doors down from a military recruiting office and once housed a mortgage company. Inside, Welcome Home Montrose central felt like a church basement. At least, that's the impression I had when I visited a few months after the opening and saw the large kitchen, the two bathrooms big enough to accommodate wheelchairs, and the function room where folding chairs can be arranged at tables for pot lucks or creative writing or photography classes, or stacked against the wall to make room for tai chi, tae kwon do and yoga workouts. The walls were decorated with photographs of vets rafting, rock-climbing and skiing, undeterred by the prosthetic arms and legs they did not hide from the camera. Certificates of appreciation from local and national groups also crowded the walls. Laptops paid for with a grant from a national big box chain were available for vets who might use one to write a resume or a paper for a college class. Books, board games and videos were ready to take home on loan. It was a home for Welcome Home Montrose, a place where vets, their relatives and their advocates could brainstorm.

The operation was trim and frugal. A local businessman charged a modest $15,000 a year for rent and utilities for the spacious headquarters and drop-in center. Monthly expenses at the start included $510 to cover childcare costs for one of two otherwise unpaid co-executive directors, and $225 to pay rent for the second. Kline and members of her founding board of directors estimated they each put in at least 50 unpaid hours a week in the early days.

In 2012, according to its first annual report, Welcome Home Montrose received $43,264 in cash donations, much of it from local businesses that contributed $100 each in exchange for stickers that could be placed in windows to alert passersby that here was a shop where vets would be offered discounts and deals. Other income included $252,000 in in-kind contributions such as housing for interns, office equipment and website design and accounting services.

When it opened in 2012, Welcome Home Montrose was supported by 70 volunteers. The number had grown to 250 by mid-2015, when registration records showed Welcome Home Montrose also had made contact with some 1,000 vets who got referrals to a job, advice about VA benefits, a cup of coffee. That 1,000 represents nearly a third of all the vets the VA says live in the county.

In 2015, county commissioners granted Welcome Home Montrose space in a small airport to set up a monthly coffee in Nucla, a farming community of about 700 people that is 90 miles west of Montrose across a long, narrow county. It made sense to have a satellite in a county of more than 2,000 square miles. Agencies that provide housing, mental health counseling and other support for veterans have pledged to attend the Nucla coffees, turning the airport into a pop-up drop-in center. In the first three months, it drew an average of 50 vets each month.

But I'm getting ahead of the story.

Kline told me: "I've had a lot of people say, 'Well, I saw that video. It was fascinating. But it didn't make me do what it made you do.'"

Kline was at a place in her life, in her community and in her town that made her particularly receptive to the faces of those wounded young men she saw on TV that Sunday morning. Her personal trajectory met her town's at a golden moment.

Kline marveled at the speed and enthusiasm with which her neighbors embraced Welcome Home Montrose, pitching in with ideas, $100 donations, services. She concluded: "People want their lives to mean something."

Chapter 4

Programs and Possibilities

One of the first places Kline showed the video that inspired her was at a regular meeting of the downtown development board. The board was in a way where Welcome Home Montrose began. Carol McDermott told me she remembered the session at which she and other policy makers and small business owners gathered around Kline's laptop screen. McDermott was a member of the development group as a representative of the city council. Before being elected to the city council, she had been a school board member, and before that a teacher in the Montrose area for 30 years.

McDermott is as warm-hearted as Kline. A freelance journalist along with her educational and public service pursuits, she once wrote a column about being asked by the Montrose Chamber of Commerce to surprise randomly chosen shoppers with $50 gift certificates. She recounted in her column that she found herself teary-eyed again and again at the gratitude with which she was met. McDermott is also pragmatic. When her city council term ended, she didn't want time wasted on a long thank-you proclamation peppered with "whereases." When her nephew enlisted, she scoured the Internet for recipes for fudge that wouldn't melt in extreme heat. She sent him homemade candy during his two Iraq tours.

McDermott said Kline has an infectious energy. When she saw Kline's video and heard her neighbor say her town could do something to help, McDermott immediately decided that students should see the video. She was a school teacher before she was a politician, after all. As Kline's project took shape, McDermott became its education specialist. On one school visit, she was accompanied by a young woman whose father was serving in

Afghanistan. The teen spoke after the video was shown, describing what it's like to have a parent away and in danger.

The students saw "another kid, they could identify with her. They started sharing stories," McDermott told me. "Kids want to be able to talk. They don't want to just be talked to."

McDermott also signed up for a Welcome Home Montrose program that matches volunteer tutors with children of men and women serving in Iraq or Afghanistan. She found the sons and daughters didn't always need help with math or spelling as much as they needed someone with whom to share their fears.

"Their families are having to make some serious adjustments," she said. "While the soldiers are gone, the community steps up."

McDermott dedicated her Welcome Home Montrose service to her nephew. She wrote a message for the organization's website in which she said that after his tours, he "returned home and serves his community as a volunteer firefighter and hockey coach. He enrolled in college, and now is a small business owner. His community newspaper gives him special rates for advertising. Welcome Home Montrose is a wonderful idea, a great way our community can thank our veterans."

McDermott's involvement illustrates how Welcome Home Montrose developed. The organization has room for any idea that might move it forward, especially if the person bringing the idea also puts in the time and commitment to make it work.

At the heart of it all is the Warrior Resource Center. Gatherings there often begin with people introducing themselves with not just names, but theaters of combat: Vietnam, Iraq, Afghanistan, Somalia, Kosovo. Even as far back as Iwo Jima.

A flyer at the front desk lists pointed questions under the heading: "Attention veterans!"

"Having a hard time adjusting to civilian life?"

"Trouble sleeping?"

"Can't talk?"

"Wish somebody understood?"

The flyer's tear-off tabs include a number for the Vet Center, a Veterans Affairs counseling project. The nearest Vet Center is an hour away, but Vet Center specialists trained in PTSD, readjustment, grief and marriage counseling visit the Warrior Resource Center regularly to hold one-on-one and group counseling. Rooms are available at the center for vets who need a private space to speak with a counselor. Other visitors on whom vets can count on finding at the center include federal and state caseworkers who can guide them to housing or cash to keep roofs over their heads.

Another poster advertises the hot line for the Center for Mental Health, a nonprofit that has sent its experts to the Warrior Resource Center to lead sessions on how to recognize the behavior of someone who is contemplating suicide.

Unlike at a federal or state office building, vets don't have to be buzzed in at the Warrior Resource Center. What a civilian might see as normal security precautions a vet might see as suspicious scrutiny.

Emily Smith, who oversees the resource center, never served in the military. But she is a military spouse. She knows from experience that a vet who feels he or she is not trusted might respond by withholding their own trust.

"The military's just its own little culture," Smith told me. "A lot of these guys feel they don't fit into society anymore."

Smith knows that pride might keep vets from visiting a social service office that also provides some of the aid they can get at her center. At Welcome Home Montrose, they feel they are getting support in the spirit of collaborative problem-solving, not as a handout. If someone is feeling frustrated and indulges in a little profanity or raises a voice, no eyebrows will be raised and Smith has no guards to call. She has instead a team composed for the most part of volunteers, many of them veterans, who come armed only with a fierce commitment to help.

At the resource center, Smith said, vets "feel accepted, they feel secure. They know that we want to give them options so they can decide what's best themselves."

The center does not always have the answers. Benefits questions can be the trickiest to parse.

"We can always research," Smith said.

Local chapters of the Veterans of Foreign Wars or Disabled Veterans of America could have resented a newcomer reaching out to the populations they serve. Far from being territorial, such groups have embraced Welcome Home Montrose and been strengthened in return. They forged partnerships with people at the project's drop-in center like a young, injured former Marine whose truncated military career had included training in refurbishing rifles. The VFW, it turned out, had a supply of dilapidated rifles it needed to get in shape for ceremonial use at funerals. The Marine stepped in.

The more established groups can suffer, unfairly or not, from stereotypes that they are only for combat vets who served overseas, only for men, only for those who have lost a limb or are retired or are looking for a comfortable bar. Welcome Home Montrose counters any tendency to segregate, which can also isolate. The drop-in center, formally known as the Warrior Resource Center, is for any and everyone who served in America's armed forces, their spouses, their children. Even their non-veteran friends can tag along to a tai chi class or lend a voice to one of the regular musical jam sessions held in the center's great room.

It's impossible to predict who or what will come through the doors of the Warrior Resource Center.

One day, it was a 12-year-old Girl Scout with so many badges on her vest she looked like a general sporting an array of medals. The girl, accompanied by her mother, had been selling cookies downtown when she saw a window sticker about Welcome Home Montrose. She asked for details, and was directed to the center, hard to miss with its giant American flag painted across the façade.

On a visit that was unannounced, almost a whim, the 12-year-old explained to the volunteer at the drop-in center's front desk that for the seven years she had been selling cookies, she has always asked buyers whether they want to pay for a box or two to be sent to men and women in the military overseas. Now, she had decided to ask buyers whether they would donate cookies for Welcome Home Montrose to distribute. The volunteer Welcome Home Montrose receptionist promised any cookies donated will be happily munched at regular coffee gatherings vets hold at the center.

"We decided to do something local this year because we'd heard about Welcome Home Montrose," her mother said.

"They're risking their lives to support us, so it's nice to do something they'll appreciate," the girl added. Welcome Home Montrose volunteers arranged for her to get a poster about the project to tape to a sales table. And now that shd has learned more about the project, she said she would be telling customers about it as she went door to door with her cookies.

"These angels show up. All we've done is give them a place to show up," Welcome Home Montrose founder Kline said.

One day, the angel was a woman who delivered thousands of dollars' worth of audiovisual equipment and did not stay long enough to get a receipt for the Internal Revenue Service. Another benefactor who had noticed on an earlier visit that a volunteer was struggling with faltering office equipment called to offer to donate a new printer.

Veterans who had trouble with medical equipment typically had to drive an hour to the nearest VA Medical Center, in Grand Junction, for repairs. Kline looked for solutions closer to home.

"Is there anybody in the community who wants to do pro bono work on wheelchairs, eyeglasses, hearing aids? Well, yeah!"

In the early days, Kline said, "none of us had any idea that the public outpouring was going to be what it is. We thought we were going to be doing most of the providing."

Instead, people were walking through the door, wanting to give.

"Open up these doors for the public to serve, and the connections will be made," Kline said.

In a struggling town, angels don't necessarily have cash. It's part of Kline's philosophy that that should not bar anyone from taking part: "If the thing to do is to give money, then all those people who don't have money don't think they have anything to give."

Sally Johnson, curator of Montrose's municipal museum, has taken to digging uniforms and other memorabilia out of her storage and using them for mini displays at the drop-in center, knowing they will find an appreciative and knowledgeable audience. The center also was the go-to place for an area resident with contacts to the Country Music Hall of Fame who wanted to bring in a big-name performer for a fundraiser to help vets. And for a hospice worker with a video made of a World War II veteran in his last hours, when he was finally ready to talk about his battlefield memories. The veteran's family knew the recording would have a place in an archive of oral histories that Welcome Home Montrose was developing.

A farmer called, asking whether any veterans might want to garden on 80 acres he's not using. A woman called, offering to write a check to cover six months' rent for Welcome Home Montrose interns. A teacher from near Denver called, saying her third-grade class wanted to send letters to troops serving overseas. She was told if she would consider wounded troops instead, Welcome Home Montrose could get them to Walter Reed, the nation's best-known military hospital.

A newly widowed woman called offering to donate the motorcycle her late husband, a Vietnam vet, had cherished. Another widow wanted to donate a wheelchair lift. Within days, word came to the drop-in center of a vet at the VA hospital who had recently had a hip operation. His doctors had refused to release him unless they were assured his house was wheelchair accessible. The connection was made, and a vet was able to get home.

A homeless vet from out of state was directed to the center almost as soon as he hit town one afternoon. Once there, he told Smith he was from the South and had had to flee his home after a difference of opinion with a roommate turned violent. He had read about Welcome Home Montrose in a newspaper, so decided to make Colorado his destination. He hitchhiked to get here. Smith arranged a hotel for the night. Then, she alerted another vet in town who had an affordable room and was willing to wait to collect rent until the wanderer's benefits checks caught up with him.

Another day, another man. He announced with little preamble:

"I'm here to see somebody about a job. See if I can get some work."

A volunteer told him about a solar company that was hiring. The wanted ad had been distributed in a Welcome Home Montrose electronic newsletter. The visitor jotted down contact information and left. He was in such a hurry to pursue the lead, he did not stay for an offered cup of coffee.

While that man refused a cup, coffee is a big draw on Thursday mornings at the drop-in center.

So many pickup trucks fill the parking lot and line neighboring streets the center looks like a popular diner. More hale vets collect older comrades and drive them in. Vets coffees are advertised as two-hour gatherings, but, center director Smith said, "the guys are here at 7:30, and stay to noon."

The first coffee morning drew four vets, Smith recalled:

"Four very sad little vets, just sitting there, thinking, 'Are you sure this is a good idea?'"

Within three years, the number grew to an average of 75 every Thursday. It must have been a good idea.

Kline from time to time will put flyers or a sign-up sheet in the room when she has word to get out about a program to benefit vets or wants to gauge interest in a new idea. Then, she leaves the room. The Thursday conversations are for vets only. Smith checks IDs when someone she doesn't know shows up, and turns away anyone who can't show proof of service. Once, that was a local politician Smith suspected wanted to transform the coffee into a self-serving fundraising opportunity.

"The most important thing of everything Welcome Home Montrose does is getting those guys together for coffee," Kline said. "No agenda, no strings attached. Just getting together and creating community.

"Militaries create warriors. Communities create citizens."

A wiry man with an assertive moustache settled with his back to the wall in a chair upholstered in a busy, grandmotherly pattern. He was Vietnam vet and retired commercial pilot Mike Bronner. I sat across a large, round table from him. How crowded is his side of the table when he's not the only vet in the room who is too anxious to sit with his or her back to the door?

Bronner had agreed to offer me a glimpse of what the Welcome Home Montrose community means to vets. He spoke to me with ease for nearly two hours. I suspect his high comfort level had to do with the setting: the drop-in center conference room where he and the four other men in his PTSD group meet regularly.

Bronner was raised in Denair, near Modesto, California, where his family grew berries, nuts and peaches. He never wanted to be a farmer himself. He dreamed of flying. He got his pilot's license when he was still in high school. He joined the Army at 18 hoping to learn to fly helicopters, but was instead assigned to be a medic. He was a Quaker, and his superiors may have assumed he would not want a combat role. But Bronner had a Ranger cousin he idolized, and was the son of a Coast Guardsman who had hauled Marines ashore at Guadalcanal. He had enlisted thinking: "I'm going to war. That's what we're supposed to do."

During his May, 1968 to May, 1969 tour in Vietnam with the 173rd Airborne Brigade, Bronner picked up dead comrades to send home and listened to the dying call out to their mothers. After his tour when he flew in to San Francisco and headed back to central California, thinking about how going to war may have affected him was not a priority. He was too busy putting his dream of being a pilot back on track. He studied aeronautics, became a flight instructor, flew private planes and crop dusters, then started working for U.S. national carriers.

"There's a lot of Vietnam veterans out there who are very successful. Some of them may not even seem to have mental problems or PTSD. But they do," he said. "When they retire, they've got all this time on their hands. They fall apart because they have time to think about things."

That time came for Bronner after major heart surgery in 1998 that required a long disability leave before retirement. He and his wife, a police crime scene investigator, were living near Colorado Springs but had been thinking about a refuge with a view. They ended up with one house in town in Montrose and another in the mountains in nearby Gunnison.

The Gunnison home became Bronner's hideout. He spent weeks alone there, nursing an anger he hadn't before given himself permission to contemplate.

"The majority of the problems that we Vietnam veterans have are caused, more than by combat situations, by the way we were treated when we got back. Just the way the country treated us like we were druggies or criminals. We've felt alone since we came home."

The teen who had volunteered to fight for his country had grown into a man who saw Vietnam as the point when his homeland "started going downhill. There hasn't been a war worth fighting since World War II. Everything's political. It's all about oil. We're just throwing away lives."

It got so his wife didn't want to go with him to Gunnison because that meant watching him check the perimeter for possible tampering with the surveillance cameras and grenades he had strung from trees to ensure his isolation. He argued with the neighbors, no easy task given how far most lived from his house. His family grew concerned he would hurt himself, or someone else.

After a particularly bitter winter in 2014, one of his three daughters drove Bronner to the VA hospital in Grand Junction, telling him it was for a flu vaccination.

"While I was in there getting a flu shot, my daughter pulled a sneaky on me, told the gals at the front desk I was really upset and she was worried."

He was referred to a counselor who prescribed an anti-anxiety medication that Bronner acknowledged did help. Bronner refused to say much during his sessions with the counselor. But he listened. He heard about Welcome Home Montrose.

"I thought, 'Well, there's other veterans over there, so maybe I better go over there and do the coffee thing.'"

Soon, he was also doing tai chi in classes at the drop-in center led by a fellow Vietnam vet.

Now, Bronner is becoming familiar with terms like "abnormal startle responses" and "hypervigilance," and realizing he has spent decades - not just his stint in Gunnison - pushing people away out of anger and fear.

The Warrior Resource Center "is what got me squared away. If it wasn't for this place, I'd still be screwed up, wanting to kill everybody."

Not that Bronner doesn't still have some anger management issues. His outrage flared when he learned county politicians might want him and his comrades to visit a government building instead of Welcome Home Montrose to see a publicly appointed outreach worker known as a veterans service officer, or VSO. VSOs working around Colorado help veterans, their relatives and survivors navigate the system for filing for federal military benefits. The Montrose County VSO had taken to holding regular office hours at the Welcome Home Montrose Warrior Resource center.

But county commissioners noted that the VSO is a county employee. They thought it made sense for the officer to spend at least some time at a government campus that also houses county health and human services offices. The commissioners argued that working at the campus would mean better communications among departments that provide resources for veterans and others, and make it easier for old soldiers to access such benefits.

At a public meeting to discuss the VSO, Bronner was blunt:

"We deserve to have the VSO located where the veterans hang out," Bronner told Montrose County commissioners at that August, 2015 meeting. "I hate the government; I don't trust any of you."

It's almost a relief to see Montrose-style contentiousness has not disappeared. This is not a fairy tale in which Welcome Home Montrose transformed residents into people who always get along and are careful not to step on one another's toes. But perhaps the project has shown them that their differences don't stand in the way of sharing goals and making progress toward those goals. Their differences, townspeople found, could be their strength if they could find unity.

"You have to build with others in the community, whether you like them or not," said Welcome Home Montrose executive director Smith. She told me she has learned to embrace having people around who challenge why she does things the way she does. Sometimes, they've offered a different approach she's ended up acknowledging was better than her own.

The August county commissioners meeting ended with a compromise: a commitment from commissioners to work with Welcome Home Montrose and ensure the VSO visited the Warrior Resource Center a few days a week as well as the government offices.

For all his bluster, it is not out of bounds to imagine the person most threatened by Bronner was himself. In what the VA called the first attempt at a comprehensive review of suicides among veterans, researchers found that between 2009 and 2012, more than 69 percent of veterans who committed suicide were at least 50 years old, while in the general population suicide is more prevalent among younger people. In both the general and veteran populations, those who commit suicide are typically male. The researchers, using data they were able to obtain from 21 states, came up with the oft-quoted estimate that 22 veterans died from suicide every day in 2010. That so many of those who took their own lives were male and older could be due to a number of factors, according to Dr. Tom Berger, who served with the Navy in Vietnam and now heads Vietnam Veterans of America's Veterans Health Council.

"Certainly, we share some of the risk factors with the younger guys," including post-traumatic stress disorder and high rates of depression and combat experience, Berger told Military.com when the VA's suicide study came out.

"A lot of guys went in, and then they came out and became a workaholic rather than deal with depression and PTSD," Berger continued. Once they retired, like Bronner, they could no longer hide in their jobs.

Once Bronner decided he was ready to get help, the PTSD support group he found at the Warrior Resource Center included Iraq combat veterans. He tries to set a good example for the younger old soldiers. In thinking of them, he helps himself.

Bronner has added his own combat souvenir, the camouflage helmet cover he wore as a teen, to the war memorabilia that decorates the resource center. It sits on a shelf outside the conference room.

"The bottom line is, you cannot fix a broken soul. You can maybe get control of your feelings. And the only people who understand that are other guys who have been there."

So, it's not all coffee and Girl Scout cookies. Smith has good reason to scoff at the made-for-television images of a wheelchair-bound vet hiding a wounded, saintly soul behind a gruff exterior. The gruffness runs deep in some vets. And those are the vets who most need her help, she said.

"When we said we wanted to help vets, we didn't say, 'certain vets,'" Smith said. "We're offering them a sense of community.

What's the worst that can come of that? I like to have faith that what you put into something is what you get out of it."

She imagines a hard case, someone already living in Montrose or a newcomer. What if, finding that a whole town offered help, he or she was no longer so angry or violent or intent on climbing into a bottle to escape everyday life?

Smith has worked late into the night to find a room for a homeless vet, only to have him go back to the street. Then, she waits for him to return.

"Who's to say how many times you should get assistance before you're ready?" Smith said. "Who decides that for another human being?"

Nationwide, homelessness among veterans is a vexing problem. The Department of Housing and Urban Development, which takes annual one-night censuses to track homelessness, found in its 2012 snapshot that 62,619 veterans were among the total of 633,782 people sleeping on the streets or in shelters. That means veterans made up nearly 10 percent of the total, though they are only 7 percent of the U.S. population.

The VA has vowed to ensure all veterans have a place to live. Its approach has included working with the Housing and Urban Development Authority to provide homes for vets who are chronically homeless and have a history of medical, mental health or substance abuse problems. Participants in the Housing and Urban Development and Veterans Affairs Supported Housing program, known as HUD-VASH, receive support from case managers to help them stay housed. During one period, the only community in the Montrose region with a HUD-VASH program was Grand Junction, about an hour's drive away. Smith worked successfully to bring HUD-VASH to Montrose.

Welcome Home Montrose takes a whole-soldier approach that includes spouses like Smith, for whom she has organized monthly lunches at the drop-in center.

Often, the meals for spouses are catered by philanthropic local restaurants. But a late October gathering was pot luck, drawing about 40 women bearing crock pots brimming with chili, foil-wrapped trays of cornbread squares arranged as carefully as chess pieces, and an astounding selection of pies.

Once the women had made their way through the buffet line, they settled at tables decorated in orange and black for Halloween. Talk was of grandchildren and children, childhood illnesses, tips for organizing the frequent moves that military families face. Names were drawn from a pot shaped and painted to look like a jack o'lantern. Lucky winners took home Halloween-themed bowls, notepads and, most ardently coveted, doilies crocheted by a popular World War II era spouse.

As the chatter died and women started collecting empty dishes and sweeping paper plates into bins, Smith rose to make an announcement: soon, the drop-in-center would be hosting weekly support groups for women, at which vets' spouses and anyone else who wanted to attend would be welcome. A professional counselor would facilitate some meetings. Smith would also be bringing in speakers on traumatic brain injury and other topics. The meetings would be a chance to strengthen the connections first made at the easy-going monthly lunches. They would be in addition to, not a replacement for, the lunches.

Now, a few female vets join the vets weekly coffees. Those women also attend the spouse luncheons, making clear they crave female company and raising the question of how many other women warriors would benefit if they felt they had a day of their own at the drop-in center, without the men.

Merry Lee Kuboske served as a Navy air traffic controller after the Korean war and before U.S. involvement in Vietnam escalated. She had a reason in addition to seeking companionship for attending both the vets coffees and the spouses lunches. She believes that, without betraying any confidences, she can help close communications gaps between the vets and the spouses.

Kuboske, her brown eyes lively under a shock of graying hair, learned about giving to her community while attending Catholic schools. She once considered becoming a nun. She saw the military as an opportunity to serve, an attitude she may have picked up from her father. He had always regretted being rejected by the Army because he had flat feet.

After high school, Kuboske worked for a time as an airline reservation clerk. Determined to do more with her life, she spoke to an Army recruiter about joining up and going to language school - she had enjoyed Latin class in high school. The recruiter apparently passed her name along to a Navy colleague who was intrigued by her airline experience. He contacted her to say she might be a candidate for flight control school. She was 19.

"I think they had anticipated I would not pass the test for the control tower and I would get a desk job," she said.

She did pass. After boot camp in Maryland and more training in California she was stationed at Moffat Field near San Francisco.

She was discharged in 1965 after completing a three-year stint. Kuboske then returned to Colorado, where she used GI Bill benefits to go to college in Grand Junction and earn a degree in accounting.

Kuboske has worked for her family's liquor, car and tourist businesses in the Colorado mountains, for a CPA in Montrose and a lodge in Telluride. She's also been president of the Ouray Chamber of Commerce, active in the Lady Elks and volunteered for a hospice. But she had never been involved with a veterans group until a neighbor told her about Welcome Home Montrose.

Many women who served, particularly those of Kuboske's generation (she was born in 1941) struggle to see themselves as on par with male veterans. They tend to stay away from traditional veterans organizations. Untraditional Welcome Home Montrose opened a door for Kuboske.

"The boys have asked me to join all the ex-military organizations," she said. And she has accepted those invitations from the vets she has met at Welcome Home Montrose.

When she was in the Navy women were not allowed on ships.

Kuboske said she is occasionally asked whether she would have gone into battle if that had been an option when she was a teen.

"I'm sure I would have. I thought I could do anything."

She sees that can-do spirit and desire to serve in today's warriors, men and women. She is grateful to Welcome Home Montrose for giving her a chance to serve them.

Kuboske has helped keep track of boating and fishing equipment during an outdoor sports festival organized by Welcome Home Montrose. She came to the drop-in center one morning to distribute toiletries, flashlights and hugs to homeless vets.

"It meant so much to be able to help those guys," she said of the men she met who served as she did and now are living on the streets. "A couple of them left some tears behind."

Sitting in waiting rooms at the veterans' hospital in Grand Junction, Kuboske ha s spoken to younger women about battlefield experiences and Post-Traumatic Stress Disorder.

"I had never pictured women on the ground having to face that," she said. "I had never talked to anyone who had PTSD. The bit they can talk about is horrific to me."

Even before U.S. Defense Secretary Ashton B. Carter announced in 2015 that all combat roles would be open to women, women had been in harm's way. They were driving trucks through hostile territory and repairing weapons, maintaining vehicles and performing other duties on the ground in Iraq and Afghanistan. Pew researchers have noted there were 42,000 active duty enlisted women in 1973 and 167,000 in 2010. By 2016, more than 160 women had been killed fighting in the war on terror. During the entire Vietnam war, eight U.S. military women were killed.

The women's support meetings Smith has planned could help put Welcome Home Montrose ahead of the curve as the military role expands even further for women.

"Programs will change," Smith told me. "It's our responsibility to keep it fresh."

Smith is fascinated by World War II. Occasionally, she will

come across military items from the '40s, a pack or a pair of boots, at an estate sale and wonder what memories are being lost. She launched a Welcome Home Montrose program to record and archive oral histories of vets, starting with the Greatest Generation.

"I hope this is the start of no longer losing their stories," she said.

The recollections that have meant the most to Smith aren't from World War II. They aren't even from old soldiers. They are from the wives of Vietnam vets in whom she finds reassurance that "no matter what's going on, you can still make it."

"These Vietnam women are amazing. They've been living with PTSD for 40 years. They stand the hard stuff."

One woman told Smith her boyfriend broke up with her, giving no reason, soon after he returned from Vietnam.

"She finally hunted him down, and in the middle of this big social dance, she laid into him. And he just hugged her. They've been together ever since. She says it hasn't been easy, that there's been a lot of times when there's been fighting. But she says it's been worth it."

The Vietnam-era spouses have pointed a way forward for her. And Smith, who is married to an Iraq and Afghanistan vet, can offer a sympathetic ear to women of her generation.

Smith hears questions like: "Is he just a jerk? Is he crazy? Why am I staying?"

Her husband provides perspective. Once, when she was describing how hard it can be to connect with a husband with PTSD, I heard him tell her gently: "This isn't exactly who we want to be all the time, either."

Officially, Smith opens the Warrior Resource Center every weekday morning at 10. She often arrives two hours before that, but visitors still beat her to the door. Closing is supposed to be 6 p.m. But Smith will stay as long as needed, as she did the evening a Vietnam vet walked in with his wife.

Smith had seen this vet's wife earlier, visiting on what the director now realized was a scouting mission. Smith got the impression the man's wife had dragged him in, because "he was fairly convinced this was not for him."

He fired questions, while his wife "just sat there with this funny little smile on her face and let him have at it."

At first, he didn't want to leave a phone number or email address, suspicious as to how that would be used. He brushed away a form Welcome Home Montrose uses to register vets who want to take advantage of discounts and special deals local businesses offer through the project. The organization checks identification against a government database of vets before issuing "dog tags" that participants can use to claim the discounts at local shops and restaurants.

"By the time we ended the conversation, he wanted his form back, so he could fill in his information," Smith said. She had persuaded him by "just taking the time to stay, to just answer questions and visit with them."

The man's wife had the last word to her husband as they left: "See? I told you."

Fridays are also late days, but not because of reluctant visitors. A group of amateur musicians, vets among them, gathers at the Warrior Resource Center at week's end. They drag the folding chairs into a circle and sit with their guitars, fiddles and harmonicas.

One Friday, an older woman sang sweetly: "Coming for to carry me home." Everyone chimed in. It was a song they knew. It was the sound of community. And underneath was a steady beat of expertise and experience, some of it gleaned formally in classrooms, some from life, and some on the battlefield.

Chapter 5

Family Stories

Welcome Home Montrose Executive Director Smith's husband is the veterans services officer who became an agenda item at a meeting of the county commissioners. Naturally, they chose a room at the drop-in center when I asked to interview them together.

In an era when an American serviceman or woman is more likely to be married than during the conflicts before 9/11, a nationwide 2011 Pew Research Center survey of 712 American veterans of the global war on terror found that among those who were married when they served, about half reported their deployments hurt their relationships with their spouses, and more than 40 percent of those who were parents said it strained ties with their children. For comparison, the Pew researchers also spoke to veterans of previous eras who were married while they served, and a third of them reported that war had taken a toll on their marriages and their parenting. Over the first decade following 9/11, the annual divorce rate among married active-duty enlisted personnel increased, from 2.9 percent in 2000 to 4 percent in 2009.

As we spoke, Emily Smith's left hand and her husband Sheldon's right were tightly gripped, like survivors of a shipwreck grateful to have found one another ashore. The couple shared with me their living, evolving lesson of how war has become part of everyday life in ways that will resonate for generations. Conflict's reverberations are often ignored or misunderstood.

As Emily puts it with fond exasperation, her husband "tends to glaze." She is talking about Sheldon's habit of leaving out some of the scarier details when he recounts his tours as a medic in Iraq and Afghanistan.

Sheldon regularly left what Emily perceived as the relative safety of his base in the Afghan capital, Kabul, to venture north 25 miles to Bagram, where the United States had a massive air base, to ferry broken computers to technicians and back to Kabul.

"You didn't actually mention that to me when you were there," Emily said of that 2012 deployment.

Sheldon is not given to putting himself at the center of his stories. The former sheriff's deputy has a direct gaze and "just the facts, ma'am" delivery. He would struggle to be dramatic even with fellow vets. At least with them, men and women who have seen combat or its impact, he would not have to fill in many details to set a scene, to make a connection. An "old soldier" in his 20s or 30s can swap war stories with one in his 80s, while cutting himself off from his own wife and children.

When he was 18, Sheldon signed up for three years in the Army with no intention of going to war. It was 1989, and he was a restless teen who wanted to get away from Montrose, his hometown.

"I didn't want to work construction. I didn't want to work fast food. And I wasn't ready to go to college."

The Army trained him to be a mechanic and sent him to Germany.

"I'd been in my unit a month when we invaded Iraq. I was, like, 'Oh, crap. I joined a peacetime army.'"

That was Desert Storm, the first Gulf War, when President George H.W. Bush rallied an international coalition that included Arab partners to rout Iraq's Saddam Hussein from Kuwait after his August 1990 invasion of Kuwait.

Sheldon was married and had children. And, as he said, he hadn't joined to fight. But he nonetheless volunteered to go to Kuwait. So did another soldier in his unit.

"They took the other one," Sheldon said. When the war was over, he thought: "Our generation had lucked out, that we had a short war."

His first marriage, before he met Emily, was failing. Sheldon finished the three years of military duty for which he had signed up and went back to Colorado. He got a job as a sheriff's deputy in

San Miguel, the county next door to Montrose that is more isolated up in the mountains and less populated.

But he found he missed military life. He had not grown up in a family that made a ritual of patriotism. He returned from Germany the kind of man who flew the flag at home. He had begun to develop a new sense of duty and honor in the Army, where he also found a new kind of family.

"They tell you what to wear, what to do and when to be there," he said. "Everyone can work together, because we're working toward the same goals. It's maybe not an easy life. But it's a simple life. And there's the camaraderie, there's the comfort of knowing that even people you don't like all that much have got your back."

So, he joined the National Guard, reporting every few weekends for a taste of military life at the Montrose armory.

He was working the night shift at the San Miguel sheriff's department on September 10, 2001. He slept late on September 11.

"I woke up to both towers down."

He immediately called Guard headquarters.

"I asked, 'When are we leaving?' We knew that we would be going."

Sheldon can't say why he was so sure this would be his time. Perhaps it was his experience in the first Gulf War, when he had wanted to go but ended up staying behind in Germany, that made him think now was his turn.

Most of us think of guardsmen as weekend warriors who respond to natural disasters and civil unrest at home, stacking sand bags after disaster strikes and bolstering patrols along the southern U.S. border. But National Guard troops have played a role in every major foreign U.S. military operation. On September 11, New York National Guard members were among the first responders at the World Trade Center. Air Guard pilots from Massachusetts and Vermont patrolled the skies that day. Since the towers fell, the Guard's war-time profile has grown to unprecedented proportions.

About a year after the 2003 start of Operation Iraqi Freedom, some 4,000 members of the North Carolina National Guard's 30th Heavy Separate Brigade set out for Iraq. It was the first complete National Guard combat brigade to deploy since the end of World War II. At times, Guard troops have made up half the combat troops in Iraq.

When Sheldon called his Guard unit on September 11, he was told to drill as normal until further notice. At a Christmas party at the armory in 2002, he learned the orders to deploy to Iraq would arrive within a month. Sheldon got the call in early 2003:

"We're going to war."

He had 36 hours to report to the armory.

As a squad leader, Sheldon's duties included alerting other soldiers in his unit. He remembered calling one who had not even had a chance to train with the unit. Another, a single father, rushed to take his son to family in Wyoming.

Sheldon was divorced and his sons were living with their mother. He called his sheriff, who said, "Go. We'll take care of you when you get back."

The first stop was Wisconsin for more training. The initial plan was to go in with the 4th Infantry through Turkey into northern Iraq. Sheldon and his comrades instead waited in Turkey through the initial combat phase, then headed in through Kuwait.

In Iraq, his base was in what had been a chemical manufacturing plant outside Baghdad. For almost eight months, Sheldon helped run a clinic that treated up to 60 people a day. The patients came from three dozen countries: American Navy corpsman, Pakistanis and Indians who were working in the kitchens, Iraqi interpreters and Japanese, British and other coalition troops.

As a member of a rapid advance medical team, Sheldon also occasionally ventured out of the chemical plant into the chaos of nearby Baghdad. His ambulance, emblazoned with a red cross, was shot at, but never hit. Rock-throwing boys who also targeted the ambulance were more accurate.

"That's war. Especially nonconventional warfare. That's how

it's done," Sheldon said of the harassment. His voice was steady.

The stretch of 2003-2004 during which he was in Iraq was a period of stepped-up attacks on non-military targets: restaurants, embassies, the offices of the Red Crescent. Concern was increasing that American troops were facing not just Saddam loyalists, but al-Qaida and other anti-Western militants converging on Iraq to confront U.S. forces and their allies. In August, 2003, a cement truck loaded with explosives struck the Baghdad hotel that housed United Nations headquarters, killing the U.N. special representative in Iraq and more than a dozen others.

Sheldon and his team responded on October 14, 2003 when a suicide bomber detonated his explosives-laden car near the Turkish Embassy in Baghdad. Along with killing himself, the attacker injured at least two Iraqi security guards. Weeks later, Sheldon was back in Baghdad following a rocket attack on a hotel that killed a U.S. colonel. Sheldon learned later the colonel was an officer he had known back at the factory-turned-military-base.

Once, Sheldon told me as his wife listened: "I realized I was scraping people off my boots so I wouldn't track them into my ambulance. That's particularly psychologically damaging to a medic."

He was detached as he related that horror. He spoke as if he were describing a scene in a movie.

Sheldon had come up with a label for his most haunting experiences: "PTSD moments." The phrase came years later. But long before he finally got a diagnosis of Post-Traumatic Stress Disorder and began to understand what that meant, Sheldon knew war had changed him.

After Iraq, Sheldon returned to Colorado and the job his sheriff had held for him as promised.

"While we were there, we all expected to die. It was weird to come back. We were like, 'It's not supposed to be like this. We're not supposed to be here.'"

Before his deployment, when Sheldon would buy a six-pack of

beer, half the cans would go flat before he got around to drinking them.

"When I got back, I was going through the big bottle of Jack (Daniels) in a week."

PTSD tends to lower inhibitions. So when Sheldon saw the vivacious woman behind the bar near the ski resort town of Telluride, "I actually talked to her, told her that I liked her. I would not have done that before. The thing about PTSD, you just do what you feel like when you feel like it."

The way Emily remembers it, she was the forward one. Sheldon had come in with the sheriff to check that no one underage was getting served. Emily teasingly demanded to see Sheldon's identification.

"My boss thought it was hysterical. So did the sheriff," Emily said.

After that, Sheldon "was pretty much a stalker, he never went away," Emily said. "I decided to keep him."

"He was cute and he was funny and he was a hard worker and he was so intelligent," Emily said, as if ticking off a list she has considered countless times. "I've always known he wasn't perfect. Over the years, it hasn't always been perfect. But it's been worth it."

She stuck with him even though his idea of a date could include showing her photos he had taken of Baghdad streets strewn with blood and body parts in the aftermath of a bombing. Only years later would she learn this was typical behavior for PTSD sufferers.

She saw his happy, easy-going moods as well as his anger. She had a friend, a former Army Ranger, whose perspective and experience she tapped. A previous job in a hospital as a radiology lab assistant also had given her glimpse of trauma and its lasting impact. So, Emily said, she was able to listen to Sheldon "without judging him as being crazy."

"You could see how much he was hurting," she said. But "I really didn't understand it."

Emily had never been near war or had close family members in military service.

Before they met, when Sheldon slept through the initial September 11 news reports, Emily was in her home with her young daughter from a previous relationship. Nadia had had her first birthday the day before. Emily was chasing her around an apartment filled with toys and discarded wrapping paper.

"The television was on. I'm sure it was on some random thing. Then, it switched to that."

From the small-town heart of the United States, it was surreal to watch the dust, smoke, bodies and then the buildings falling as little Nadia fussed for cartoons.

"It was like movie footage. It was hard to even imagine that something like that could happen."

She was working at the hospital then. Later that day at work, Emily found colleagues frantic, trying to reach relatives on the East Coast. She never imagined the unimaginable would come any closer than watching a friend's relief at getting a call through. She never thought September 11 would come home.

"It was so far away. In the center of the country, we just feel so protected."

The war came closer when she met Sheldon. When she married him in 2005, Emily discovered that "the whole family is in the military." In minor ways, such as making plans around the weekends Sheldon was scheduled to drill with his Guard unit, only to see his schedule change. In major ways, as the invisible wounds inflicted on Sheldon by the trauma of Iraq became increasingly apparent. His moods swung. He sought solace in alcohol.

"We'd been living with PTSD at our house," Emily began.

Sheldon finished her thought: "And we didn't know what it was."

PTSD wasn't in the news, at least not that Sheldon noticed, during those first years of conflict. Unlike regular Army soldiers who might return together to the same base, the men and women of Sheldon's Guard unit dispersed when they returned from Iraq. He had no one to compare notes with, no one to tell him that what he was suffering had a name. He felt he had no one to talk to. He told his wife he needed to fix himself.

News of PTSD eventually began to reach them. Sheldon started to see a therapist.

"The drugs didn't work. They made it worse," Emily said.

Then the couple heard about new units designed to help returning soldiers resume civilian lives. Sheldon applied to the closest one, at Fort Carson, a five-hour drive on the other side of the Rockies. He heard he'd been given a place in 2007, the day after his and Emily's son, Xavier, was born.

Emily said at Fort Carson she began to realize her family was part of something enormous happening in America. She saw soldiers with grievous physical injuries and with invisible, traumatic brain injuries. Other spouses told her about behavior with which she was familiar by then.

Soldiers "would go home and play a video game for 18 hours straight, then go to formation. Or they would crawl in a bottle and sober up just for formation. It wasn't just our family that faced those things and dealt with it."

"All the things that were so terrible, so hard, it put them into perspective."

Upon arriving at Fort Carson with Sheldon and their son and daughter, Emily was asked to join the FRG. She did not know what the initials stood for, or that she would soon learn a whole vocabulary of military acronyms.

FRG is Family Readiness Group. The Army wife running Fort Carson's when Emily arrived explained it would be a place where she could learn basics like how the chain of command worked and where to find support services. Emily was already getting a sense of the rhythm of Fort Carson, where the day started with a flag raising and soldiers would stop their cars and get out to salute.

After only a few months, the woman who had welcomed Emily

into the FRG moved on with her family. Frequent transfers are another basic of military life. Emily took over FRG, and helped shift its focus in a way that necessitated an acronym change: WSG, for Warrior Support Group.

The idea, Emily said, was to help families help their men and women who were struggling, untethered from home and from society, after seeing combat. She worked to improve communications between soldiers' superior officers and their families, so that the entire village that was Fort Carson could support its warriors. Years later, Emily looked back to what she learned at Fort Carson to launch the Welcome Home Montrose support group for military spouses.

Emily, Sheldon, Nadia and Xavier would spend over two years at Fort Carson. Sheldon began to heal his PTSD. Then, world events intervened.

Sheldon heard that his Guard unit was being deployed to Afghanistan. U.S. involvement there had been dragging on for nearly a decade. Sheldon felt he knew the challenges. He wanted to be with his old comrades.

Afghanistan, whose Taliban regime harbored al-Qaida as that terror group was planning the September 11 attacks, has a brutally shattered history. So violent and fragmented that, as veteran war correspondent Dexter Filkins wrote in his aptly named memoir of America's war on terror, "Forever War," some Afghans then embraced the Taliban's "beards, the burqas, the whips and stones … Anything but the past." The Americans were another in a series of invaders, and not all Afghans saw reason to welcome them as liberators.

To go, Sheldon had to abandon Fort Carson and its Warrior Transition Unit to rejoin the Guard. He and Emily decided she and the children should move to Montrose, where her husband had extended family.

Emily had come into her own as a leader at Fort Carson. The family had found a network of support among other military families. Now, when they needed them most, they were walking away from others who understood what they were facing.

It was selfish of Sheldon to leave his family, and reckless to risk further damage to himself amid growing evidence that repeated deployments increase the severity of PTSD. But what is a hero without a measure of recklessness and selfishness as well as selflessness? Emily's and Sheldon's story offers no simple answers.

A Vietnam veteran I interviewed while researching this book urged me several times to read *Warrior's Return* by Edward Tick, a psychotherapist based in New York state who has worked with vets from several wars since the 1970s. Tick's book, which takes a long view of the scars on individuals and societies left by wars, gave me a different perspective on Sheldon's choice.

"Greek mythology tells us of the dilemma of Achilles," Tick wrote. "The warrior was given the choice between brutal service and early death with fame and honor or a long but dull and routine civilian existence without honor. Achilles chose the first. Many vets find the return to the ordinary boring and meaningless and make their version of Achilles's choice by reenlisting for another deployment or by staying home but refusing to participate in the ordinary."

Tick's observations allowed me to see the heroism both in Sheldon's quiet determination to seek a second deployment, and in Emily's support of that decision.

Sheldon wanted to be with his Guard unit because he thought some of what he had learned in Iraq would help his fellow soldiers, especially younger ones who had missed the first deployment.

"It was my unit, the unit I'd spent so many years with. I knew there's things you would see that you would never un-see."

He wanted to try to provide the good leadership he believed could lessen the impact of PTSD. Iraq, he said, had been "such a horrid, twisting time. In Afghanistan, I wanted to protect soldiers from the horrid stuff that I could change. This was my opportunity to make sure others didn't go through that."

If nothing else, he would be living proof that they could survive.

"As much as I really didn't want him to go, you could see how important it was for him to go with his friends," Emily said. "It was very important for him to want to go."

In January of 2011, as Emily and the children moved to Montrose. Sheldon went to a U.S. military headquarters installation in the Afghan capital of Kabul.

Emily remembers his deployment as, in part, a year of waiting. She couldn't just pick up the phone or ping Sheldon on Skype when she wanted or needed to talk. She had to wait until he had a chance to get in touch.

Unable to talk to him at will, she put energy into doing for him. Emily learned to preserve food so she could send him cans of her green chili with turkey. For good measure, she shipped cornbread in the jars. She used bubble-wrap "like a crazy person."

Sheldon teased: "The chili was awesome. The cornbread was … meh."

Other goodies could be sent at a reasonable cost in flat rate boxes. Emily boasted that she became a master of squeezing as much as possible into those packages, turning it into a puzzle game you might call military spouse Tetris. Once, though, she arrived at the post office to discover her painstakingly packed box was actually slightly bigger than a flat rate container. The figure on the cash register was astounding.

Emily sent the package anyway, joking that she thought to herself: "I'll just sell a kidney to make up the difference."

For Sheldon's 40th birthday, she packed a joke gift: an inflatable walker.

Sheldon was away as well for his son Xavier's potty training. Sheldon did manage to schedule an R&R to make a surprise visit home for Nadia's September birthday.

"The kids were so excited," Emily said. "Then, he had to go back. And Xavier did NOT understand why he wasn't home for his birthday. And Christmas."

When the little boy turned three in December, Xavier opened his presents as his father watched via Skype, the computer resting on the kitchen table.

Xavier and Nadia also had a large photograph showing Sheldon in uniform. Flat Daddy, he was called. He was especially dear to Xavier. Flat Daddy was carted up Pikes Peak. Once at a restaurant, a thoughtful waiter served the image a drink. Sheldon made electronic recordings as he read children's books that Xavier would play as he gazed at Flat Daddy.

Sheldon had his own way of making his family tangible. He sat down every day with an old-fashioned pen he dipped in ink. The letters he wrote were sealed in envelopes with wax before he sent them to Emily.

"It was carving out that time to stay connected even though we were on different sides of the world," said Emily. She didn't have the patience and her toddler and budding teen ensured she did not always have the time for rituals of inkwell and melted wax, but she did reply to Sheldon with handwritten letters.

The headquarters camp that was Sheldon's home in Afghanistan was named for Army Captain Daniel Eggers, a Special Forces detachment commander who was killed near Kandahar in 2004 by an improvised explosive device. That tribute was a reminder of the risks even though, other than those trips to Bagram, Sheldon didn't mention them to Emily until years later. While he was there, Sheldon described his Afghan deployment as uneventful. He was operations NCO for two clinics and the supply officer.

The camp was also home to Canadian, Italian even Mongolian troops.

"We trained the Mongolian security force in lifesaving skills. They were really tough. They were a lot like the Gurkhas, the Nepalese guys we had in Iraq."

That's as close as Sheldon said his Afghan tour came to resembling his time in Iraq. Commanders didn't allow his team to venture out to donate clothes or offer first aid to Iraqi civilians on humanitarian missions, let alone go on "crazy medical missions like we were doing in Iraq."

He learned the Canadians keep the rhythm when performing CPR by singing "Another One Bites the Dust." Americans sing "Stayin' Alive." The Italians invited him for pizza they topped with olives and tuna, an exotic combination for Sheldon.

"He was spoiled rotten," Emily said. "But he still missed home."

Testament to that were inked letters strewn about his quarters to dry.

Because his second deployment was relatively calm, Sheldon may have thought his return would be smooth. But getting home was no straight shot, neither literally nor figuratively. He was first flown to Kyrgyzstan, then had to spend a few weeks transitioning in at Fort Lewis in Washington state.

"It was really hard knowing he was in the U.S. and we couldn't see him," Emily said.

By the time Sheldon returned to his homeland on January 17, 2012 America had been at war a decade. The sheriff had enthusiastically assured Sheldon his job would be waiting in 2003 when the memory of 9/11 was fresh and his deputy was headed to "axis of evil" member Iraq. Since then, news from the Afghan front had grown more somber and more confusing. Fervor and fear were fading in America in the face of economic concerns closer to home.

The years at Fort Carson had meant more time away from the sheriff's department, which, when Sheldon first got back from Afghanistan, had no money in its budget to hire him. A few weeks later, another deputy quit and Sheldon was slotted in. He sometimes felt his colleagues saw him as an intruder

The San Miguel County seat is an hour's drive over twisting mountain roads to Montrose. The commute added to the stress of Sheldon's return. He was initially unable to find full-time work closer to home and was reluctant to uproot his family again.

Their son Xavier still tenses whenever his family goes near the airport, which shares a patch of land on the edge of Montrose with the National Guards post. For Xavier, airports are for saying farewell to daddy.

"It was amazing how much he picked up on," Emily remembered. "He would ask if Daddy was going to die."

"It's funny, he doesn't have those conversations with me," her husband said.

"Which is crap," said Emily with the characteristic blunt humor that helps her carry the burden of being the parent who stayed behind.

"She has to be mom AND dad too much," Sheldon said.

"He still works a lot with the kids. It's still sharing them with him," said Emily, quick to rise to her husband's defense. She added, though, that they have to work at reminding the children that dad is back and his authority as well as hers must now be part of family decision-making.

Re-establishing a relationship with a preschooler who knows you are mortal is easy compared to re-inserting yourself into the life of a teenage step-daughter. Sheldon bought Nadia a car. It was not quite a bribe. For one thing, the 1970s VW wasn't exactly running when Sheldon found it. He planned to work side-by-side on it with Nadia, in hopes of getting it and his family ties back in shape by the time Nadia was old enough to drive.

When he was in Afghanistan, Sheldon took pains to use pen and ink to write Emily. She responded with hand-written letters, eschewing emails. The romance of that story adds to their image as the perfect couple, both blonde and fresh-faced, with matching athletic gaits. Their personalities are more complementary than similar. Emily is humorous, direct and quick to smile. Sheldon, 10 years her senior, is contemplative.

When Sheldon first got back home, between worries over work and commuting and the kids, there never seemed time for marriage. They have begun to realize mindfulness is necessary now that they are together again, perhaps even more so than when they were apart.

In 2015, in part thanks to lobbying from Welcome Home Montrose, county officials upgraded the position of veterans service officer from part- to full-time. Sheldon had held the part-time position, squeezing in hours around his sheriff's deputy shifts. The upgrade allowed him to quit the sheriff's department, easing the strain commuting had put on his marriage.

On the days the VSO works out of the Welcome Home Montrose drop-in center, Sheldon is in an office 25 feet from Emily's. The couple at first worried they were going from the frying pan of too little time together to the fire of too much. But Emily said it is working out, in part because while their goals at work are similar, they are separate.

"We don't answer to each other," Emily said. "But we can come together."

And, she said, Sheldon is around to make sure she gets out to lunch every now and then.

War is part of Emily and Sheldon's marriage. Their son has never known a world without the vast, international conflict in which the United States is embroiled and his sister's earliest memories are colored by it. Not every American family shares such an experience. Those that do and those that have been spared can all draw strength from the way the Smiths rise every day and try to see to the possibilities and beyond the fear, heartache and uncertainty.

"It's a unique opportunity to start your life over," Emily said. "To decide: How do we want to be, moving forward?"

Chapter 6

Expertise

A visitor joked that if he were looking for a serial killer, he could come to the Warrior Resource Center and someone would say matter of factly: "Well, are you looking for someone who prefers to use machetes or firearms?"

In all seriousness, an outsider might wonder how the drop-in center is able to offer such a wide range of services. City folk have lots of resources. Small towns have people who know their bench is shallow so they have to step into a variety of roles. Like Sheldon Smith, serving as a sheriff's deputy in one county and a veterans services officer in another.

It was Sheldon's wife who told me that serial killer story. She said Montrose "just has such a diversity of expertise and experience." She has seen a lot of that embodied in people who started by visiting on vacation, then returned again and again for brief visits until retirement allowed them to settle permanently.

John Bish was initially one such casual visitor to Montrose. He is a tall, calm Vietnam vet who wears his white hair combed back like a country music star. His eyes, under heavy, gray brows, are friendly and attentive.

Bish is an avid pilot who grew up in Camden, New Jersey and joined the Air Force before the Vietnam War.

"I wanted to make the Air Force a career, and they made a war for me," he said.

He didn't have much to say about Vietnam, except that he flew as a forward air controller, a key position in which a pilot operating close to the action directs attackers in the air, ensuring their fire hits the enemy and not their own fighters. Bish, speaking quietly but with evident pride, described the job to me as "looking out for the ground troops." He was assigned to the 4th Infantry Division.

"I don't have many military stories because I feel everything else I did is more important," he said. "But my experience in the military, my combat experience, makes me welcome here" at Welcome Home Montrose.

Bish can occasionally be found taking a shift at the Warrior Resource Center's front desk, a job that is something like air traffic controller, directing incoming offers and requests for help.

When he's not out front, Bish might be using an office in the back for counseling sessions offered without charge.

After Vietnam, he was a flight instructor at the Air Force Academy, across the Rockies from Montrose in Colorado Springs. He got a degree in counseling while he was there. When he retired from the military, he found a job as a probation officer in Austin, Texas.

A few years later, when his mother had a fall that left her unable to care for his father, who had Alzheimer's, Bish moved back to New Jersey to be close to his parents. He had grown up knowing his father as a caring man who didn't shirk his family responsibilities, but who struggled with anger and anxiety he tried to hide. It was only years later that Bish's mother told him the man she knew before World War II had not had that rage and fear.

"I wondered what had happened to my friend, because this doesn't seem like the guy I married," she once told her son.

"It was called shell shock back then," said Bish, whose father served in Europe and would complain about losing four years of his life to war.

"He didn't put us on his lap and tell us stories. But we got bits and pieces," Bish said. "He was almost flippant about getting a Purple Heart. He would say, 'A bullet ricocheted.'"

"He was angry for a very long time."

Bish eventually moved his parents into an assisted living facility. The transfer entailed disposing of four containers of old bikes, refrigerators, fencing supplies and other items his dad had collected over the years. The hoarding will be familiar to many who have lived with survivors of trauma.

Bish described his father's collection as "an eyesore to my mom, but interesting to me." His nonjudgmental attitude was needed when illness left his father increasingly more suspicious and physically aggressive. The son found he could calm the elder vet, responding without fear or any urge to hit back.

His parents settled, Bish again looked for work. This time, it was as a counselor at a state-run substance abuse center for adolescents in New Mexico.

What Bish calls his "mosaic" of experiences put him in a position to mentor across generations. At Welcome Home Montrose, that can mean young vets barely out of adolescents who are self-medicating their post-Iraq PTSD with alcohol and marijuana, as well as older vets who like Bish's dad had hid suffering for decades.

Bish came to Welcome Home Montrose almost by chance. When he was living in New Mexico, he often drove through Montrose on the way to visit a friend in nearby Grand Junction. On one trip, Bish read an article about the vet project in the Grand Junction newspaper. That inspired him to drop by the Warrior Resource Center.

"I stopped here right after my 70th birthday and just started crying," he said. His were tears of joy.

He found on that visit that Welcome Home Montrose was planning an outdoors festival. Bish glanced down the list of events and saw "equestrian therapy." He had grown up with horses and once lent a hand to a friend in Texas who was rescuing wild horses. He volunteered to help out at a stable outside Montrose where vets could learn to look after horses as a way to care for themselves.

After that, Bish returned to New Mexico long enough to retire from his counseling job and pack up. Once he had moved into an apartment in Montrose, Welcome Home Montrose founder Kline asked him to take a course in Mental Health First Aid. The internationally recognized approach to recognizing and responding to signs someone is suicidal includes specialized training for those who know veterans.

Bish has subsequently trained people in the course in Montrose and the neighboring, even smaller town of Olathe.

Bish has been called in to counsel veterans when their friends and family grow concerned about the possibility of suicide. He sits in on a PTSD support group that meets weekly at the Warrior Resource Center, sometimes leading it when the counselor who drives in from the VA hospital in Grand Junction can't make it. The group members talk about their fears, nightmares, their gripes. Bish said his contribution can consist of getting the conversation going, directing vets to go on without him, then discretely bowing out.

Kline calls Bish "that guy, the guy who's got your back."

Center director Smith could be Bish's daughter. They share broad, open faces and reassuring manners. But her expertise is different than his. While Bish knows when to bow out, Smith knows when to wade in.

Smith has taken on tasks like battling the bureaucracy to ensure that vets could use federal housing vouchers to help pay the rent in Montrose. Before Smith intervened, that benefit was only available one place in the region, the population hub of Grand Junction, an hour away. She's helped persuade three organizations to provide boxes of food vets can take home, an alternative to dining at a soup kitchen that can save the pride of an old soldier. She was the one who got the Veterans Administration to send a counselor to the drop-in center.

Smith first came to Welcome Home Montrose not to help, but because she was the one in need of aid. The leader of the Montrose VFW post connected Kline to his nephew, who is Smith's husband, when the couple was looking for a place to live. Kline directed Emily and Sheldon Smith to an organization that offered housing advice for vets.

Kline also needed a hand at the time. She had recently learned that Montrose would host a stage of the USA Pro Cycling

Challenge, which would bring thousands of spectators and more than 100 professional cyclists to town. Kline had not yet started Welcome Home Montrose. She was in the planning stages and saw the race as an opportunity to remind people of the needs of vets in their midst and what they could do for them. She had proposed a secondary event for wounded vets the day the pros were in town. She asked Smith if she had any ideas for organizing a cycling race.

"Emily said, 'Oh, sure,' like it was no big deal. It was a really big deal to me," Kline said.

Smith, who is only half-joking when she calls Kline the "four-star civilian," tackled the request like she had been given orders from an officer. When her family lived at the Fort Carson Army post near Colorado Springs, she had helped create a safety net for soldiers. She had dreaded leaving the close-knit community she had found at Fort Carson to come to Montrose. Perhaps she also dreaded losing a sense of mission. Welcome Home Montrose became her new purpose.

Smith's work at Fort Carson had included event planning. She came back to Kline two days after getting the request about the bike tour with an outline of an adaptive cycling race and a list of committees that would be needed and the number of people that would have to be recruited for a variety of tasks. Smith broke down work such as manning the start and finish lines, distributing refreshments and cleaning up into goals with deadlines. She proposed series of committee meetings, laid out on a spread sheet in oh-one-hundred-hour military-time increments. She ended her report with a designation: "unclassified."

"That's how I met Emily," Kline said. "She had it unbelievably figured out. I kept on calling her, saying, 'I need a little help with this, I need a little help with that.'"

Smith responded to each call, even though when the idea of Welcome Home Montrose was first outlined to her, she scoffed - in detailed terms.

"It's insane," Smith told Kline. "You would double your

population. Some of these people aren't interested in small town life. Some of these people are at a place where you might not want them around."

Kline heard exactly the kind of tough questioning she thought she needed to ensure her vision could be transformed into a workable reality. She talked Smith into joining the project.

Kline's ability to recognize and exploit talent is one of the reasons for the success of Welcome Home Montrose. In landing Smith, she got a lifetime of skills and a personal passion. Smith has been working since she was in high school, when she cut lenses for an optician. Later, she worked in a hospital radiology lab, as a paralegal and a bartender. At home, she juggles a toddler and a teen, which speaks of her patience and flexibility. At Fort Carson, she honed her attention to detail and people skills and developed a familiarity with all things military that would serve her well at Welcome Home Montrose. Her sense of community may be her most important asset.

"I've always wanted everyone to be involved," she said.

In a promotional video that was made for Welcome Home by a colleague who knows Smith well, photos of the Smiths flash by as the Lady Antebellum song "I was here" plays:

"I want to do something that matters.

"I want to try to touch a few hearts in this life."

From the vantage point of her desk at the resource center, Smith has learned people in Montrose care deeply about vets. She had seen them come out in force to see off fighters, her husband among them, headed to Afghanistan. When her husband and his comrades from across the country returned to a nearby National Guard base, crowds appeared to welcome them back. Small towns don't always embrace outsiders, Smith knew. But this patriotic town did not see vets, wherever they were from, as outsiders.

"Montrose is bigger than just the small town where everyone knows your name," she said. "But it's still a small town."

A small town in which Smith has become well-known because

of her work with Welcome Home Montrose. Supporters of a children's advocacy group saw her as a celebrity, so they asked Smith to take part in a dancing with the stars style fundraiser. Smith knew the group as one that had helped veterans' families, so she couldn't refuse outright as she wanted to. Instead, she said she'd have to check with her husband, assuming she'd be able to hide behind his shyness. Instead, he said: "Why not?"

That's how Smith and her husband ended up being coached by a choreographer who worked with the town's community theater. Their son teased his parents so charmingly during rehearsals that the choreographer, recognizing a natural ham when she saw one, suggested he should try out for the 2016 summer musical. Their daughter tagged along to the auditions, where Smith and her husband were dragooned to read a few lines as well. The entire family ended up cast in *The Velveteen Rabbit,* about a stuffed toy that becomes real because of his connection to a small boy.

Smith remembered sitting backstage in full makeup, looking at her family and wondering, "How did we get here?"

Small towns can offer opportunities to connect in ways city dwellers may never know.

Welcome Home Montrose has not always taken Smith to unfamiliar places. Smith became so well known as a bureaucracy buster, a family in neighboring Olathe asked for her help when they held a memorial service for a man who went missing in Korea in 1951.

Sergeant Eugene Putney's niece, Cyndi Duran, recalled that a radio he bought his parents in 1948 sat in her grandparents' kitchen throughout her childhood.

Though she never met him "I always knew I had an Uncle Gene. He was that present in my grandparents' home," Duran said.

Putney was a supply truck driver with the 2nd Infantry Division during a Cold War conflagration that the United States saw as part of an international battle against communism. The Korean War began in the summer of 1950 when soldiers from Soviet-backed

North Korea crossed the 38th parallel into South Korea. U.S. troops arrived within weeks of the invasion to support the South. Three years and some 5 million deaths later, the war ended. But the Korean peninsula remains divided.

A niece Putney never had a chance to meet mourned him. Faraway wars can have enduring impact at home.

A man who had fought alongside Putney told the family "Uncle Gene" had died in his arms after being shot in the chest, stomach and leg in a fierce battle. Both the witness and Putney were taken prisoner after that fight. The army, though, said the account could not be verified. Putney's parents died with neither the closure of having his remains identified and sent home, nor official word of what had happened. He was one of four sons they saw off to war and the only one not to return.

In 2014, Putney's sister and brothers decided it was time, even without a body, to place a marker for him alongside the graves of their parents. They turned to Smith for help arranging a gravestone from Veterans Affairs.

Mourners who filed into the clapboard Olathe Assembly of God Church on a hot summer day were handed packets of gum. They were told that the last letter Putney's parents sent him contained gum and candy. The parents' letter and treats, which had been sent as birthday presents, were returned as undeliverable.

For the long-delayed memorial service, relatives decorated the church with patriotic bunting and streamers in vases and photographs of a 19-year-old Putney. He had not yet grown into his ears or his military cap. His smile was slight. He looked like someone who would have teased his niece.

"I hope this heals your heart," a tearful Duran told her aunt, Oneta Ballard.

"My family deserves closure," Duran continued, turning to other mourners who included great grandnieces who had taken up the patriotic theme by layering on three tank tops each, in red, white and blue.

If tank tops might have struck some as too casual for church, others might have seen them as genuine and unpretentious. And they certainly suited the weather once the group made its way to the cemetery.

There under a blazing Colorado sun, facing the gravestone Smith had helped secure, Ballard cried as a guard of honor presented a folded flag "on behalf of a grateful nation." Welcome Home Montrose volunteers could be spotted among the seven riflemen who fired a 21-gun salute and the three flag bearers standing at attention under an ungentle sun.

Taps sounded over the gathered generations. I had come to Montrose following 21st century wars home. In the cemetery that day, I was reminded how many wars had preceded the war on terror. And I caught a sobering glimpse of future conflict.

The bugler for Putney was a teen girl, an ROTC student from the local high school. In Putney's day, it might have been hard to imagine a woman fighting alongside him. Toward the end of 2015, Defense Secretary Ash Carter made an announcement that was historic if long-expected: the U.S. military would allow women to serve in all combat roles, even as Army Rangers, Green Berets, Navy SEALS, Marine Corps infantry, Air Force parajumpers.

By the time Carter made his announcement, many women had already been in harm's way driving trucks and serving in other support roles in a war with no clear forward lines. With the pool of volunteers so small, women were stepping up.

With an end to our war on terror evidently so far off, it is all too easy to see the girl bugling in the Olathe cemetery taking her place on the front lines one day. And crucial to see her coming home, perhaps sharing a cup of coffee with her elders at Welcome Home Montrose.

Chapter 7

Word Spreads

Gary Love is the man I first saw on Kline's computer screen carrying his son Todd to a roaring river. In 2011, the elder Love came across a newspaper article about the beginnings of Welcome Home Montrose. He was suspicious when he saw Kline quoted as saying she was inspired by seeing the Loves on TV.

Love tracked down Kline's phone number and called. Kline invited him to see for himself. She raised money for his plane ticket from Maryland, where he had moved from his home in South Carolina to be close while his son was recovering at Walter Reed National Military Medical Center.

Love visited Montrose in December of 2011.

"He came out a skeptic. And he left as an ambassador," Kline said.

Love took up the story when I met him a few years after his first visit to Montrose. He said he was not so much skeptical as unclear why someone who did not know his son and lived so far away could be inspired to act.

For years, Love would remain a bit baffled that his son had played a part in Welcome Home Montrose. His son was not trying to point the way for anyone, Love said.

"He just does what he does," Love told me, adding he believes he has cried more than the younger man ever has over the wartime injury that left his son without his legs and left arm.

"As a father, it tears me up to see that my son, at 25, will have to spend the rest of his life with no legs. He proves every day that he can live it. He says he was bored with legs and God evened the playing field," Gary Love said. "As a fellow Marine, I can't be prouder of him."

"I've got a video of my son walking on his hands (one a

prosthetic) on a treadmill. Not for any reason. Just because. He figures out how to get around," the father said.

"The word hero is thrown around quite a lot. My son would say the people who helped him the day he was hurt are heroes. Heroes do extraordinary things under pressure. The young men that come back with their physical and mental injuries, it's what they do after that makes them heroes. If you reach out and help other people be better, then you're a hero. Stepping up to the plate and being what God asked you to be no matter what, that's what makes you a hero."

After Team River Runner taught his son to kayak, Love continued to volunteer for the group. He helped on outings even when his son was not along.

"I'll pick these guys up, I'll tote them to the end of the world. I'll get them up on skis and pick them up and get them on again if they fall over. I'll jump in the water if they flip over on their kayaks," Love told me. "You can't do it because you feel sorry for them. You've got to do it because you respect them."

Gary Love served three years in the Marines and is the son of a career Marine. He grew up near Parris Island, South Carolina, which has been a Marine post since the late 18th century. Love is one of the many examples of vets I interviewed for this book who have a tremendous capacity to continue serving their families and their communities long after they have taken off their uniforms.

After serving in the Marines, Gary Love went on to operate high-rise construction cranes.

"I've always been a rough and tumble type of guy," he said. "Compassion wasn't one of my strong suits."

When his son came back from war, Gary Love cared for him as he had done in the early days of fatherhood. The elder Love spent two years at his son's side at Walter Reed. Now, the resilient Todd Love is living an independent life. Gary Love, back home in South Carolina, said the reservoir of tenderness and patience he discovered he had at Walter Reed served him well as he cared for his aging, ailing mother.

Love the father and Kline the mother each are able to tap into parental instincts and mentor young people who are not their own children.

Love told me that while Kline's challenges do not compare with the wounds of war, he has observed her at the hard work of persuading others her idea was not crazy. He has seen the time, energy and money she has devoted to Welcome Home Montrose. He has seen her persistence.

"Melanie saw what was going on with my son ... and that inspired her to get off her bum and do something. She's the hero of Welcome Home Montrose. She won't say that. But most heroes don't say that."

On his first visit to Montrose in 2011, Love spent several days watching Kline meet with members of the Chamber of Commerce and city administration, often showing them the video in which he appears with his son. The drop-in center did not exist at the time.

"A fresh concept was all it was when I came," he said.

But it was enough to move him to phone Jared Bolhuis, the man who had introduced his son to kayaking. Bolhuis is the age of Love's son. Love took a fatherly approach, saying: "Jared, this is some cool stuff going on. You need to meet Melanie." Bolhuis trusted the elder Love enough to contact Kline. She told him: "Hey, you helped us. You inspired us. Come out and see what we're doing."

Chapter 8

A Newcomer

Bolhuis, a native of Zeeland, Michigan, population 5,000, came to Montrose for a weekend in April 2012. He thought as he flew out that what he had heard from Love about Kline and her project could not be as good as it sounded.

"What I found out was that Melanie was, honest to God, a big-hearted woman who wanted to help," he told me. He did not think she understood what she was getting into, but he saw she was determined to try.

After that brief fact-finding visit, Bolhuis returned to spend the 2012 summer learning more about Montrose. On Memorial Days when he was a uniformed Marine in the nation's capital, it wasn't unusual for strangers in bars to offer him drinks. It seemed to him like every day was Memorial Day in Montrose.

"People are so supportive of the military here," Bolhuis said. "There is just something about this community, about the individuals, that is so powerful. I don't know where they get it from out here. I don't know if it's in the water."

By the time the Warrior Resource Center opened in September of 2012, Bolhuis was no longer a visitor. He was co-executive director of Welcome Home Montrose, a lofty title with no salary attached. Fortunately, Bolhuis receives military retirement benefits. Kline did find a donor to pay rent for his apartment.

Bolhuis's title lacked a job description, leaving him free to make of it what he could. He made videos that Kline used to tell the story of why and how Montrose was reaching out to vets. Bolhuis had been treated for war injuries at a military hospital and worked as a patient advocate while there, walking fellow soldiers and their families through the hospital bureaucracy. That gave him expertise when men and women in Montrose wanted help signing up for VA benefits.

"I may not be a Marine anymore, but I'm still fighting every day for my brothers," Bolhuis told me at one of our first meetings, when he was new to his role as executive director.

Bolhuis could have stepped off a recruiting poster: tall, blond, and blue-eyed. That helped make him a compelling figure when he appeared on behalf of Welcome Home Montrose, telling his own story in classrooms and board rooms. It can be disconcerting to hear his story, which should belong to a much older man, one with filme noir instead of heartthrob looks.

Weeks into his deployment in Afghanistan in 2008, he told me in a tone as emotionless as a Raymond Chandler character's: "I got blown up."

His job as a gunner had left him fairly exposed in a turret when his unit was on the road. A 120-mm mortar exploded five feet from his truck. The concussive wave knocked Bolhuis out. Less than a month later, a 500-pound bomb exploded 40 feet from his truck. Again, he was left temporarily unconscious.

Bolhuis did not seek treatment because he did not want his eight-month deployment to be cut short. He loaded up on pain medication to fight migraines and tried to ignore periods of confusion. He did everything he could "to stay in the fight."

When he got home in November 2008, the damage done by his two close brushes with explosives was invisible. But he began to notice problems he had been too busy in Afghanistan to think about: bad balance, bouts of memory loss.

"It was kind of a lost feeling. Constantly," he said.

He might have continued to ignore the symptoms if not for a buddy's wedding in Michigan. He was the best man. One moment, he was standing next to the groom. The next, he was waking up on the ground.

Bolhuis had been a member of a Marine ceremonial unit in the nation's capital before he was deployed to Afghanistan. He could not believe he had blacked out while performing a ceremonial duty of sorts at the wedding.

"Learning how to stand is what I was trained to do," he said. He had to face the fact that something was very wrong.

After the wedding, Bolhuis went to a hospital for an MRI. In early 2009 he was sent to Walter Reed, the premier national military hospital near Washington in Bethesda, Maryland. He would remain there for more than three years.

His diagnosis included traumatic brain injury, or TBI. The advanced armor that soldiers wear and in which their vehicles are wrapped means they can survive onslaughts of bombs and bullets that would have killed fighters in earlier wars. But under attack, the most crucial organ is knocked against the skull and left bruised and battered. Civilians know the mildest form of TBI, a concussion, from playground and sports field accidents. More severe injuries can result in changes in personality and affect thinking and moods for long periods. The most severe TBI can result in death. Experts are able to do little more than treat the symptoms with medication for anxiety, convulsions and other after-effects; surgery; and rehabilitation therapy.

Bolhuis also has Post Traumatic Stress Disorder, or PTSD, sometimes called the signature medical issue of the post-9/11 wars. The impact on the mind of the horrors of war can leave PTSD sufferers with inescapable flashbacks to the traumatic event, emotional numbness, sleeplessness, anger that is hard to control.

At Walter Reed, doctors and therapists "did what they could," Bolhuis said. "I've been through basically every treatment the military could offer."

Some of his symptoms receded or responded to medications. But years after leaving the hospital he still had memory lapses and trouble following a long-range task through from assignment to completion. In the end, the military told him he would never be well enough to continue as a Marine. Bolhuis had joined at 17, three days after his high school graduation. He initially signed up for four years, with every intention of doing 20. At 24, when other young men are starting their careers, Bolhuis was retiring on medical grounds.

"A 24-year-old with a pension," Bolhuis said, shaking his head at the cruel absurdity. "My dad and I joke that I retired before he did."

While he could joke later, the news initially left him in tears.

"I was fighting to get back in the infantry for two and a half years," he said. "When they finally told me I was done, it was the biggest kick in the gut I'd ever had.

"My entire future had disappeared."

He had seen his future as part of a tradition. Military service is "the family job," Bolhuis said. His mother Jackie had been an accountant in the Army Reserves and her sister was active duty Army. His two younger sisters repeated the pattern set by their aunt and mother: one joined the Army National Guard, the other active duty Army. Both Bolhuis's grandfathers and a paternal uncle had served. His father did not, but met his mother when he took a few ROTC classes while in college.

"Every branch of my family tree has someone in the military," Bolhuis said.

When he was 10 or 11, he told his Army aunt that he wanted to grow up to be an Army sniper.

"She said, 'Do you want to join the military?'"

"Yes."

"Then join the Marines."

"Why?"

"Because no one will ever hold their head higher than the Marines."

In high school, he came home from classes one day and told his parents he had stopped by the office of a Marine recruiter. The recruiter, he said, would be by that night with permission papers for them to sign.

In many ways, Bolhuis is typical of members of the force that America has sent to the front lines of the war on terror. The

Washington Post and Kaiser Family Foundation pollsters found in a 2014 survey that almost six in 10 Iraq and Afghanistan vets came from non-urban areas. Many might say, like Bolhuis, that the military is a family tradition. More than four in 10 are children of vets and half had grandparents who served.

"This generation's veterans are more diverse than any other contingent America has shipped to war. Thirty-five percent are non-white, more than one in 10 are women and a quarter are now 40 years or older," the pollsters also found. "But much of the force remains homogeneous: Half are Southerners, two-thirds lack a college degree ...."

Bolhuis's mother Jackie thought the Marines were a good option for a young man who did not seem ready for college, even though it was 2004 and the nation was already years into a war on two fronts with no clear end in sight.

After the Twin Towers fell on September 11, 2001, Operation Enduring Freedom was launched with a U.S.-British bombing campaign on October 7, 2001. The target was Afghanistan's Taliban, the extremist Islamic regime that was harboring al-Qaida, the multinational terror group responsible for September 11.

President George W. Bush accused the Iraqi leader Saddam Hussein of possessing and making weapons of mass destruction and supporting al-Qaida and other terrorist groups. Operation Iraqi Freedom was launched on March 19, 2003, with attacks by U.S. and coalition forces on Baghdad.

Jackie Bolhuis believes that "people who don't have any experience in the military tend to freak out when their kids join."

But she had always looked at the military as a job. Yes, one that could be dangerous. But civilian life also has dangers.

Her son did not head immediately from high school into danger. During his first four years, he was assigned to the Alpha Company at Marine Barracks in Washington, D.C. Duties included taking part in funerals at Arlington National Cemetery, laying wreaths at the Tomb of the Unknown Soldier and parading at the

Marine Corps War Memorial.

After completing his first four years, Bolhuis signed up for another four. Almost immediately, he was deployed to Afghanistan. His mother had known at the back of her mind that deployment orders would come one day. And that day, she would no longer be able to think of the military as just another job. The Bolhuises, like the Smiths and the Putneys and so many families, were being changed by war.

Because Bolhuis is so young and so insistently upbeat, it can sometimes seem he was not deeply affected by war and injury. His demeanor can be a shield. So can keeping his distance. During his years at Walter Reed, he would visit his parents in Michigan, but waved them off when they attempted to come to him in Maryland.

His parents, who had seen him collapse at the wedding, heard very little from him about his injuries or treatment.

"He always told us everything was fine, that it was no big deal," Jackie Bolhuis told me.

When he was still being treated at Bethesda, visits home were sometimes punctuated by shouts for help at night. He had left his bed to go to the bathroom, and fallen.

"There were a lot of things that had to heal in his brain," his father David told me.

David and Jackie would come to learn that their son's withdrawal from his family was a symptom of depression. His father, an aerospace engineer, had done enough research on his own into 21st century battlefield injuries to worry about what disappointment over the end of his military career could do to his son.

"It's not hard for these guys to get lost," David Bolhuis told me.

If he had come home after leaving the hospital, Bolhuis "would have crashed," his father said. "He needed to find a way to help people."

Instead of going home to Michigan, Bolhuis accepted an offer of a basement apartment from the Team River Runner founder.

Team River Runner is the Maryland group with whom Bolhuis was working when Kline saw him on TV offering a fellow wounded Marine an adventure on the water.

Bolhuis had initially come to Team River Runner to learn and build on boating skills he had learned as a child. He graduated to trainer for the organization. He once wore goggles blacked out with duct tape to race around an obstacle course set up for boaters on a lake. He wanted to experience what kayaking was like for the blind vets with whom he worked.

Coming to Montrose can be seen as a step on a journey Bolhuis began with Team River Runner.

Bolhuis continued to have dark bouts in Montrose. And as when he had been in Maryland, he kept his family at a distance. He would not respond to calls, cell phone texts or emails for long periods

"I think a lot of it was due to the medications," his mother said.

She would prepare for a visit to Montrose, only to have Bolhuis ask her to postpone at the last minute, saying he was too busy.

His parents got around that by "dropping in" for a day or two on their way to see one of his sisters, who was living in Utah. At each visit, he would be happy to see his parents and proud to show them around town. They also were reassured to see that he had support from many people in Montrose.

"From the moment we met everybody, we just loved them," mother Jackie said. "There's a lot of great people out there who watched out for him."

Dave Bolhuis found Montrose to be the kind of town where strangers would ask how he was, not as a routine greeting, but out of genuine interest in his answer.

In the early summer 2013, Bolhuis's Welcome Home Montrose colleagues had invited two dozen Iraq and Afghanistan war veterans to town for a festival of fly-fishing, rafting, hiking and other outdoor activities they dubbed Mission No Barriers. Volunteers were needed as guides, cooks, drivers, messengers and more. Jackie and Dave came to pitch in.

"We were super-excited. We were going to be involved with something he was involved in and we were going to be with him," his mother said.

Instead, they found that Bolhuis was in a moment when he seemed to be pulling away from Welcome Home Montrose. His parents still got to as many events as possible, appointing themselves official photographers, taxiing people where they needed to be, inflating rafts, "just seeing a need and doing it," Jackie Bolhuis said.

Her son, remembering that visit, said: "I get my willingness to serve from both my parents."

That part of his personality survived what war had done to him.

As co-executive director of Welcome Home Montrose, Bolhuis brought the skills of a platoon leader, able to rally enthusiasm in himself and others to quickly complete a contained task. But much of the painstaking duties fell to his partner director, Smith.

"I'm a great ideas guy, but Emily's the one who can make ideas happen," Bolhuis said.

He was restless at a desk, and management duties such as making plans for others to follow were a challenge for someone with TBI. He had to give up to co-executive director post after a few months, though he remained a fluid and engaging spokesman for Welcome Home Montrose and a frequent visitor to its drop-in center

Bolhuis tried many roles in Montrose, including one on stage. At a friend's suggestion, he auditioned for a community theater production of *A Few Good Men,* and got a role in the military courtroom drama. His parents came out from Michigan to see his stage debut. According to a local newspaper's critic, Marine defendant Lance Corporal Harold Dawson was "played to perfection by Jared Bolhuis." A soldier again, if only on stage.

In the fall of 2014, I drove 30 miles outside Montrose to catch up with Bolhuis. He had been taking silversmithing lessons from

Kline's sons. They had put him to work a few days a week behind the counter in their Ouray jewelry shop. I found Bolhuis at his affable best, teasing a browser into buying a silver necklace.

Bolhuis was commuting from Montrose to Ouray, once a silver mining camp that now survives on tourists drawn by its Old West charm. The day I met him there, as his dog reclined at his feet, Bolhuis spoke of giving up his Montrose apartment and moving to Ouray. He had his eye on an apartment in a century-old building that housed the jewelry store. He also was considering buying and running Ouray's ice cream parlor.

When I visited the next month, I heard about a new plan. A Costa Rican adventure tourism company had offered Bolhuis a job as a whitewater guide. First, he was to travel to California and South Carolina for courses in swift water rescue and other specializations. He had traded his station wagon for a heavy duty truck to haul all the gear he and his dog would need for a combination camping and learning cross-country trip. He was considering taking a stab at learning Spanish.

With his medical and retirement benefits, "I could stay at home playing video games all day. But I need to be doing something. I need to be helping people."

He had not quite shaken the lost feeling. But he had learned how to stand again and seemed intent on running toward some goal. But he needed to find a way to focus.

Chapter 9

A New Idea

The first time I saw Bolhuis on Montrose's river, I also saw the healing power of the waters.

The air temperature was in the 40s on an overcast winter morning. I did not want to imagine how cold the Uncompahgre River was, let alone dip even a finger in to check. But Bolhuis's exuberance warmed the gloom. The former Marine pulled his kayak from the roof of his station wagon, stripped to the wet suit he wore under his clothing and pulled on a helmet.

He hopped into his craft, slipped into the rushing current and darted around boulders and over drops. I watched him execute an expert roll in a "come on in, the water's fine" gesture that failed miserably at convincing me that it was a good day for boating.

Bolhuis had been an avid boater in all kinds of weather since he learned to kayak as a child. When his own sense of purpose had been shattered by war wounds, he found Team River Runner. The adventure sports project for wounded vets helped Bolhuis reconnect with a part of himself he had thought was lost and to discover he had abilities he had never imagined.

I had seen Bolhuis on the water before, of course: with Team River Runner on the Potomac near Washington in the video that inspired Welcome Home Montrose. In Montrose, Bolhuis again found focus through water.

The stretch of the Uncompahgre River that runs through Montrose is about as wide as a country road. The United States Geological Survey classifies the Uncompahgre as a tributary of the Gunnison River. The Uncompahgre, its name taken from a Native American Ute phrase that can be translated as "red waters," flows for about 75 miles across southwestern Colorado from Lake Como in neighboring San Juan County to join the Gunnison River in

Delta, a town 20 miles north of Montrose.

In Montrose, the Uncompahgre reaches a point where it acts as the border between manicured ball fields and playgrounds on one side, and on the other a roughly groomed trail that takes hikers up a rise. This stretch had for years been the focus of a proposal to create a whitewater park to boost tourism in the region. The idea had ebbed and flowed without ever gaining much momentum. Moving forward required unity among city and county officials who had found it tough to cooperate.

Bolhuis and other vets proposed to those officials that the water park serve disabled as well as able-bodied enthusiasts. The energy and fresh perspective brought by Bolhuis and others rekindled interest in the project. County commissioners pledged to work with the city. Soon the city manager had approved the engineering contract for initial work on the river. People were coming together because of Welcome Home Montrose.

"Welcome Home Montrose is about taking care of veterans AND building community," Bolhuis said. "The veterans coming into the community are bringing just as much as they are getting. The people that we're bringing in are becoming part of this community."

But first, action had to be taken to address concerns from the state's wildlife division about the impact the water park would have on fish. Work began in 2013 to build trout habitats upstream on a quarter-mile stretch. During the winter, before spring snow melt raised water levels, heavy equipment rumbled at the task of re-grading the river bed and placing boulders that formed fish homes.

Montrose got encouragement along the way. In 2013, the National Civil League recognized the community as an All-America City, a designation dating to 1949 that celebrates "trail-blazing efforts to bring all aspects of the community together to tackle the most pressing local issues."

Montrose Mayor David Romero would later acknowledge that

"one idea behind the Water Sports Park was to make Montrose a more welcoming place for our vets. ... This was a major contributing factor to Montrose receiving the All-America City Award." The achievement is touted in red-white-and-blue banners around town and celebrations in 2013 were held in front of the Welcome Home Montrose Warrior Resource Center.

The paradise for fish that was the precursor to the water sports park was completed in February of 2014. Then, construction on the park began. Pipes diverted waters in stages to allow work on the river bed. Changes to the river included arranging boulders to create new channels and smoothing drops.

It all was completed within budget and about two months ahead of schedule, achievements that would be cause for celebration on any large project in a community of any size. By early 2015, all that was left was work on ramps that a kayaker using a wheelchair could use to slip into and out of the water, final touches on nearby recreation trails and making the site look pretty.

Bolhuis didn't wait for the finishing touches. On January 24, 2015, he launched himself on the official maiden kayak run through the park. Bolhuis said the three years of attending city and county council meetings and consulting with community members, bureaucrats and designers all seemed worthwhile once he was on the water.

"I would be honored beyond belief to be able to do a first descent anywhere," Bolhuis told me, sounding boyish and almost breathless in his excitement. "To be able to do a first descent on a whitewater park that I helped design, pass the legislation for and got it built, that is an absolute dream come true."

For his maiden run, Bolhuis used one of the longer kayaks designed to get down a river quickly and efficiently. He splashed first over a steep slope that, had he been on a shorter play boat, he would have sat on doing flips and twists, playing rodeo cowboy on a bucking steer. The second obstacle was gentler, creating a wave that "you could bring a surfboard and stand on as long as you wanted," Bolhuis said. The third was another abrupt drop.

If landscaping equipment had not still been strewn in and alongside the course, Bolhuis would have repeated that alternating series through the park's last three obstacles. Halfway was enough for him to get a feel for the flow. He could see where amateur kayakers could work on their skills and, especially in the summer when the dam-fed river would be higher, where more advanced boaters could be challenged.

Water enthusiasts would not necessarily have to be equipped with kayaks.

"The waves were pushy enough so that Joe Blow in his inner tube with his buddies and tub of beer can still go straight through," Bolhuis said.

On a Saturday morning a few months later, Bolhuis demonstrated more than competence on the river. The park was still not officially open, but Bolhuis was kayaking. He noticed a small boy was playing, jumping from rock to rock across the river. The Montrose Daily Press reported the next day, March 15, 2015, that Bolhuis saw the boy slip.

"I pulled off the course and paddled to where I thought the current would take him," Bolhuis told the newspaper. "When I got there I saw purple, the color of his shirt. I reached down, plucked him out of the water and laid him across my kayak."

The child, estimated by Bolhuis to be 4 or 5 years old, was conscious. A woman, probably the mother, carried the boy away before Bolhuis could learn his name. The newspaper quoted a witness, Nathan Brewer, as saying the child was fully submerged and in the water for 30 seconds.

"It was a well-executed heroic move," Brewer said of Bolhuis's reaction.

"We want everyone to enjoy the park, but it can be dangerous," Bolhuis said. "We just want parents to watch their children and for people to be careful around the water."

Ensuring that the park had something for everyone was a key

consideration throughout the design process to which Bolhuis contributed. Once the park was completed, its accessibility features included a wide trail along the banks for nearly 2,000 feet that was paved with concrete to make it wheelchair-friendly. Improvements also were made on 1,900 feet of dirt trail and new signs were posted. A new sidewalk linked handicapped parking to the trail. Benches of rock and concrete were added where spectators could lounge and kayakers could rest between runs along the course, which was more than 1,000 feet.

"Montrose now has its very own Water Sports Park," the city said on its website. "The park has been designed with all citizens in mind, from ankle waders to expert kayakers."

A chill, steady rain fell on May 16, 2015 when the city celebrated the park's completion with small-town fanfare. Members of several 4-H clubs kicked things off with a pancake breakfast. By the time the last syrup-sodden bite had been eaten, about 100 people, including vets from across the country, had gathered for a ribbon-cutting ceremony. The ceremony started with a Junior Reserve Officer Training Corps color guard: four solemn young men bearing the U.S. and POW/MIA flags. A half dozen musicians from the Montrose Community band played the national anthem while some in the crowd saluted and others placed hands on hearts.

Mayor Romero referred in a speech to the days when city and county officials seemed to be competing, applying separately for state grants to develop the park.

"Believe it or not, we teamed up," Romero said. "The theme these days is partnering up and getting a lot done."

A state agency funded by lottery players gave the park a coveted grant of about $260,000. The city boasts on its website that the project was one of eight selected from 51 proposals from across the state, and "strong intergovernmental collaboration involving the Recreation District, County, and City distinguished the proposal from others in the extremely competitive grant cycle."

In all, a total of $1.1 million was raised from state and other funders for the project, the mayor said on the day of the ribbon-cutting ceremony. As he spoke, rain became increasingly hard to ignore. The mayor opened a khaki umbrella and kept speaking.

Welcome Home Montrose founder Kline was then invited to address the crowd. She singled out Bolhuis when she took her turn at the microphone, set up in front of a low, pale stone wall on which "Montrose Water Sports Park" was carved.

"Jared made a promise that it would be an accessible water park where anyone could play and heal," she said. "And he kept his promise."

A wet-suited Bolhuis was focused on getting in the river. He already had his kayak helmet on when the mayor called him up. The former Marine tucked his headgear under an arm and moved to the front of the applauding crowd to be given a certificate of appreciation and a key-shaped lapel pin.

Once Bolhuis rushed to put his helmet back on and find a friend to hold his key to the city, he splashed into the river along with other wounded vets representing Team River Runner who had traveled from around the country to be part of the celebrations. Brightly colored kayaks resembled the petals of some giant, flamboyant flower scattered on the waters like an offering. Boaters whooped and one shouted "on me" to guide two blind comrades. Cameras flashed and a little boy on a pedestrian bridge over the water waved an American flag as big as he was. It was a moment Bolhuis had looked forward to almost as much as he had once anticipated coming home from Afghanistan.

Later, over chicken tacos at Kline's home, Bolhuis showed off his certificate proclaiming him a recipient of the Montrose Citizen's Award. But he was no longer a citizen of Montrose. He would be leaving the next day for Michigan, where he had for several months been living with his parents.

Before that taco dinner, the last plans I'd heard Bolhuis making involved working as a river guide in Costa Rica. That had been scrapped as impractical. He was now headed for college in Florida. He had not been ready for college right after high school, nor when he tried a few classes after he was injured at war and had left the hospital.

"Sitting next to the kid with his feet up on the desk texting all the time drove me mad," he said of his last academic foray.

He still might find that irritating. But now he might be better able to concentrate on his own goals, not on what was happening around him. His mother credited that to what he had accomplished in Montrose.

"It was really good for him to go out and have some big-picture ideas and be able to see them play out," she told me.

In Michigan days could go by with Bolhuis having little to say to his parents. But on other days he was open and talkative, slowly closing the gap that had opened when he was in the hospital and then in Colorado.

After the years in Colorado, his memory had improved and blackouts and bouts of vertigo were less frequent.

At 12, he had come home one day announcing he had gotten himself work washing dishes and busing tables at a restaurant. He commuted the mile to his first job on foot or by bike. As a 17-year-old, Bolhuis had consulted a Marine recruiter and decided to sign up without first discussing his plans with them.

"He would find something, he would do it, and, and then he would tell you he had done it," his father said.

His parents glimpsed something of his old independence when he returned from Colorado, living with them for the first time since he was a teen. But they also saw him stumble at simple things, like paying bills.

"It's tough for him to remember normal, month to month activities," his father said.

His parents faced challenges as well.

"The last time he was in my house was 10 years ago," his mother said. "He is an adult, but I'm still a parent. I struggle with when not to parent too much."

His father added: "It is a big learning experience, and I think it will continue to be for some time. You have to let him go on on his own and just give him guidance. That's the hardest part. You can't catch them all the time."

The celebrations at the river will be an important touchstone for Montrose and for Bolhuis. In the future, both will find energies and spirits flagging and will face crises. It will be crucial then to look back on better times as proof of what is possible.

For all the welcome and support Montrose offered, it would not be home for Bolhuis. Not yet.

Water always finds a way. Bolhuis said his course might someday bring him back to Montrose. Perhaps one day when the tourism industry he envisioned develops around the water park, he will return to open a kayak outfitter business.

"With all my experiences and all the time I've put into this community, this is my home," he told me during his time in Montrose, speaking firmly, as if describing a vision he saw in his mind. "I want to raise a family here one day.

"I really look forward to the day when I have kids and they're able to understand: 'Daddy built that - the river park and everything that Welcome Home Montrose helped start.'"

Chapter 10

Seeing Potential

Let's return to 2014, when Bolhuis's water park was still a muddy, boulder-strewn construction site. That was about the time Bill Glasscock first saw it. The veteran river guide and water rescue expert was also a ski instructor and lived in the nearby resort town of Ridgway. He had heard about plans to develop the park, but was vague on the details. So, while in Montrose on a grocery run, he wandered down to the Uncompahgre River to have a look.

Glasscock had seen projects in other towns of Montrose's size. Those had only a few of what are known as features, the drops or mini water falls created by placing boulders or pouring concrete. On the banks of the Uncompahgre that day amid the heavy equipment, Glasscock quickly grasped that what Montrose had in mind was ambitious. The park would be twice as long and have twice as many features as he had expected. As a resident of the region with an interest in its waters, Glasscock also was familiar with the Gunnison Tunnel, the early 20th century infrastructure project that brought water for irrigation six miles from the Gunnison River to the Uncompahgre River.

Glasscock knew the Gunnison Tunnel would keep bringing water to the Uncompahgre months after the rush that rafters love had subsided at other Colorado river towns, places where snow melt running down from the mountains created the kayaking thrills.

"I saw there was a potential for big business in this town," Glasscock told me. "I thought, `Holy smoke, there's a door here somebody's got to be knocking on.'"

Glasscock's enthusiasm for adventure sports had made him a comfortable living and given him an exciting life. But it had not left him with the kind of savings he would need to start a business.

Like Welcome Home Montrose founder Kline, he would need collaborators.

Glasscock's turned to Erik Dalton, a friend and owner of Jagged Edge Mountain Gear, a well-known sportsperson's outfitter in Telluride, the region's resort town. Dalton put in the money. Glasscock, as shop manager, contributed the time and expertise. The two moved quickly to open a shop to rent and sell equipment to river enthusiasts. They did not even have a name when Glasscock addressed a Montrose City Council meeting in April 2015 when officials were discussing establishing a permitting process for commercial rafting at the park. Glasscock praised the city for creating a park that was attracting new business and urged attention to such details as bathrooms and parking.

A month after Glasscock spoke to the city council, he and Dalton were in business as Montrose Kayak & Surf. The shop is located off Main Street in a part of time I knew well from vistis to the nearby rail station that houses the municipal museum. The wiry Glasscock, who wears a cap with his shop's logo over his shaggy, graying brown hair, has a showroom the size of a three-car garage. It once housed a bike shop and before that a silk screen enterprise. The entrance is decorated with a string of Tibetan prayer flags. The tiny silk banners were dyed in more muted versions of the hues of the kayaks and stand-up paddle boards stacked like so many oversized toy soldiers against the back wall. Glasscock commutes from Ridgway for days that can easily stretch to 10 hours or more each. The house next door that came with the business property is a place to crash after particularly long days.

Glasscock has enjoyed watching the river be embraced by people like the members of a hardworking Montrose farming family. When they showed up to rent equipment they told him they usually reserved recreational activities for the winter, when three generations would ride snowmobiles together. They came into Montrose Kayak and Surf one summer weekend morning determined to try something new. After an afternoon at the water park, they came in to return rented stand-up paddle boards and report to Glasscock. He was told a favorite moment was "when grandma fell off that board the second time and came up sputtering and laughing."

They asked to book equipment for the next weekend.

Glasscock has customers from Denver and other parts of eastern Colorado. They are often visiting relatives in Montrose when they come in to his shop.

"Now, Montrose residents have a new way to show visitors a good time," he told me, optimistic and energetic, as we sat on the front steps of the house next to his shop.

He was riding a wave that swelled in part thanks to Welcome Home Montrose. While one new business does not a revival make, Glasscock's enterprise is among several developments in Montrose that are worth a closer look as we consider that Welcome Home Montrose emerged from an effort to put the town on more secure financial footing.

Montrose Kayak & Surf had been in business about a year when I met Glasscock in 2016. Before sitting down to speak with him I had done my traditional storefront survey. The coffee shop where Welcome Home Montrose founder Kline once held court was among the Main Street businesses shuttered since my last visit. Also no longer: a warehouse-size discount liquor store with a drive-up counter.

I counted among new businesses a gallery selling high-end oil paintings; a cafe that also served breakfasts featuring delectable biscuits and homemade bread; an Italian restaurant that a chef from Telluride was running with his wife and daughters; and a brew pub. For the first time in years of visits, it seemed to me that the grand openings outnumbered the bleak closings.

I shared the results of my storefront survey with Lance Michaels, a retired banker who had recently taken over as executive director of the Montrose Downtown Development Authority. He had recently submitted a monthly report to the city that for the first time in his 22-month tenure included a net gain of a half dozen downtown businesses.

Michaels came to the development authority job after a career in banking that had taken him all over Colorado. His last decade as a banker was in Montrose. He had seen the town in good times, when home loan seekers would tell him Montrose fit all the criteria they were looking for in a place to retire. He heard so many people tick off the mild winters and access to a good hospital and to an airport he began to wonder if they all weren't referencing some checklist published by the American Association of Retired Persons.

Some of those aspiring retirees were building second homes they planned to use for vacations before easing into them as primary residences. They helped fuel a building boom. So did new shopping centers anchored by big box stores on the south side of town, convenient for people in Montrose's smaller, more rural neighboring communities. Trucks hauling supplies back and forth to Telluride, which also was expanding, kept service businesses in bigger Montrose booming. By some estimates, Michaels said, as much as 70 percent of the city's economy was dependent on construction in the period from 2004 until the bubble burst for Montrose in 2008.

"The bottom line is, we've struggled," Michaels said, looking at me through his rimless glasses. But now, "we have what feels like the opening of a new door. I kind of feel like we're hitting a stride on the positive.

"It's certainly fair to say we're overdue. We're long overdue for something good to happen to us. Maybe some economies just have to go through it to get to it."

If in a few years Welcome Home Montrose revives the internship program for veterans forced to retire early by injury or illness, the town might be able to offer them more and more varied job opportunities.

Michaels saw Welcome Home Montrose as having demonstrated

that a small town can be more than the sum of its parts. The elements must find a way to work together.

"I think Melanie (Kline) started something that's very synergistic for Montrose," Michaels said.

Webster's defines synergy as a combined or cooperative force. Like the force that got the water park built after years of divisiveness. Or the engine behind one of the new Main Street businesses, Proximity Space, whose 2015 opening showed Montrose was in tune with the new sharing economy.

Proximity Space is a co-working venture that offers high speed Internet and is open 24 hours a day. The city put $150,000 into the public-private initiative and city leaders keep regular hours there to answer questions from constituents and take part in and contribute to a collaborative atmosphere they hope will bring entrepreneurs together in new businesses. A local credit union paid fees to allow four high school students to use the space, whose managers also were working with Colorado Mesa University to give students access at night and on weekends when the library on the school's Montrose campus is closed. Proximity Space attracted freelancers like marketing specialist Laura Williams, who told *The Montrose Mirror* that after moving from Michigan, she felt lucky to have found "a small town with this kind of big city amenity."

Michaels, the development group director, believed the city's commitment to Proximity Space helped get the attention of the federal government. In May 2016 the U.S. Department of Agriculture and the U.S. Environmental Protection Agency announced Montrose was among five communities that would get technical assistance aimed at ensuring steps they were taking to get connected would improve their economies. Georgetown, Delaware, was getting help under the program known as Cool & Connected to expand public Internet access. Leon, Iowa, and Tullahoma, Tennessee, were getting help to build free downtown Wi-Fi zones. Toledo, Washington, was to experiment with using broadband to draw tourists. And in Montrose, the focus was to be on leveraging broadband and other downtown assets, including a farmers market that operates twice a week near City Hall, to promote local food access, development and tourism. Georgetown, with 6,800 people; Leon with 1,900 and Toledo with 700 are much smaller than Montrose, while Tullahoma is of comparable size.

The kind of people who talk about being cool and connected include a young man Michaels met at Proximity Space who had neither a car nor any interest in acquiring his own wheels. That was not the only way in which the generation entering the workforce now is different from his own, Michaels told me. When he was starting his career, "I looked for the job. I didn't look for the community. Today, people are looking more for their quality of life."

They can find it in Montrose, Michaels said, echoing some of the discussions at that long-ago meeting that set former development authority board member Kline on the road to founding Welcome Home Montrose.

Not that Michaels is ready to declare Montrose completely through the bad times. He spoke with a banker's caution, and used the phrase "the bottom line" more than once. He worried, for example, about issues such as a lack of affordable housing. The Montrose campus of Colorado Mesa University does not have dormitories, creating even more need for homes at the low end of the scale even as, at the higher end, some of the residences built for retirees go unoccupied.

That car-free young man that Michaels had met at Proximity Space may have noticed that it's an easy walk from the shared working hub to a large grocery story, the main post office, the weekly farmer's market, the art deco cinema that shows first-run movies, restaurants, brew pubs and cafes. Michaels has seen young hipsters charmed by the city's historic buildings, like the grand stone annex where the Downtown Development Authority office is located next to the even grander brick City Hall. Getting some of the building stock in shape for downtown living takes investment. Michaels was concerned that his former colleagues in banking, burned by an economic crisis still fresh in the minds of many, have been hesitant to give housing and construction the loan boost he believes the sector needs now.

Michaels also believes too many people use his town as merely a place to pause for gas, groceries and beer on the way to more storied destinations down the road, such as Telluride with its winter skiing and star-studded end-of-summer film festival. The natural attractions of Montrose should make visitors pause, but is possible to enter and leave town without even realizing a river runs through it. Michaels spoke of his town's status as the gateway to the hiking and camping paradise that is the Black Canyon of the Gunnison National Park, as well as to motor cross trails across the eerie adobe hills, to trout streams, to biking paths. All that "should be making people fly into our wonderful airport and put their heads in our beds," Michaels said.

He included on his list of Montrose amenities the water park that Welcome Home Montrose helped get built. The city of Montrose has made the park the centerpiece of a one-day festival it hopes will help keep tourists in town for a few days beyond a pit stop.

Stacey Ryan, program director for the Montrose Office of Business and Tourism, oversees the festival dubbed FUNC for "fun on the Uncompahgre," a moniker that allows newcomers to avoid trying to pronounce the name that once twisted the tongue of a president. Ryan's office is funded through an excise tax on hotel stays. So she has a vested interest in the festival, which is intended to be an annual event.

The first FUNC Fest was held in August 2015. The clear skies over that inaugural fest contrasted with the rainy day in May when I had watched Bolhuis and other disabled vets open the water park. By holding the FUNC Fest in August, Montrose was showing off its water park's long season. Similar events that are held elsewhere in the state are scheduled in May and June. Thanks to the Gunnison Tunnel, irrigation water for agriculture is released into the Uncompahgre River from spring through fall.

"The Montrose story is about water. It started with the tunnel. If it wasn't here, we wouldn't be here," Ryan told me.

Before moving to the city's tourism development agency, Ryan ran the Montrose County Fair. Before that, she grew up in a ranching and farming community in California's San Joaquin Valley. Her personal story gives her empathy for the farmers who built the economy of early Montrose.

"It's come full circle in a beautiful way," she said. "It started with agriculture. And now recreation is benefiting from agriculture."

We were talking under a sleek gazebo - sheet metal roof supported by steel poles over a concrete patio - near the edge of the water park. The spot was an inviting vista of groomed lawns on which children ran and ducks waddled, a contrast to the disarray entrepreneur Glasscock first saw. Ryan's back was to a nearby playground and baseball fields beyond. She directed my gaze to the river.

"This was brought to you by a farmer. Thank you, local farmer."

As we finished chatting, a half dozen colleagues arrived to hold a staff meeting. Several smiled as they realized a mud swallow was flitting back and forth over their heads from a nest she had built in the gazebo rafters. As I watched the bureaucrats in blue jeans greet each other warmly, I thought it was the kind of professional environment that would attract the kind of young people looking first for quality of life, then for a job. The kind of young people that Michaels, head of the development authority, was beginning to understand are attracted to Montrose.

Ryan's team did not see the FUNC Fest as a city project. They could erect portable toilets, ensure electricity hookups and a sound system were in place and hire a seasoned race director. But for success, they needed it to be the community's event. They needed unity.

They put out the word, and community partners responded. One group organized rubber ducky races for children on a stream that feeds into the river at the park. The authority that runs park and recreation facilities throughout the region also had kids in mind, bringing in a dunk tank and a bouncy castle. A mountain bike club mapped out a course that climbed the mesa overlooking the park and took cyclists on a challenging ride. Bands played as families lounged on blankets on the grass. More than 1,000 people attended.

Ryan had a diverse audience in mind: "The idea is to make it accessible to everyone. We want to bring in the tourists. We want to bring in the community. We want to bring in the vets. We want the adaptive sports element."

I had heard such collaborative, inclusive language from Welcome Home Montrose founder Kline. It is a leadership style particularly suited to small towns, which do not have the luxury of overlooking or undervaluing any resource or talent. I asked Ryan her opinion about something else I often heard from Kline, her mantra that the possibility of failure was no reason not to try something new. Small towns have to be willing to innovate, or they will fall further behind, Ryan agreed. She saw the right spirit in two high school students who decided to build their own craft for a FUNC event meant to be a relaxed river parade. While others floated by in inner tubes and rafts picked up at a big box store, the teens put together a "boat" composed mostly of duct tape that Ryan had difficulty describing.

"Whatever it was, it didn't float," she said. "But they had a great time."

She noted that the teens walked away from their disaster on the water. She hoped that was instructive for townspeople who did not have much experience kayaking. They could see that the waters weren't too deep or too fast to be forgiving of amateurs. Not that Ryan is sanguine about the dangers of water sports. She welcomed the Bureau of Land Management when it proposed setting up a booth at the FUNC Fest to hold safety workshops. Signs posted along the water park caution users to play responsibly.

The river was certainly challenging enough to attract more serious boaters from far afield. At the first FUNC Fest, an Argentinian took third place in the women's standup paddleboard competition, behind racers from Durango and Glenwood Springs, Colorado towns with deeper whitewater traditions than Montrose. FUNC Fest also featured men's standup paddle board and kayak races and competitors from around the country.

On a quiet Sunday afternoon at the park months after the inaugural FUNC Fest, I found a couple of hard-core kayakers in wet suits plying the Uncompahgre in trim crafts that can cost $100 or more. They and a standup paddle boarder working hard at a treadmill-like maneuver on the water were outnumbered by young men and women in swimsuits lazing their way down the river in $10 neon-colored tubes they probably picked up at Walmart. Several older couples sat on the new stone benches built into the banks. The graying men and women dipped their toes into water that was the temperature of melted snow, their backs warmed by the sun. A courtly gentleman in a cowboy hat, jeans and boots was showing his lady companion how to use a piece of exercise equipment placed on a nearby trail that was also part of the renovations undertaken for the water park. Strolling parents held hands with toddlers. Hispanic and white families gathered around barbecue grills. I don't know that I had ever seen such a diverse crowd at any other spot in Montrose.

Ryan told me the FUNC Fest drew a similar diversity of ages, ethnic groups and economic status. She attributed that to the role the park has played in Montrose for generations. Now, people who grew up playing baseball in the park can take their kids kayaking on its river.

City Engineer Scott Murphy, who had been in charge of the water park's design, told me he has been surprised at the impact it has had. Not that he didn't expect water sports enthusiasts to flock to Montrose. It's that so many people come merely to watch them that was unexpected.

"Ninety percent of the people are just there for the atmosphere," Murphy said.

Once they come to see the water park, they come back, again for reasons Murphy had not foreseen. Children who are being homeschooled come to read on the stone steps set up for kayak race spectators. Amateur artists set up their easels on the banks. Murphy said he did not have attendance statistics, but had a metric he felt was important. Park managers had been accustomed to clearing trash only on weekdays. Since the water park opened, they have had to adjust schedules to ensure cleaners work on Saturdays and Sundays as well. Otherwise too much trash piles up between Friday and Monday.

Welcome Home Montrose did not create a resource by championing the water park. The project reminded the community of a resource it already had but needed to develop. Similarly, Welcome Home Montrose did not transform townsfolk. They did not stop crowding into City Council meetings to fuss over grievances old and new. But they did find that their differences did not have to be fatal. Montrose is no utopia and is too pragmatic to want to be one. It instead is striving to be the best of all possible Montroses.

For the water park, "with the whole Welcome Home Montrose Project, it all came together," Ryan said. "It helps us set ourselves apart."

Ryan included an area for vendors at the FUNC Fest, giving local businesses a chance to reach new customers. She'd like to see an enterprising teen set up a pedicab business to bring people and their crafts that have floated down river back to the start of the water park for another run. I imagined how welcome that would be for a blind or paraplegic veteran drawn to the park by a Welcome Home Montrose event.

"You'd have to check with the city about permitting of course," Ryan said of her pedicab business plan, and laughed.

"There's a lot of potential for this to grow," she said. "It'll be neat to watch."

Glasscock, the new kayak shop's manager, joined vendors at the first water festival. When Glasscock saw the water park under construction, he did not know much about Welcome Home Montrose. He soon learned. His grand opening was a barbecue fundraiser for Welcome Home Montrose. He displays the red-white-and-blue Welcome Home Montrose window sticker that alerts veterans his is a business that offers them special deals, in this case a 15 percent discount on equipment rentals and purchases.

Glasscock also displays the Welcome Home Montrose commitment to creating opportunity. He talks up the Montrose banner making company that created his shop sign. A local graphics expert designed his logo: the shop name and a kayaker's silhouette in black and white accented with a stylized red wave.

I notice a striking pair of silver cuffs on Glasscock's wrists. They have the handcrafted look, if not quite the style, of pieces Welcome Home Montrose founder Kline might have hammered out at her jewelry bench. It turns out they are vintage pieces from a shop Glasscock's late mother Jean once ran. She bought an Indian craft business on Route 66 in Arizona in the 1960s to help her family through a financial setback. Her son said she had little knowledge of the wares or customer relations when she started, but she learned quickly.

"I have some retail in my blood from her," he told me, as I contemplate how much leadership that enterprising, creative women like his mother and like Kline have contributed to small towns.

The first summer, Montrose Kayak & Surf started with one paid employee: Glasscock. Just as he was beginning to realize he couldn't do it alone, a young woman showed up and announced that she had moved to Montrose because her mother lived in town and that she needed a job. She had worked at two REI stores, was a stand-up paddle boarder who wanted to learn to raft.

"I said, 'You're hired,'" Glasscock recalled.

His first year in business, a friend of Glasscock donated her time helping him answer emails. The second summer, the friend had been promoted to paid (but part-time) web site manager and marketing director, and he was looking at bringing her on full-time. Glasscock added a second shop assistant, a college student, for the second summer. That season he also hired two high school students to manage weekend equipment rentals on the lake at a park in Delta. Delta is a neighboring farming community that like Montrose had been hard-hit by the recession.

Glasscock got his start as a whitewater guide in Moab, the eastern Utah town of 5,000 that is near a fistful of national parks and offers river trips, biking, hiking and other adventure pursuits. Moab, a three-hour drive from Montrose, began marketing itself as an outdoor sports mecca after its mining industry faltered. The Utah town now is a world famous destination.

"I don't think Montrose wants to be Moab. Moab's out of control," Glasscock said, "We want to be healthy, not trampled (by tourists.) But we have a long way to go before we have to worry about being trampled. We have to work on healthy."

He sees himself as helping Montrose toward that goal. And, nearing 60, his new business was helping him envision retirement.

"Montrose is in turn helping me grow and perhaps have a more secure future."

Chapter 11

Limitations

The Water Sports Park that is contributing so much to Montrose's sense of itself and to its economy is an example of what vision and compassion can achieve. Another idea that came from Bolhuis is a sobering reminder that good intentions sometimes are not enough.

At Welcome Home Montrose and before that at Team River Runner, Bolhuis did what he felt he was meant to do if he couldn't be a Marine. He was helping warriors and former warriors. If he could realize his dreams in Colorado, Bolhuis thought, perhaps others could as well. That idea became the Dream Job Program in which Welcome Home Montrose brought wounded vets to town to take up unpaid internships. One vet shadowed a high school teacher, another helped the city plan events and a third was placed at a farm.

Those dream jobs were envisioned as transitions from military to civilian life. If nothing else, the young men and women would have a bit of civilian work experience for their resumes at a time when, according to the U.S. Bureau of Labor Statistics, the national unemployment rate was 20.4 percent among young veterans of the conflicts since 9/11. That compared with 15 percent of nonveterans in that category.

Dream Job was a high-stakes workshop in which townspeople and newcomers explored the vulnerabilities and strengths of both sides.

Though much smaller in scale, Dream Job was not dissimilar in ambition to the Homestead Act. Like that Civil War-era piece of legislation meant to spur settlement of the West, Montrose's internship program offered opportunity and support to people with a pioneering spirit. And it brought to the community much-needed energy and dedication. An old soldier can be measured by

. his wounds or her medals. Dream Job wanted to take stock of vets' possibilities.

Townspeople rallied around the project. That included taking a keen interest in the young people who moved to Colorado to take part. Friendly Montrose residents would make sure to pause for a chat if they saw one of the newcomers on the street or at the supermarket. Welcome Home Montrose scheduled the vets to speak to schools and community groups that were eager to have them as guests.

"They became the poster child Wounded Warrior," Welcome Home Montrose founder Kline said, rueful in hindsight. "Here's the lesson we learned from the Dream Job program: we put them in the spotlight way too much. They lost their anonymity and they resented us for it."

Smith, looking back several years later, saw that in a town the size of Montrose, the interns "were never offstage. It really hindered their transition." Smith, as executive director of Welcome Home Montrose, provided the organizational and networking skills to make Bolhuis's Dream Job a reality.

Not that the interns didn't appreciate the neighborly interest and support. But for someone struggling with the paranoia that is often a symptom of the aftermath of trauma, being recognized by strangers who know your face from the local paper can be disconcerting.

The experiment drew attention from further afield as well. Glenn Beck invited Kline, Smith and a Welcome Home Montrose board member into his studios and interviewed one of the interns via satellite. Beck, looking his most folksy in suspenders and a denim shirt, closed the 2014 interview with high praise, turning to Kline and her colleagues to tell them:

"You guys are like a little slice of Mr. Smith Goes to Washington. You restore my hope … It's not as hard as it seems to just do it ourselves, do it the right way and do it for the right reasons."

I'm among the journalists who wrote about the interns. A few years after my 2014 *Stars and Stripes* story was published, none of the three former interns responded to my requests for follow-up interviews for this book. They had all received my story warmly when it appeared. In the intervening years, perhaps they had come to believe they had already given journalists and the world enough of themselves. In this book I will give them the anonymity that might have lightened the burden on them during their time in Montrose.

One had a resume that resembled Bolhuis's. He was a former Marine whose Midwestern family had sent several generations to war. He was an Iowan who joined the military straight out of high school. Weeks into his 2009 deployment in Afghanistan, shrapnel from a home-made bomb explosion severed his left arm and tore into his organs. When I met him in Montrose three years after the bombing that maimed him, the slight, dark-haired Iowan could manage a sardonic joke about his deployment: "I enjoyed it so much, I figured I'd leave part of my arm there to keep fighting while I went home."

He had spent much of the three years before our interview being treated and recovering at Walter Reed, the military hospital where he met Bolhuis. Each would medically retire from the Marines before the age of 30.

Bolhuis's parents said that by not coming home to them from Walter Reed, their son made a start at healing. The Iowan went home to his parents from the hospital in the spring of 2012. His mood was dark.

"I was really feeling sorry for myself. I grew up in a military family. I had no plans for my future other than the Marine Corps."

He was jostled from his funk by a phone call from Bolhuis who offered him the opportunity to try out any civilian job he could imagine as part of the Dream Job program.

Considering possible futures led the Iowan to contemplate his past. He remembered a high school history teacher who had a knack for sharing his passion for his subject with restless teenagers.

With that teacher in mind, the Iowan thought perhaps he could revive the sense of purpose he feared he had lost when he retired as a lance corporal.

He told Bolhuis: "I want to not just teach, but to make a difference."

He had hit upon an area of particular concern to small towns. In 2014, Robert Mitchell, a Colorado Department of Higher Education official, described the situation to Colorado Public Radio: "I don't use the word crisis very often but we are on the brink of crisis in the rural school districts."

Another education official told the radio station about planning a career fair at which 25 rural districts hoped to try to lure talent. Only three people signed up ahead of time to apply for teaching jobs, so the event was cancelled. A district near Grand Junction, the Montrose region's population hub, tries to lure teachers by offering to pay for a master's degree if a new teacher promised to serve in the district for five years.

Montrose County school officials who were among Welcome Home Montrose's supporters arranged for Bolhuis's friend and fellow retired Marine to shadow a high school history teacher.

The former lance corporal said that after his injury, he had found it hard to open up to anyone who had not seen combat. He suspected that civilians saw him as dangerous. In Montrose, he was paired with a high school history teacher who was also a member of the National Guard and had served a tour in Iraq. The Iowan found a mentor. That initial connection helped him make others. Again, Montrose showed its uncanny ability to bring the right people to the problem.

The high school teacher had, along with his wife, founded a center that combines mental health therapy and caring for horses. After years of avoiding counseling, the former Marine began to visit the horses regularly.

"I've never believed in talking about your feelings with a shrink. I thought it was bull crap," he said. "I'd see a shrink in the military. I'd see them once, and never go back."

In Montrose, "stepping into the community and seeing how welcoming the community was and how willing everyone was to help, it just made it possible for me to come out of the shell that I had been in since my injury.

"It was just finding something else that I could be passionate about. I honestly believe that was the best form of therapy I'd ever received after three years in the hospital with nothing to do but wait to get out of the Marines."

His only teaching experience had been outlining tactics to junior Marines. He had thought his infantry training would mean little in a civilian job. But he came to see the discipline and patience he had honed in the Marines were important at the head of the classroom. As one of 10 siblings, he certainly was used to being around young people.

For an hour-long class on Iwo Jima, he spent a week consulting Department of Defense archives and watching documentaries. He brought in as a guest speaker a World War II vet he had met in Montrose. For show and tell, he offered his own Purple Heart.

The work may have been as much for himself as for his 10 students, who were 15- and 16-year-olds. He wanted to know what he could learn from people who had fought in the 1940s.

And he wanted the students to find purpose in history and to understand the import of the phrase "freedom isn't free," easy to say and difficult to understand.

"What is it that we thank our veterans for?" he said. "Anyone can go to war and say, 'Let's kill all the Muslims.' If you don't know what it was for, then what was it worth? It's not just killing people because they made us angry. It was actually for a bigger reason, for freedom and liberty, to stop tyranny. If it goes unappreciated, it won't be long before we don't have freedoms."

He had a capacity for empathy that could serve a teacher well. He felt particularly compelled to mentor students the age he was when he joined the military.

"They're the ones that are taking the next step, the step that will not only determine their future, but their children's. They're the ones that most need molding in the right direction. Teen age wasn't that long ago for me. I remember how confused and scared I was."

Teaching, like soldiering, required hard work and idealism. But for all he brought to it, he found it was not his calling. He left Montrose with plans to go to college and vague thoughts of channeling his desire to serve into politics, another field where he believed a deep knowledge of history could be useful.

Montrose gave him a luxury he may have thought he had forfeited: the freedom to make youthful mistakes; to be uncertain; to change his mind. The emphasis when he was in Montrose was on the dream, not the job. Perhaps any occupation would have been transformative, especially if it gave him a chance to help others.

"You kind of get comfortable in the military. It's a safe feeling. Getting out, it can be kind of intimidating," he said. "I was in a whirlwind of a mess when I first got here. I wasn't ready to accept that I was out of the military. I learned that things can change. I discovered that it (civilian life) is not so bad. With the experiences I've had, the stressors of civilian life don't seem so stressful."

Life in Montrose "helped bring me into my own."

Another intern believed that if she stumbled, Montrose would provide a soft place to land. She was a redhead with an open, round face and stars tattooed in a falling pattern down her neck. After a troubled childhood near Morristown, New Jersey - a town with about the same number of people as Montrose - she joined the Navy right after high school in 2006. Two years after signing up, she suffered a stroke doctors blamed on an arterial disorder that had not been previously diagnosed. She retired from the Navy at 24 after two brain surgeries and years of therapy. The vision on her left side was impaired. She suffered memory loss and periodic severe headaches.

She, like the Iowa Marine, had met Bolhuis at Walter Reed. She was between brain surgeries. He suggested she come to Montrose for a dream job when he saw her at a fair showcasing sports in which the injured could compete. She was initially skeptical.

"I kind of looked at Jared like he had five heads."

After his initial proposal, Bolhuis wandered off to see more of the fair. By the time she saw him again later that day, she had reconsidered. Maybe this was a chance to raise awareness about women in the military and to tell the stories of young people who had been willing to put themselves in harm's way, even if they never got to the battlefield. If she went to Montrose, others like her might follow.

Because she wasn't injured in battle, she said, "It took a lot for me to realize I was a wounded warrior. A wounded warrior is someone that's ill, injured or wounded. A lot of people forget that."

She had worked in a Navy galley and once had hoped to be a chef. The memory problems that persisted after her stroke made her doubt her ability to work in a professional kitchen where the pressure can be as high as the heat under a saute pan. So, the former sailor told Bolhuis she would like to try event planning. Many events involve food and putting a program together requires a cook's attention to detail.

Welcome Home Montrose found her a job and a home in one place. She was given quarters at an assisted living facility where she also was put to work leading activities for patients. She found the setting, though, too much like the hospital where she'd already spent years. And living with patients with memory problems only made her more sensitive about her own. Welcome Home Montrose stepped in and she was moved to City Hall.

"It's a really small town, so there aren't a lot of events," she said wryly. She helped organize team-building staff picnics and community parties for children and she raised funds for foster children with a dodge ball tournament. When she was a kid, she had been placed in foster care and later adopted.

Some of the event planning she did in her last months in Montrose was the long-distance organizing of her own wedding. Before coming to Montrose, she had met a Marine with traumatic brain and other injuries at a sports tournament for wounded warriors. She left Montrose after her internship to marry him and settle in Wisconsin.

The third Dream Job intern did not look like a stereotypical soldier. He had studied graphic design in college after high school and played in a band. When I met him in Montrose, he had the shaggy sandy hair and glasses of a hipster strolling the streets of Portland or Brooklyn. But he told me, "If someone were to knock on my door right now and say, 'Cut your hair, suit up,' I'd go."

He still had what he called a "fierce, almost manic motivation that never goes away for a lot of servicemen."

He had gone to a Marine recruiter in 2008 seeking goals.

"At that time, I probably wanted to save the world," he said. "I wanted to do something with my life other than work until you stop. That wasn't happening for me in college."

The Marines sent him to field radio operator school. He had recently finished the training when he had a stroke followed by a series of grand mal seizures. Memory loss was a lingering side effect. Doctors still don't know what caused his stroke. He was to spend the rest of his four-year Marine commitment in the hospital, where he often sat outside in a smokers' area chatting with Bolhuis.

It sounded like more idle talk when Bolhuis called to ask: "What would you do if I told you I wanted to move you to Colorado in six months and set you up in whatever dream job you want?"

"I was a smartass," the former Marine from Pennsylvania recalled. "I said, 'Sure, you let me know when you have that all set up.'"

Bolhuis explained it was set up. The Pennsylvanian wondered whether a small town could really be so committed to vets. Bolhuis seemed to have found something there. The third recruit gave

Montrose a chance.

He told Bolhuis he wanted to learn to grow food, which he saw as a step toward living mindfully and independently and a way to be in charge of his own hours.

"You can't eat money, and it doesn't make up for lost time with friends."

He was matched with an organic farmer who raised herbs, tomatoes, garlic and chickens in greenhouses outside Montrose. The farmer sold his food at local markets, and encouraged sharing produce and ideas with other small growers.

Arriving from Pennsylvania, the ex-Marine was calmed by a natural setting that evoked timelessness, endurance and strength.

"When something is bothering me," he said, "I just look around, and whatever is bothering me isn't anymore."

Caution signs on the two-lane highways leading in and out of town warn drivers to watch for wildlife. The pale, smooth adobe hills, like waves turned to stone, could be from some distant planet that is starker and more serene than our own. I wondered if the Pennsylvanian has ever, as I have done, become so caught up meditating on the undulating adobes that an hour's jog easily becomes two. The Pennsylvanian told me that when his friends back East saw the photos from Colorado he posted on Facebook, they asked if Montrose was real, as if such a place could exist only in Photoshop.

I have ventured on foot to the edge of the region's most dramatic spot, the Black Canyon. I also was lucky enough to get a ride in a small plane from a Montrose pilot eager to show off the area's treasures. We swooped over the mesmerizingly sheer walls of the gorge.

The young man who showed such appreciation for this scenery brought his bride, who is an artist, to Montrose. He had married her in Pennsylvania after his stroke. They remained after his internship, she working as a graphic designer, he growing mushrooms for sale at markets and local restaurants.

Because he and his wife stayed, some might consider him the most successful Dream Job intern. Unlike the others, he had gone to college before joining the military, so arrived in Montrose a few years older and perhaps in a better position to consider settling down.

His colleagues took important lessons with them when they left. The Marine from Iowa acknowledged there's something to be said for learning you don't like the classroom before spending your GI Bill benefits on teacher's college. The sailor from New Jersey went on to urge friends to apply for Dream Job internships because she knew they would find people in Montrose ready to lend a hand, like the neighbor, also a vet, who gave her rides when she needed to get to medical checkups an hour away at the closest VA hospital. She also pointed out that because she was working for free, no one could fire her when she found it was difficult to read or to sit for long periods at a desk or when she was crippled by headaches. That took pressure off when she most needed to be as relaxed as possible. Based on her experiences in Colorado, she decided she should find a way to work for herself, perhaps as a freelance wedding planner or photographer. That way, she would never have to call in sick.

"It's scary going out there, saying, 'I'm going to try to work, but I'm not sure I can,'" she said. "I have all these things that I can't do normally anymore. It sucks, but it's just one of those things you have to overcome."

She worked in Montrose to train herself not to focus on the "dis" in "disability."

"Focus on the second part. What is your ability?" she said. Hers, she said, was the power to help other wounded warriors.

Bolhuis, who recruited the three, could be considered the fourth intern.

His mother said Bolhuis had never minded being in the spotlight. He had performed ceremonial duties as a Marine and had already been on national television talking about another effort to help wounded vets, Team River Runner. He was able to cope with requests for interviews about the Dream Job program better than the three friends he brought to town. But, then, it was his project, born of his own experiences.

"I spent three years in the hospital. Then, all of a sudden, I was just driving out of the gates," he said. "The purpose of the Dream Job program is to get our wounded veterans back into the civilian world."

Over the years I visited Montrose after first coming to report on Dream Job for a newspaper article I heard lots of speculation about whether the broader experiment that is Welcome Home Montrose could be replicated anywhere else. Some say another small town would be the best host because the family atmosphere of such places ensures everyone will pitch in and make it a success. But Dream Job might take a city instead of a village. An urban center offers educational, professional and medical resources. More importantly, the interns would find a level of anonymity in a metropolis that was unavailable in Montrose.

One reason Dream Job may have drawn so much enthusiastic attention is that it is the aspect of the Montrose experiment that seems most easily transferred. Not every town has a folksy Main Street and great-grandfatherly World War II vets to welcome those who fought in America's latest war. Cities can't offer vets the opportunity to disappear into the great outdoors. But, as hard to believe as it might sound to him, Bolhuis knew not everyone wanted to live in a place like Montrose.

"Some people want a high rise in New York or a flat in Chicago. Communities can develop excitement around what they have," Bolhuis said.

Some of Bolhuis's friends have told him their ideal career would be at a New York investment firm. While Bolhuis cannot imagine being happy there, he could imagine a Dream Job program in Manhattan, with perhaps a Welcome Home New York cafe where veterans-turned-bankers could stop for a cup of coffee and a chat with an empathetic listener on the way to the office.

A big city offers opportunities that small towns lack. Montrose took on Dream Job despite some very real shortcomings. In retrospect, it's fair to ask whether good will and intentions would have been enough if any of the interns had faced a medical crisis, physical or mental. But at the time, it seemed there was nothing to do but get on with helping the town's fragile but determined guests.

Bolhuis got to town only a few months before his first recruit arrived. Townspeople volunteered homes. Jobs were lined up through word of mouth.

The former sailor's stroke left her unable to drive. She commuted by bus, but the town's transportation system doesn't operate in the evenings, not unusual for a community of its size. She suggested that the next interns be housed close to downtown Montrose, where they could walk not only to work, but to shops, restaurants and the movies.

When the former Marine from Iowa finished the six months the internships were scheduled to last, he still felt uncertain about his future. He was given another six months. In retrospect, a transition plan that could have included career and education counseling for all three should have been in place.

The Marine from Iowa did find his way to equine therapy through his mentor. That broke a path that can be followed by others who think they are too tough to need help, both because he set an example and because he told VA counselors how helpful he found it to care for the horses. Since his stay in town, Welcome Home Montrose has added a range of mental health programs to the services it can tell vets about. A VA therapist keeps regular hours, several support groups have been formed, and suicide prevention workshops have been held at the center. Still, vets as well as civilians in Montrose and across rural America remain under-served by mental health care professionals, a challenge too big for one small grassroots organization.

"It was a pilot program, and everyone expected there to be issues, even the participants," Bolhuis said. "It had its hiccups, but it was a major success."

If it was a success, the challenge is to build on what has been accomplished. The first interns gave Montrose a place to start, said Welcome Home Montrose Executive Director Smith.

"We were so lucky with the individuals who came out to participate. They were honest and gave us great feedback," she said. "This is somebody's life. It could be a great experience, it could change someone's life for the better."

I suspect Smith will be a formidable gatekeeper when reporters request interviews with the interns who follow the first class, whenever they come. She may get fewer requests, as the second time around is rarely seen as being as newsworthy as the first. The first interns paid the price of being pioneers and that will ease the experience for anyone else.

Smith was concerned her small town would not be able to provide some of the training and educational opportunities future interns might want or decide they needed after arriving. Imagine accepting Montrose's offer, putting your belongings in storage and moving to Colorado for six months. Wouldn't you tough out the experience even if it was not what you expected, even if it might mean wasting valuable time?

"Are we going to have them feel trapped?" Smith said.

The 2012 participants relied largely on their military retirement and medical benefits for expenses beyond housing, and some struggled financially.

Since 2012, the Dream Job project has been on indefinite hold while Smith and others consider how far Welcome Home Montrose organizers could go to ensure participants attend therapy sessions and take prescribed medications. How to respond if a participant breaks the law while in Montrose? What behavior could lead to expulsion from the program? For organizers who believe deeply not only in second chances but in as many chances as it takes, even asking such questions can seem like breaking a promise.

Smith said Welcome Home Montrose needed to have funding for a staffer dedicated to coordinating the next class of Dream Job interns. Too much is at stake not to get it right.

"I would never want to do harm," Smith said.

A structure for recruiting and choosing participants was also needed. Should the internship program focus on the most vulnerable, those wounded on the battlefield? A nationwide 2011 Pew Research Center survey of 712 veterans who have served since 9/11 found that half of those who saw combat have had difficulty readjusting to civilian life, while only a third of those who did not see combat had a similarly tough re-entry. Nearly six out of every 10 combat veterans also told the Pew interviewers that they are gripped often by irritability or anger, compared with three out of 10 noncombat veterans. More than half the combat veterans have experienced strains in family relations, compared with less than 40 percent noncombat veterans.

Whoever comes next, whenever they come, they will be asked to be prepared to act as consultants to Welcome Home Montrose.

"We do need their input," Welcome Home Montrose founder Kline said. "Our programs are in our infancy. We're definitely not ready to say, 'This is how you do it.'"

"When we first started, we were pretty naïve. We were enthusiastic, but we were naïve," she said. "We've learned a lot about the services that we need here."

Smith said Montrose remains enthusiastic about Dream Job. She has seen businesspeople in town struggling to meet payroll who are reluctant to say no when asked for cash donations for some of the programs her grassroots organization offers for vets. The Dream Job program is different. It does not require cash.

"It allows people in the community to share their expertise and mentorship," said Smith, who has seen, as word of the project spread over the years, more and more people come forward with key skills.

The first group of interns arrived from different places and mental spaces. But they were united in a desire to serve. Their Montrose hosts also wanted to serve.

People need other people to grow. Or, as the Pennsylvanian put it when he compared raising tomatoes to share with neighbors in Montrose to his years in the sterile hospital:

"You can't heal in a concrete building. You can't develop as a human unless you're treated as one."

Chapter 12

Hometown Heroes

Tim Kenney gave me directions by phone to his Toads Guide Shop on Montrose's Main Street. I set out on the five-hour drive from Denver expected a get-to-know-you chat with him, perhaps over a cup of coffee. After I arrived in the early afternoon I noticed as he shook my hand that Kenney seemed to be sizing me up, with particular attention to my feet.

"So, are you ready to go fishing?" he asked.

He supplied the equipment, including overalls and waders. His earlier appraising glance was very much for a purpose. I didn't catch any fish. But I got acquainted with Kenney at his most assured and patient, standing in the Uncompahgre River.

Kenney is a veteran of the war on terror and a key contributor to Welcome Home Montrose. His idea for an outdoor festival for vets is only a small part of what he has brought to the project. And what it has given him.

When Kline started Welcome Home Montrose, she was thinking of bringing former fighters from far away to heal in Colorado. She would come to learn of the many vets already in Montrose who needed help to feel at home.

After taking me fishing, Kenney drove me to his 100-year-old farm house on the 80 acres on the outskirts of town. His home is as cozy as something out of a child's picture book: clapboard walls under a steeped roof, with a tiny duplicate house for kids to play in set in a stately tree out front. Kenney has 15 cows. To get home, we drive along pastures where deer graze calmly.

"Hunting season's over. They're safe now for the year," Kenney said mischievously, using his chin to point at the deer.

We also pass a Marine Corps flag flying over a neighbor's home. A young man in that household had recently finished basic training. If you know the people, you can see war in the landscape of Montrose.

"War is easy," Kenney said. "You know what you're going to do every day: sleep when you can, eat when you can, fight when you can."

Coming home is the challenge. Kenney was hard on himself about the worry he put his family through when he was away. He wondered whether he would be able to provide for his wife, three daughters and son and whether he would ever be able to contribute as much as he could before he was wounded, physically and psychologically. He is haunted, as well, by memories of men who died or were seriously wounded fighting alongside him. Some of his peers did not survive their homecomings. One December's holiday mood was darkened by news of the suicide of the soldier who drove Kenney's team in Afghanistan.

Kenney grew up in Tomahawk, Nebraska. He got away from his small town to the University of Nebraska on a wrestling scholarship. He says ruefully that he didn't make much of the opportunity.

"I mostly wrestled and partied," he said. "It wasn't for me. All I was doing was getting into trouble."

He was also in ROTC, which might have given him self-discipline and led to a career in the military. But a bar brawl got Kenney kicked out of the officer training program and he left university after three years without a degree.

His sister graduated from the Air Force Academy and went on to become a lieutenant colonel. When he came to see his sister graduate in Colorado Springs, Kenney met and fell in love with another cadet. He and Trish, who graduated from the Academy with an engineering degree and served five years in California working on satellites, started a family. Kenney found discipline and purpose. He speaks often of his church and even more often and proudly of his daughters and son, the boy adopted from Ethiopia after the girls were mostly grown.

After their stint in California, the family moved to Trish's home state of Colorado. She grew up in Grand Junction, an hour from Montrose. They bought a ranch outside Montrose, she managed real estate and he worked as an outdoor guide and outfitter. They were able to give their children the small town life they treasured.

Then came the 9/11 attacks, and something stirred in Kenney. He tried to volunteer to fight, the same impulse that drove thousands of younger people. But Kenney was a father and husband, with family and job responsibilities. And the Army told him he was too old.

As the war dragged on, the maximum age was raised. Kenney was 42 when he enlisted in the Army. He said his wife struggled to understand why he would leave his family and put himself in harm's way. His explanation:

"I felt guilty more than anything," he said. "All the kids dying, and I'm living this great life with my family."

Truth is, Kenney may not understand why he signed up. Perhaps because he finds it difficult to connect with his pre-war self, that man who was free of regrets, uninjured and confident.

Kenney completed basic training at Fort Benning and was assigned to a reserve unit in Colorado. Determined to fight, he talked his way into a Vermont-based Army National Guard infantry unit. He reached his goal, deployment in Afghanistan in 2010. Not long before that, his adopted son had arrived.

Kenney was a gunner, getting knocked around a few times in the truck when rocket-propelled grenades exploded close by, injuring his back. He refused to be sent to a hospital, fearing that would lead to the end of his combat time.

"I was still able to function," he said, saying many others who fought faced worse.

"A lot of combat guys get jacked up in a lot of different ways."

Once Kenney completed his 11-month tour, he no longer avoided the hospital. At Fort Carson, back in Colorado, 2011 was for him a year of surgeries. He had to relearn to walk after operations on his back and right shoulder.

He also had to relearn to be a part of his family. His wife and children had to get to know a man who was not as physically capable as the one who had left them a year before. One who was moody, given to self-medicating with alcohol.

One of his daughters had overheard the father of a friend discussing Kenney's back injuries. The man said Kenney had been fighting a "senseless war."

"A big part of me feels guilty for putting them through the war," Kenney said of his family. "But I also want my kids to know that freedom's not free."

Kline said Welcome Home Montrose became a place where people who opposed the war and those who supported it could come together.

"These kids that go serve make us rise above our political divisions," she said. "I don't care how you feel about the war, about the current administration or the last ones. These are our kids."

Kline's executive director, Smith, said the importance of the goal helped bring people together and then showed them their strength was in their differences.

"You have to build with others in your community whether you like them or not," Smith told me. "You have to open yourself up to people who are different from you. You need people around you that are going to challenge why you're doing things the way you are and maybe offer a different approach that is better."

When Kline is talking with a young vet who might remind her of one of her sons, she seems to struggle. She asks herself whether she's hovering too much, or too little. She knows she can't make decisions for others. She can only offer choices. But the impulse to mother them is strong. Compassion helped create Welcome Home Montrose.

A parent himself, Kenney doesn't need mothering. If he's ever sensed anything patronizing in Kline's attitude, he doesn't show it. He's thankful that when he found himself unmoored by PTSD, Kline was there. Her Montrose jewelry shop is conveniently across Main Street from his fishing and hunting guide business.

Kline "hooked me up with a Vietnam vet," Kenney told me after our fishing expedition. "Now, he and I are talking."

While many people in Montrose had offered kind words to vets, they lacked direction when it came to taking action, Kenney said. Kline is "the first person that I know about that didn't just talk about it. She did something."

"Welcome Home Montrose pulled our community together like nothing ever has."

He connects with other vets over the coffees at the Welcome Home Montrose drop-in center. He harbors guilt over killing Afghanis who might have been as young his own children. He finds talking with his peers eases his pain.

Kenney went to war a fierce patriot and returned with his idealism bruised. Since coming home, he has deployed his loyalty and generosity of spirit not in aid of larger national issues, but to help those closest to him: his family, his neighbors, his comrades. He counts Kline among his comrades, even if she did not go to war.

"There's a lot of guilt going on for people who didn't serve," Kenney said. Kline's project is "a way for people to relieve some of the guilt."

Like Bolhuis, an outsider who came and helped bring Montrose the water park, Kenney finds waters healing.

Kenney had worked on his own to organize fishing and hunting trips for friends who had been wounded at war. Then, he joined forces with Welcome Home Montrose, and was able to expand those ad hoc trips into what was dubbed "Mission No Barriers."

For its debut in 2013, Mission No Barriers welcomed 20 men and women from around the country to test river rapids in kayaks, borrow all-terrain personal vehicles to explore the countryside, fare better than I did at fly-fishing. Welcome Home Montrose signed up more than 200 volunteers and more than 100 business, service groups and churches to help that year. Days were packed from sunrise tai chi classes to sunset drum circles. The vets struggled to take advantage of all the activities.

"The responsibility of the whole thing was spread throughout the community," Kline said.

The community did not simply set out to show vets a good time. It wanted to learn from them what it would mean for the town to take on the mission of ensuring the disabled faced no barriers. In 2013, after wheelchair-bound visitors who came for Mission No Barriers pointed out they had found it difficult to cross at some key downtown intersections, Welcome Home Montrose pushed the city to install more curb cuts at intersections. Since then, Kenney said, "I've had people in wheelchairs who are not veterans come and tell me, 'Thanks, man. For 10 years, I've had to go around the block (in search of a curb cut). Now, I can cross the street just like anyone else.'"

"Little things like that, every day, these people deal with," Kenney told me. "These are things our organization brings to the forefront."

"It's not just the veterans who benefit from what we do. Everybody benefits."

Welcome Home Montrose has helped the city think about how it can be more of a home to anyone. Once, City Manager Bill Bell told me, he would have considered it enough to require city playgrounds, for instance, to meet the minimum requirements to be deemed disabled accessible. After Welcome Home Montrose came to town, Bell took a closer look and determined that the chief attraction of those requirements were that they were cheap. Now, the city is spending 20 to 30 percent more to ensure disabled children can actually play on the equipment, not merely get themselves to the edge of the ground, he said.

"If we want to be a no-barriers community, that's the only way to do it," Bell said.

Progress takes time, as *The Montrose Mirror* noted in 2016, three years after the first Mission No Barriers.

"Many barriers remain - not only for veterans, but for all residents who face mobility challenges and the need for accessible housing, sidewalks and services," the online newspaper reported.

Tracy Morton, disability program benefits manager for the nonprofit Center for Independence, which advocates for people with disabilities across western Colorado, told the *Mirror* about a downtown Montrose corner that was particularly difficult for wheelchairs to negotiate. When she brought it up at a meeting with city officials, "they told me there is only so much money."

Morton, whose organization helps the disabled find housing and overcome other accessibility problems in the region, added that she understood such questions can be particularly difficult for cash-strapped small towns.

"If you think Montrose has challenges, Gunnison can be very tough," she told the *Mirror*, referring to a nearby mountain community. "There was a blind lady up there who was basically trapped in her house whenever it snowed - it was very unsafe."

Like the Center for Independence, Welcome Home Montrose is dedicated to ensuring such problems aren't forgotten. Mission No Barriers can be a tool, helping shine a light.

While thought had been given to making Mission No Barriers an annual event, wiser heads questioned whether it made sense to ask a small town to give so much every year. Opting to go biannually looked even smarter when it became clear the water park would be ready in 2015. In the interim, Kenney renovated the bunkhouse outside his house. He had first built the low, wooden structure that was a cross between a barracks and a log cabin to host the buddies he took fishing.

In the pay-it-forward spirit of Welcome Home Montrose, a trio of vets who had been guests in 2013 returned as volunteers for the second Mission No Barriers, in May of 2015, when it coincided with the opening of the water park.

The returning volunteers were older. Two had served in Vietnam. They spent the week in 2015 teaching younger vets to fly fish. Kenney gave angling lessons as well, determined that everyone he took into the river caught a fish. Archery and kayaking were also on the schedule. Horseback riding got rained out. May is an uncertain month when it comes to Colorado weather.

Val Roberts is a veteran of both Vietnam and Desert Storm who lives in the Denver area. He was one of the volunteer fishing instructors. He marveled at the pot luck lunches and dinners Montrose residents threw for the visitors. He met people who weren't just saying "thank you for your service" or writing a donation check.

"They're actually there. It's hands-on. There's a real personal touch. You get a chance to sit and meet and talk with folks," Roberts told me. "I've spoken to World War II vets all the way to young folks. You feel like part of the town."

As the activities wound down, Steve Baskis, a third-generation soldier, sat at a rough table in Kenney's bunkhouse. A savory aroma floated in the dim room as, in a lunchtime assembly line, vets stacked ham and cheese on bread and one of the 150 volunteers who were part of the second Mission No Barriers grilled the sandwiches on a small stovetop.

Baskis, who is from Normal, Illinois, was among the 20 disabled vets that Team River Runner brought to Montrose to take part in an event he said had an invitingly homemade feel.

A sense of adventure is part of what drove Baskis to join the Army in 2007, soon after he left high school. He had grown up marveling at photographs of the Sphinx and the Pyramids taken during World War II by his grandfather, an Army Air Corps flight engineer who had been based in North Africa.

"His stories and his pictures intrigued me as an 8-, 9-, 10-year-old. And just hearing what his generation did, I was influenced and inspired by those men and women," he said.

Baskis trained at Fort Hood in Texas and was in Iraq by the end of 2007. His father, who never spoke about his Army service in Vietnam, did not support the war in Iraq. He supported his son's decision to serve, but told him as he prepared to deploy "not to come back a different person." The father, who did not elaborate, must have known that what he was asking was impossible. And he must have wanted it fervently.

Months after reaching Iraq, a roadside bomb exploded near Baskis's armored vehicle, killing a comrade and leaving Baskis blind and with injuries to his skull, right leg and left arm.

"I had a good friend who died next to me," Baskis said. "That reminds me more than anything that it could have been worse. I could have died that day."

I had stood on the banks of the Uncompahgre earlier that day watching Baskis slip into warm clothes after running the river. He dressed deftly, feeling for shoes, collapsible cane, dark glasses in a mesh bag the size of a pillowcase. At one point, he accidentally scattered his things, but recovered without requesting or needing help. He offered me his left hand to demonstrate how his circulation had been compromised by his war wounds. His hand was cool and thinner than his right. The thumb was at an unnatural angle.

"The blindness is bad," Baskis told me as if he were describing personal details no more interesting than his height and weight. "But it's my hand that makes kayaking a challenge."

Since being injured, Baskis, thin with a shadow of a beard and close-cropped, dark hair, has skied, picked his way up rock faces, climbed mountains in Nepal and trekked in the French Alps. Often, it's organizations like Team River Runner that make his improbable adventures possible. In Bend, Oregon, at the U.S. Paralympics Road Cycling National Championships, he and a partner won a bronze medal in the men's tandem road race in the blind/visually impaired category.

"When you have a physical injury, when you're given, just like in the military, a mission to do and you have to go through the process of training and working with a team and pursuing a goal, it gives you focus and a sense of accomplishment," Baskis told me.

He'd kayaked in a man-made waterway, but had only been on a river once, in Yellowstone with Team River Runner, before plunging into Montrose's Uncompahgre. After a week in Colorado, he laughed to hear himself talking like an expert.

"It's great water, Class III water," he said. That's moderate but challenging, according to the industry leaders at Rafting America.

On his travels, Baskis hates when strangers in airports, seeing his dark glasses and cane, approach to offer help. He feels he is being pitied. On the water, he may take a tumble, but he can find his own way, and even give direction. After a run in Montrose, he was eager to tell anyone who asks how it went, mistakes and all.

"I flipped over. But I rolled back."

"All the athletics I've pursued have ... enabled me," Baskis said. "When you're told you can't drive, can't do certain things, when you can go down the river and even roll (over) and come out, it's empowering."

"To come out and do this, it inspires other people," he said of Mission No Barriers, Kenney's baby. Baskis has made it his mission, he said, "to make people aware of what is possible. So that if something happens to them, they know."

Baskis knew he was in Colorado for more than playing in the water. He was serious about the responsibility of helping Welcome Home Montrose improve.

"I've been to a lot of different events put on by non-profits the last six-seven years that I've been blind. Montrose stands out," he said, citing depth and breadth of involvement. He had put his finger on something: Welcome Home Montrose had brought its diverse community together.

Baskis had only one complaint: the water park requires boaters to get out on the bank opposite where they got in, then make their way back across the bridge to their gear and vehicles. It might not seem like much to an able-bodied athlete, but it is an extra hurdle to someone who might need a wheelchair or a guide to get across the bridge.

Kenney, unsurprisingly, had also noticed that it was a problem to have the put-in on one bank and the put-out on another. When Kenney renovated his own home outside Montrose, he had changed plans for a traditional, step-up porch in favor of a level entrance. He was thinking of a vet friend who was a quadriplegic. He had seen the friend prepare for an evening out by checking online photos of restaurants to see whether he would find them accessible.

"How'd you like to go through life like that? Every place you go, you have to research to see if you can go in," Kenney told me, and I caught a note of incredulity in his usually easy drawl.

If Kenney could have his way, his quadriplegic friend would not have to check the Internet before visiting any place in Montrose.

Volunteers were on hand in such large numbers for the opening of the water park that anyone who needed one had a hand getting to and over the bridge after making their river run. But Kenney wondered aloud about what it would be like when the helpful crowds were gone.

The disabled are "a group of Americans that really have been forgotten. Equality should be for all. Access should be for all," he said.

He cited the federal Americans with Disabilities Act. I had heard Kenney rail against big government. I was tempted to tease him. But I knew it was a serious matter, an issue of equity. Kenney is as fiercely fair-minded as he is anti-authoritarian.

Kenney had heard that budget constraints had dictated where boats went in and where they exited the water park. I brought the question to City Engineer Murphy, who had been in charge of the park's design and already gotten an earful from Kenney. Murphy said money was not the issue. Instead, he had had to take into account where construction of platforms and railings that would suit disabled boaters would have the least impact on a delicate wetland ecosystem. So many concerns have to be balanced to make progress.

Eventually, the dust-up over put-ins subsided. Kenney did not want to focus on criticism:

"What I don't want to do is take away from the fact that it was because of Welcome Home Montrose, it's because of Melanie Kline, it's because of Team River Runner that we have the newest white water park in the country, and one of the most handicapped accessible parks in the country," he told me. "I need to look at the positive as well. It's amazing what we have accomplished."

"That should be an encouragement to cities everywhere. You can make a change."

The fighting in Iraq and Afghanistan is not the first to bring veterans to Montrose, and to define the town.

Cleo Elliott is among the regular visitors to the Welcome Home Montrose drop-in center's weekly coffees. He is a 93-year-old World War II veteran who has seen how war can brutally reverse the natural order of death. Elliott is mourning his grandson killed on August 19, 2006, as his U.S. Army convoy rolled through eastern Afghanistan.

"His vehicle ran over one of those roadside bombs. What do they call them? IEDs," Elliott told me.

His grandson Corporal Christopher Sitton and a fellow soldier were killed instantly. Sitton had been in Afghanistan five months as a medic for the 10th Mountain Division. He looks boyish in a candid shot that accompanied his obituary in the *Military Times* and only a little older in the formal portrait the local papers used. He was 21.

"That was my only grandson," Elliott said. "It kind of tears a family to pieces."

Elliott wasn't there to protect his grandson. He is there to help his family put itself back together.

Three years after graduating from Montrose High School, Elliott's grandson had joined the Army to earn money for medical school.

"He wanted to be a sports doctor," Elliott said with pride. "That was his goal in life. He joined to get his education, to get started."

Elliott, raised on a farm in east Texas, only got as far as 10th grade himself. But that was at a time when a young man from a small town didn't need to go to college to get a start in life. Elliott left high school to go to a technical school where he learned to build the planes the military used to train pilots.

"In 19 and 44, February, I joined the Marine Corps," he told me. He was not able to explain that decision any more than Kenney was able to tell me why he joined to fight in Afghanistan.

"I don't know why," he said. "It was just an idea I had. I knew a lot of people who had been drafted. But I joined."

He was 24. After boot camp in San Diego, the Marines sent him to tank maintenance school. After he learned to replace treads even under fire he was off to Guam and then to Iwo Jima.

I was sitting in Elliott's dimly lit living room in a small house he keeps so clean the tracks of his vacuum cleaner made a pattern on the light rug. With the words "Iwo Jima" he took us on a mental journey to a place of chaos. The name brought to my mind the image of Marines raising an American flag to mark their capture, after a hard battle, of Mt. Suribachi in 1945. Elliott gave me a glimpse of how agonizing the fight was before that moment of victory was immortalized in a photo that has become among the most iconic images of World War II, if not of all wars.

The U.S. capture of Iwo Jima, which gave it a strategic air base, came after a 36-day assault. Admiral Chester W. Nimitz said, "Among the Americans who served on Iwo Island, uncommon valor was a common virtue."

Historians say of the more than 20,000 Japanese defenders, only 1,083 survived, and more than 6,000 Americans were killed.

Elliott told me in his comforting drawl: "Just on Iwo Jima alone, I don't know that I could ever tell everything that happened there."

For most of his life, Elliott had said next to nothing about his experiences on Iwo Jima. His grandson's death triggered something in him. Elliott began talking about World War II. As he shared his memories, friends he had made at Veterans of Foreign Wars gatherings dug for details and began contacting politicians and military leaders. Because of their efforts, Elliott was awarded three Purple Hearts and a Bronze Star in 2012.

"Corporal Cleo Elliott, a member of C Company, 3rd Tank Battalion of the 3rd Marine Division, went ashore during the amphibious assault and was badly wounded in the leg by a grenade as he negotiated the beach. His wound was treated and he continued in the assault with a bandaged leg. Thus he is awarded his first Purple Heart," his citation reads, describing events on Iwo Jima in February, 1945.

The citation goes on to detail Elliott's attempt to rescue a crew from a burning tank, resulting in wounds to his arms and hands that earned the second Purple Heart and a Bronze Star. The third was for a bayonet wound received a week later when, arms still bandaged, he was assigned to a defensive position in expectation of a Japanese counterattack.

Just as hometown vets like Kenney had helped make their town welcoming for visitors like the Team River Runner extreme sports enthusiasts, Elliott was able to offer succor to a newcomer. Soon after one of the young medically retired warriors arrived in Colorado for the Welcome Home Montrose internship program, he was invited to Elliott's medal ceremony. The two struck up a friendship that is a testament to the sense of family that Welcome Home Montrose has helped develop among vets and between vets and those who never served in the military.

The Afghanistan vet from Iowa understood the Iwo Jima survivor from Texas who had been reticent for so many years about battlefield horrors and heroism. What happens in war, the Iowan told me, can only be fully comprehended by those who have been there. It doesn't matter which field or which war.

The Afghanistan vet had in his 23 years seen the kind of horrendous death and injury only the young witness. We send only the young to war. It had been seven decades since Elliott had had experiences similar to the Iowan's. But he and his young comrade always had something to talk about when they drank coffee together at the Welcome Home Montrose drop-in center. It was Elliott the younger vet brought into a high school classroom to help with a history lesson.

Elliott never thought he deserved medals.

"The man died that I pulled out of the tank. So I didn't tell anybody."

He makes two fists, showing hands still a blush red decades after he was burned on Iwo Jima. His hands are slightly too big, like the hands of a larger man. They get cold easily, he said, but that "didn't stop me from working. It never did stop me from making a living.

"I could make a living anywhere because of the way I was raised," said Elliott, a wiry man with a full head of hair he wears swept back from his long face.

He stands strong and straight despite his years. I'm surprised when he pulls up his pants legs to reveal mottled skin and another war story.

"I've got glass and sand and rocks in my legs," he said. It was a landmine explosion that rammed debris into his body. He and a comrade he believes was only 17 years old had been running under fire on Iwo Jima when the other soldier stepped on the mine. Elliott ducked, surprisingly flexible, as he told me the story, illustrating his posture while fleeing.

The explosion cut his companion in half.

"I couldn't stop. I wanted to stop. But you've got to keep going if you want to stay alive.

"I guess I missed it this much, getting killed, more than one time," Elliott said, holding his hands a foot apart.

At almost 95, his scarred legs could still carry him on a mile and a quarter daily walk.

"I've been doing that now for more than 30 years. It becomes something you look forward to every morning. And you've got to really walk, not just drag along. It's the best thing you can do for your health. I can still walk, I can still get on with it."

He brushes aside his war as "an experience." Emily Smith might accuse him of glazing, as Sheldon Smith does when he recalls his time on the front lines of the war on terror.

"I saw some foreign countries and I got back home," Elliott told me. "I've had a good life."

"Most of my scars have grown over pretty well," he said. "I'm not bitter. Some of the guys are bitter as hell. They don't think they were treated very well. But I think I got just about everything I needed or wanted out of the Marine Corps."

On August 6, 1945, the United States dropped an atomic bomb that devastated the Japanese city of Hiroshima. Three days later, it dropped a second atomic bomb on Nagasaki. Tens of thousands of civilians in those cities were killed. Japan surrendered on August 15 and formally signed a truce on September 2, 1945.

In the aftermath of the atomic bombings, Elliott made his way from Asia to America, first by Merchant Marine vessel to California.

"It made more speed than I had ever seen a ship make," he said.

After docking in San Francisco, he took a train to San Diego where he was discharged. From San Diego he caught an overnight bus to Dallas, where he had left his wife Gladys to go to war.

"I called my wife. She came to the bus station. And we started a new life."

He could, he said, have sought an educational loan, one of the benefits of his service.

"If I had been younger, I would have probably have needed to go to school. But I had so much experience while I was in the Marine Corps, I could have gone in almost any direction. I didn't need any loans. I got back to work as quick as I could."

He went back to the aviation company for which he had worked before the war. It was now refitting cargo planes into passenger planes and selling the craft to airlines across South America.

Elliott didn't stay long in aviation or working for someone else. He became an automobile mechanic. He owned his own garage and a home in Dallas and a 36-acre farm in East Texas by the time he retired. He'd once thought of retiring to the farm with Gladys. But by the time he did stop working he was a widower. He sold the farm and followed Judy, his only child, to Montrose.

Gladys, who died of cancer in 1981, was the love of his life. Not that Elliott would ever let such a flowery cliché cross his lips.

"I've been a single man now for 33 years. I was such a busy man, I didn't think about remarriage."

His son-in-law is a mining engineer who travels around the country to consult. Judy runs a business maintaining the vacation homes of wealthy people who visit the area only in the winters to ski. His daughter's business, Elliott said, exploits a resourcefulness she gets from him and his wife, and that he got from his father. His granddaughter, who now works with her mother, has that family spirit, he said.

"I keep telling her she's not going to get married if she stays so independent."

He moved to Colorado two years before his grandson was killed.

In the obituary, his family remembered Sitton as a generous, outgoing young man who was a musician and Eagle Scout and loved hiking and rafting. On September 3, 2006 after a memorial in his high school gym, he was buried with military honors in Grand View Cemetery on the outskirts of Montrose. At the funeral a general handed his relatives the young man's Bronze Star, Purple Heart, Army Good Conduct Medal and Army Medic's badge.

Elliott has his own plot picked out next to his grandson's. Elliott, a member of the VFW honor guard, is often at the cemetery for ceremonies for the fallen.

"At the funerals, I always do the same thing. I hold the flag. I stand at attention and hold the flag," Elliott said.

George Lawrence, a Vietnam vet who is active in the VFW and

Welcome Home Montrose, always asks Elliott if he wants to sit during the services. Elliott always refuses.

"He just does what it takes. That's the philosophy that he's passed on to all of us," Lawrence said. "It's quite an honor to stand next to that gentleman."

After each service, Elliott pauses for a few minutes at his grandson's grave.

Elliott is quietly dismissive of any suggestion that he bears scars from World War II more deeply hidden than those he showed me by pulling up a pant leg or memories that haven't faded in the face of hard work and long walks. He describes PTSD as a phrase he has heard but sees no connection to, though the empathy he shows younger vets makes me wonder if he really sees the disorder as a characteristic of this century's war, not his own. He wants me to believe PTSD is as foreign a concept to him as women in harm's way. When he speaks of his grandson's death, he often adds that a female comrade died in the same explosion.

What to make of Elliott's half century of silence about the bloody tumult he saw on Iwo Jima? And of his breaking that silence only after his grandson died? He spoke then only to other old soldiers who he says "have seen things they don't like to talk about to other people who are not vets."

The ghosts that haunt you can rise up at surprising times. They would lay you low if you did not have comrades to lean on. The worst things that have happened to him, Elliott told me, did not happen on Iwo Jima.

"They are my wife and my grandson dying.

"But you have to get on with life.

"You can't just sit around and cry."

Elliott is gentle, humble, resilient. I believe those innate qualities were deepened by his battlefield trials. His comrades from other wars were no doubt shaped in similar ways by their service; it only remains to be seen how their experiences will influence their characters and lives over the coming decades.

Elliott could be an older version of Kenney. Both are no-nonsense men. Kenney can be gruff, but not without humor. His brusque manner and jokes don't hide an essential kindness and generosity. When he joined forces with Welcome Home Montrose, he told Kline: "You be the nice one. I'll be the hammer."

"They let me off the chain every once in a while when someone needs to be attacked."

It's Kenney who speaks up at community meetings when he hears grumbling that Welcome Home Montrose was established for outsiders.

"Why don't you guys just shut up?" he'll say.

Kenney also has heard the gripes of Vietnam vets who say they were not welcomed home as warmly as those who fought in Afghanistan and Iraq.

"And they weren't. And shame on us as a country," he says.

But the past can't be changed. Kenney and Elliot live their shared belief that all that can be done is to try to make the future better.

Chapter 13

Revisiting Vietnam

A tall, white-haired Vietnam vet moved gracefully. He was a fish in water.

"In the Army, they always said 110 percent. Here, we want 70 percent."

Lee Burkins was leading a class through the soothing, disciplined movements of tai chi. His students were dressed in sweats or jeans and gathered in the common room of the Welcome Home Montrose drop-in center. Among them was the restless Afghanistan vet from Iowa who had befriended World War II vet Elliott.

Burkins put a bit more command in his tone. He knew his audience.

"This is going somewhere. You will get stronger."

Kline said that once she started talking to her neighbors about her vision for reaching out to Iraq and Afghanistan veterans, "I ended up getting vetted by a lot of vets."

Vietnam vets paid particular attention. They wanted to know whether she might want to exploit younger vets for personal or political gain. Or they were concerned she'd end up hurting someone by raising hopes impossibly high and then dashing them.

Whatever drew them, the Vietnam vets ended by making a commitment to Welcome Home Montrose that is proof individuals can survive conflict and its aftermath. And their very presence demands that their fellow Americans confront how deeply war has shaped our nation and its citizens.

Kline told me the question of what Vietnam vets have brought to Welcome Home Montrose is a big one. Three were on her founding board of directors, while others like Burkins led outreach efforts.

"As I met with organizations and service groups, mostly it was the Vietnam veterans and their wives who volunteered and gave their time," Kline continued. "They are acutely aware of the need for acceptance and camaraderie after leaving the military.

"I learned so much from them, gaining insight into the way that war affected their lives. I witnessed the unbreakable bond they share from it and am so proud that they have a place to meet, gather and support each other.

"They are *everything* to the success of WHM."

The bond seems natural between those who fought in Vietnam and those who fought in Iraq and Afghanistan. Perhaps it's the parallels in their experiences of war. Both generations know what it is to fight on ill-defined fronts and grapple with a sense of danger any- and everywhere that haunts them even when they return home. Veterans of Vietnam and those of the war on terror also see similarities in the political and social divisiveness linked to conflict in both eras.

The beginnings of America's entanglement in Vietnam can be traced to the 1950s as the United States tried to fill the vacuum left as French colonial power waned. The French era ended in 1954 with an international agreement that split Vietnam at the 17th parallel, with Ho Chi Minh heading a Communist government in the north and Western-backed Ngo Dinh Diem in power in the south.

In 1964, amid contested reports that U.S. warships off North Vietnam had come under fire, Congress passed the Gulf of Tonkin resolution authorizing President Lyndon Johnson to "take all necessary measures to repel any armed attack against the forces of the United States and to prevent further aggression."

Hostilities dragged on for a decade. President Richard Nixon signed a peace treaty in 1973. In 1975, North Vietnamese forces entered Saigon, sealing the failure of an American war on Communism. Vietnam was reunited the next year under Communist rule.

The war on terror began with the 9/11 attacks orchestrated by al-Qaida, a militant group espousing its own extremist version of Islam. The initial U.S. response was against Afghanistan, where an extremist Muslim movement known as the Taliban was harboring al-Qaida fighters and leaders. Even as American boots hit the ground in Afghanistan, contingency plans targeting Iraq were being drawn up at the behest of the Bush White House. Analysts produced an argument around accusations, later to be disproven, that Iraqi dictator Saddam Hussein was stockpiling a terrifying arsenal. In late 2002, the U.S. House of Representatives and the U.S. Senate voted to approve resolutions authorizing Bush to use force against Iraq.

Some in the Vietnam generation saw parallels to the Gulf of Tonkin in the controversy over Iraqi weapons of mass destruction.

American-led Operation Iraqi Freedom was launched in 2003 and quickly led to the toppling of Saddam, who was executed by Iraqi authorities. Anger and fear flared among members of his Sunni Muslim ethnic group. Chaos followed, as is inevitable after the disintegration of a brutal dictatorship. Iraq, a country I visited as a journalist when Saddam was in power, was none-too-integrated to begin with. It had a bloody modern history cobbled together by colonial powers when the Ottoman Empire collapsed in the early 1900s. Sunni Muslim-controlled Iraq's war over oil and territory with neighboring Shiite Muslim Iran dragged on from 1980 to 1988 and killed hundreds of thousands on both sides. Saddam's invasion of tiny, oil-rich Kuwait in 1990 ended within months with his defeat at the hands of a U.S.-led coalition. A frustrated Saddam then unleashed terror on his political rivals and his country's Shiite Muslim and Kurdish communities.

War correspondent Dexter Filkins writes that since Operation Iraqi Freedom was launched "the U.S. destroyed the Iraqi state and began spending billions of dollars trying to build a new one." Nuri al-Maliki, the Shiite who became Iraq's U.S.-backed post-invasion prime minister, showed little capacity for building a democratic post-Saddam Iraq.

A new threat that called itself al-Qaida in Iraq rose following Saddam's fall. Its splintering produced the Islamic State, which is so extreme in its interpretation of Islam and the perceived need to confront the West that al Qaida proper's leaders have disassociated themselves from the group. The Islamic State also is known as ISIS, ISIL or Daesh.

"In an earlier time," former U.S. Defense Secretary Gates wrote in his memoirs, "people would speak of winning or losing wars." The long Vietnam War ended. But this is the time of "The Forever War," as Filkins titled his book on the conflicts touched off by 9/11.

A forever war without boundaries. The official U.S. military toll counts deaths and injuries in nearly three dozen countries, Iraq and Afghanistan, but also Djibouti, Syria, Pakistan. Halfway through 2015, that toll was more than 6,000 dead and more than 50,000 wounded.

"You have these guys who see their buddies blown up, they see friends who lose limbs and in the end they say, 'What did we accomplish?'" Vietnam vet Frank Anderson told me, adding that the violent deaths and dismemberments of friends and a haunting sense of failure "weigh on vets' minds."

Anderson was among those three Vietnam vets on the founding board of Welcome Home Montrose. He is rarely seen without a black baseball cap emblazoned with the 101st Airborne insignia. The cap shadows the parts of his face not already hidden by a graying beard and moustache. Nothing hides his smile, but that masks dark preoccupations.

As in Vietnam, the United States in Iraq has allied with a government whose stability and trustworthiness has come under question. The battleground is home to people roiled by anti-colonial passions and divided by religion, ethnicity and history. In Vietnam then and the Middle East now, war has pitted American military might, particularly from the air, against an enemy that can blend in with civilians and launch guerrilla attacks from any direction.

"War on terror?" said 27-year Marine veteran Gary Gratton, who fought in Vietnam. He paused to expel a hard breath, a venting of powerful, complex emotions.

"There's no way to win that," he said, resuming his critique of America's latest war. "You're not fighting a country. You're fighting radicals in that country. How can you win that?"

Gratton was talking about Iraq and Afghanistan. But he also was offering a description of Vietnam, a conflict that lasted over a decade and saw the deployment of nearly 9 million servicemen and women in an era of draft and more than 90,000 Americans killed.

Gratton spoke to me at the Welcome Home Montrose drop-in center. It's a place where he spends plenty of time volunteering to support younger vets.

When he was young himself, in July of 1966, Gratton and two buddies reported to Parris Island, the Marine installation in South Carolina. They were straight out of high school, like Bolhuis decades later. The year 1966 saw heavy fighting in Vietnam. It was the year of Lo Ke and Con Thien, of operations Crimp, Hastings, Attleboro. More than 6,000 Americans died in Vietnam in 1966.

I have to look up the names of the places where the Vietnam vets tell me they fought. I am mortified, thinking they can see my ignorance and are put off by the blank look in my eyes when they share words that for them are at the core of their personal histories.

A mental health worker in Montrose told me that she doesn't follow the news from the Middle East and that she was surprised that Iraq and Afghanistan vets in town do, and do so with intense concentration. After that conversation, I approached Bolhuis, the veteran Marine who settled in Montrose at Kline's invitation after returning from Afghanistan with traumatic brain injury. I ask Bolhuis how it feels (that perennial journalist's question) to talk to clueless civilians.

Bolhuis told me he knows plenty of vets who get fired up watching the news. He's not one of them. He even skips over the political messages on his Facebook feed.

"I can't tell you what the latest ISIS attacks were," he said, referring to that group too militant for al-Qaida that emerged in Iraq. "War is not my realm anymore. When I do catch a story about ISIS, I get angry. I get sad. I get a little bit scared. But there's absolutely nothing I can do about it anymore, except support the troops that are there."

Bolhuis was born in 1990, weeks before the outbreak of the first Gulf War, which would end before Bolhuis had his first birthday.

"I feel sorry for kids today," Bolhuis said. "I remember growing up in peacetime. I didn't grow up seeing pictures of wounded veterans on the TV. Now, we have an entire generation with that. With the whole global climate, it's not looking like that's going to change any time soon."

He does not expect the civilians to understand war in the way he does. But he also has seen that people like Kline can find ways to shoulder the costs of freedom.

Kline didn't grasp the scope of what war had done to fighters "until she saw the kayak video," Bolhuis said.

"Now, she's an expert. Not on the war, but on how to help vets. You don't have to be a political expert or an expert on war games. You just have to have a heart."

Others can take on the task of military expertise. Kline has different priorities than parsing a confusing array of players in far-away places. Here's how my friend Borzou Daragahi, a perceptive journalist who covers the Middle East and its conflicts, summed up the terrain in a tongue-in-cheek Facebook post in 2014:

"The PYD's YPG, an offshoot of the PKK, is being backed by the KRG (which includes the skeptical KDP and the more enthusiastic PDK) against IS (or the ISIS or ISIL) despite the hostility of the AKP, which would like the DOD to back the FSA, which the USA suspects of being too weak compared to the IF and JAN. Got it?"

It's a relief to hear Bolhuis say we civilians don't have to get it. Even if his answer wasn't what I'd expected. That's why journalists ask dumb questions: because assumptions will always be dumber than any question. Bolhuis got me back to focusing on what the experts know.

Experts like Gratton, a trim man with thinning hair and a soft chuckle. They offered me insight into another time and were patient when I struggled to understand.

Gratton said when he was growing up, he knew no one who opposed the draft. A friend who initially took a college deferment dropped out to join and was killed on his first patrol.

Gratton grew up on a farm east of Cleveland. As a boy, he showed short horn beef cattle at fairs. He idolized his father, who was a former Marine, and other World War II veterans.

"Dad, back then, had the Eisenhower jacket. I loved that jacket. I wore it until it was in shreds," Gratton said.

"Every Memorial Day, my dad would tear the house apart looking for some part of his uniform to wear in the parade. At first, it was mandatory that the kids come. Then, it was voluntary. Right now, just talking about it, I get choked up, knowing that those guys gave their lives to protect our freedom."

While fighting in Vietnam, Gratton heard reports from home that convinced him that his generation of soldiers would not be idolized. He extended his service a month and a half.

"We were afraid to go home. We were hearing there were riots going on," he said.

He was an angry 21-year-old when he finally returned. He settled in Ravenna, Ohio. So he was nearby in 1970 when National Guardsmen fired on student anti-war demonstrators at Kent State, killing four people. Gratton raised a banner in his yard: "National Guard 4, Kent State, 0."

He had wanted to join the state highway patrol after Vietnam. But he withdrew his application because of the possibility he would be called on to confront protesters.

"I said, 'I don't want no part of riots.'"

He came to believe, though, that his view of protesters had

been shaped by news that "had been sensationalized several times over" by the time it reached him in Vietnam. And he came to see the protesters as patriots who loved their country as much as he does. In later years, when a nephew spoke out against the Gulf War, he was philosophical.

"There's two views to everything," he said. "I pick the military view of things."

Any personal skepticism, he said, has to be put aside when a political decision has been made. It is a soldier's job to go to war when the country calls.

In the 1970s, though, Gratton didn't spend much time on reflection. Like Elliott after World War II, he got to work, not as a highway patrolman but as a truck driver. After two years behind the wheel, Gratton (former combat engineer, son of a bricklayer, grandson of a general contractor) had saved enough to open a construction business.

The business, though, quickly collapsed. Gratton, by the time his business failed also had lost his family, a wife and three sons, through divorce. His wife went to Florida with the boys and he got a motorcycle and drifted. His wandering took him to Colorado. For a time, he worked on a ranch near Steamboat Springs in the northwestern part of the state.

"I grew up with cows," he said. "I understood cows."

He decided he needed the structure of the Marines again.

"I went back in to make a career. And I made it."

The career took him around the world as a construction engineer, aviation radar technician, explosives instructor. The Marines, he said, valued education and he took classes here and there, joking that he crammed four years of college into 10.

He earned a degree in vocational education. He also married again. His second wife had two daughters about the age of his sons. He repaired his relationship with his sons, the eldest of whom would one day join the Navy.

He had fallen in love with Colorado during his stint on the

ranch. He would bring his family to the state on vacation from wherever the military had posted him. It was on one of those trips that he first encountered Montrose, and thought: "This is a nice town."

He moved to Montrose in December of 1996, a day after retiring. Retirement did not mean he stopped working. Vets, as I learned working on this book, burn to serve and Gratton was no exception. He took a spot on the board of directors of the local chapter of Habitat for Humanity and later directed the program, which is dedicated to housing the poor. Combining his vocational education studies and his construction background, Gratton developed a training course for Habitat volunteers who build houses. He has also helped out at a food bank, and he and his wife co-led a group formed to ensure newcomers feel at home in Montrose. He is a deacon at his church, and writes its newsletters.

"I served my country for 27 years," he said. "Now, I want to serve my community."

He first encountered Welcome Home Montrose before it was launched. He heard Kline was speaking to people active in the community about what her program might look like.

Then, "I had no idea it was going to grow into what it is," he said.

Now, Gratton is at the Welcome Home Montrose drop-in center several days a week. He puts to work the expertise at navigating red tape that he honed during his years of active duty. He helps vets sign up for VA health and pension benefits, learn about the GI Bill and look for jobs. And he talks to them from his own experience about the benefits of mental health counseling.

He got an Afghanistan vet to participate in a project Welcome Home Montrose has championed to provide walking sticks with hand-carved eagle heads to vets as a way to honor them. The younger vet told Gratton, a man who understands postwar anger and anxiety, that when he is carving, he doesn't think about his rage.

"He is so excited that he is doing something for someone else," Gratton said. It is a lesson in the power of giving.

Like a lot of Vietnam vets, George Lawrence believes his generation of fighters "didn't receive good treatment, and I'm going to make damn sure that doesn't happen again."

Lawrence, a plain-spoken 70-year-old who is not above the occasional joke about adult diapers, was born in Silverton, a mountain mining town in the nearby San Juan range. He was raised in the western Colorado region he still calls home.

"When I got back from Vietnam, I was told by my stepfather I couldn't join the VFW because I wasn't in a declared war," Lawrence says of his own homecoming.

For decades, that was fine with Lawrence. He didn't want to sit around trading war stories. He found others who were equally reticent, like a high school buddy he had not realized had been to Vietnam until they were nearing retirement. The friend had had no idea Lawrence was also a vet.

"A lot of us just wanted to be left alone. There are still some who feel that way."

His war had started as a community experience. On Valentine's Day in 1968, Lawrence set off on a bus from Montrose to Denver to be inducted. He knew almost all of the 20 or so other young men on the bus on the same mission. They were from Montrose or the nearby towns of Olathe or Delta.

Lawrence was 24, almost too old to be drafted. He'd been in college but dropped a few courses and suddenly found himself no longer considered a full-time student and therefore eligible to be called up.

His basic training was at Fort Gordon, Georgia. Lawrence recalled it being hard to get his bearings without the San Juan Mountains as his lodestar. From Georgia he was sent to Fort Bliss, Texas, where he went to language school, and then to Qui Nhon, on the South China Sea.

The flight over was "the first time I'd ever seen the ocean. I couldn't believe how flat it was," he said. "The closest I'd ever come to going to a foreign country before that was going to Utah."

His duties at Qui Nhon included guarding an Armed Forces Radio Network station. He'd picked up enough at language school to be able to speak a bit to some of the Vietnamese camped nearby.

"Everybody around our compound were all refugees in their own country," he said. "When you look back on it, we didn't need to be there. Seems like we're doing the same thing again. I don't know why our government keeps making the same mistakes and expecting different results."

Lawrence returned from Vietnam to Montrose in October 1969. He wore a uniform designed for a hot, humid climate, not late fall in the San Juan Mountains. The shock of feeling the cold is as much as he'll say about any discomfort upon return. Lawrence makes his own transition sound easy. He finished college, earning a degree in recreation. He became the first director of the Montrose regional recreation district, organizing softball games and swim meets.

Lawrence also has worked in mining and in tourism in Alaska. Into his late 60s he was a groundskeeper at a Montrose golf course. And when he reached his 60s, he encountered a new VFW. He was not the only Vietnam vet to find some members of the organization were hostile in the 1960s and 1970s. But attitudes softened. Lawrence not only joined, he became a leader in Post 784.

He wanted his post to be active in finding ways to help vets, whether it was forming honor guards at their funerals or distributing walking sticks to the frail. Increasingly, Lawrence is seeing fighters joining the VFW who had been part of the 1989 U.S. invasion of Panama or the 1990-1991 fight to evict Iraq from Kuwait.

"These younger guys are stepping up," Lawrence said.

What would become the VFW was started at the dawn of the 20th century as a local organization before the term grassroots became common. At a time when there were no Veterans Affairs hospitals or veterans' pensions, the VFW was founded by Americans who had fought in the 1898 Spanish-American War, in which Spain relinquished to the United States Cuba, Guam, Puerto Rico, and the Philippines and the 1898-1901 U.S. battle against nationalists in the Philippines.

VFW lobbying helped lead to the creation of what would become the U.S. Department of Veterans Affairs, GI bills and service memorials, including monuments honoring those who fought in Vietnam.

Some in groups like the VFW, long established as forums for veterans, might see Welcome Home Montrose as a rival. Lawrence counters it could as easily be argued that maybe Welcome Home Montrose arose to fill a void because "the VFW and the American Legion aren't doing their jobs."

Lawrence isn't interested in such a debate. He focuses on "anything we can do to help veterans, no quibbling allowed. It's better than sitting on your butts doing nothing."

"If everybody just focuses on the main thing, which is helping vets, then it works out fine."

Lawrence always seems to be at the Welcome Home Montrose drop-in center. One morning finds him delivering an elderly vet who needed a ride to the weekly coffee. Other times, he is organizing a crew of volunteers to build a wheelchair ramp, keeping track of fundraising projects like one to buy a chair equipped with tracks instead of wheels that can maneuver hiking and hunting trails. He helped bring to Welcome Home Montrose the cane carving project that has helped Gratton's young friend ease his anger. Lawrence's gruff humor ensures informality at the drop-in center during the monthly ceremonies at which the elegant sticks are presented to vets.

The Montrose cane project was inspired by an effort Lawrence heard of in Oklahoma. He believes similar canes were carved by Civil War veterans for other old soldiers. For Lawrence, the canes are a link to a tradition of veterans working for one another.

The Civil War left the United States with some 2 million vets.

The internecine conflict also galvanized efforts to help wounded warriors, according to a VA history that recounts how many of those efforts were led by veterans themselves. The Grand Army of the Republic, formed by former Union soldiers, became the largest veterans group of its time.

I met vets of Korea and World War II as well as of Vietnam in Montrose. As I explored the town's history and its people's stories, I saw scars of the earliest wars that made America a nation. I heard anger and bitter disappointment. I also saw reason for hope in faces like Lawrence's, round and with a neatly trimmed beard and moustache.

Lawrence looks like an affable coach in the baseball cap he usually wears. He still sees some of the kids for whom he once organized softball games and swim meets around town. They have their own kids. Lawrence, who has two sons and two grandchildren, knitted together a small-town life after Vietnam. The war set Gratton on a path to a career in the military. In the story of tai chi instructor Burkins, we see how war can launch an individual on an odyssey whose destination may never be quite clear.

Burkins grew up on the East Coast. As a boy, he hunted and fished and once worked in a gun shop. He enlisted in the Army rather than wait to be drafted, thinking that would put him in a position to choose what role he would have in Vietnam. He hoped to go to armory training at a facility he knew in Aberdeen, a small town near Baltimore. Instead, he was sent to infantry training.

A Green Beret came to speak to the infantry class. Burkins liked what he heard.

"I want to be my own boss," Burkins told the Green Beret recruiter.

Burkins would go on to serve with the 5th Special Forces Group. He worked in Southeast Asia with the Military Assistance Command in Special Operations. He wrote in a memoir about the pain of coming home from Vietnam and the anguish of being unable to disagree when he heard anti-war activists calling vets baby killers.

"It was criminal what I did," he said of his war experiences. "But it was sanctioned by the government."

Back home in 1973, Burkins wanted a break not only from the war, but from his old life. He identified two places he saw as counter-culture meccas at a time he wanted nothing to do with anything mainstream: Boulder, Colorado and the Willamette Valley in Oregon. He set out from Maryland and, because he hit Colorado first, settled in Boulder.

"I was angry. I was raging. And I needed a new place," he said. "I was a pretty miserable son of a bitch."

He brought something he had learned as a soldier with him, an interest in Asian martial arts. He had injured his knees pursuing the sport. He heard about a teacher at the University of Colorado at Boulder who was an expert in tai chi. Tai chi, he was told, was a martial art that could promote healing. Curious, he found a book.

"There is a great joy to be discovered in the practice of tai chi," Burkins said, quoting a line from the book he read some four decades ago. When he first read it, "I thought to myself, 'Man, I could use some joy in my life.' And, I wanted to heal my knees."

He embraced tai chi. He went from student to teacher.

"It's just what I do. Tai chi teaches you how to be a human being."

But he remained restless, moving from Boulder to Hawaii at the suggestions of a friend who lived there. In Hawaii he found a passion to add to tai chi, lobbying in support of Vietnam veterans.

"There was no help available to Vietnam veterans from anyone but ourselves until the early '80s. We grouped together, learned the federal laws governing veterans' care and took the VA to task for many years before they began to help us with our wounds."

He pestered politicians, VA bureaucrats and journalists.

"It sort of became a way of life for me to find vets who needed help and assist them."

In his memoir Burkins recounted his struggles with PTSD and for the dignity of a diagnosis. He said he was sneered at for seeking psychological counseling. He did get it. He credits that along with the mental and physical discipline of tai chi for his continuing recovery.

He left Hawaii and his work for veterans. Back on the mainland, he supported himself giving tai chi classes as he traveled across the country. He ended up in Denver, where he also worked with vets but turned more of his attention to environmental advocacy. In Denver, he met and married a woman (whom he later divorced) and together they decided to move to the Montrose area. They were drawn by the mountain views and open spaces. They also were glad it was near an airport big enough for large planes when they wanted to travel or have visitors.

A young videomaker shared my fascination with the contrast between the turmoil of Burkins's past and the beauty of Montrose. In *Warrior Within,* a short documentary about Burkins that Jacob White made for a film class at the University of Texas, scenes of southwestern Colorado's dramatic skies and canyons are juxtaposed with still photographs from Burkins's collection of images from his war days. His pictures show helicopters and heavily armed men.

The Montrose scenes are shot in autumn, a particularly beautiful time in the region. The reds and golds appear super-saturated. A young Burkins poses with a skull in one black-and-white photograph. Burkins still has the lean face and intense, light-colored eyes of his younger self. It is the older version of the man who looks more carefree.

"If you had known me 40 years ago, you see me coming, you turn around and go the other way," Burkins told White.

Explaining his transformation, he told White that tai chi exercises "help us expose the body and most importantly the mind that's in this body."

When Burkins began teaching tai chi in Montrose only a few

vets attended his classes. He didn't seek out other vets. For a decade or so, that was his quiet life.

Then, Burkins read a small item about Welcome Home Montrose in a local paper. He thought anything so ambitious would need all the help it could get. So, he sought out Kline. He helped her write funding requests and navigate the legal and official channels he had first mapped while in Hawaii. Later, he began teaching tai chi at the Welcome Home Montrose drop-in center. He leads his 90-minute classes twice a week. Among his students is Bronner, the Vietnam vet who for decades hid the anger war and returning from war had fired in him. When he finally let the anger show, it scared him and his family. Coming to Welcome Home Montrose and to Burkins's classes has given Bronner refuge from rage.

"Lee's been through some crap in his day. He has a way of calming you down," Bronner said. "I figured out it's better to let things go than go out and shoot 15 people and destroy your own life in the process."

Burkins classes are open to all: vets and their spouses, community members. One day, Burkins would like to add a class for combat veterans only.

In Vietnam, he said, he learned how to hurt people. With tai chi, he began to learn how to fix people, starting with himself.

"When I am trying to heal myself, when I am meditating or whatever, I keep in mind that this is for the healing of everyone. I'm not separate. As good as I feel, I want to share it with everyone. If you've got some pain, share it with others," he said. "A lot of vets, they struggle with themselves. As you struggle to help yourself, realize that you're helping others. Just realize that."

Burkins had lived in Montrose 16 years before Welcome Home Montrose was born. In those 16 years, he said, he did not know any vets in town. Or, at least, no one he knew was a vet. He did not bring up his service and they did not bring up theirs.

"Welcome Home Montrose brought me out of the woodwork. It brought quite a few vets out of the woodwork, out of the woods,"

Burkins said. "They've rejoined the community."

In his past, Burkins believed he could get better in isolation. His sense of community and understanding of its power have grown and deepened on a journey home from Vietnam that took decades.

Burkins believes that part of what vets can contribute to their community is an understanding of the toll of war that might slow any rush to possible new conflicts.

"It's society that leads us into wars. We, especially as combat veterans, we have a lot we can say," he said. "War is such a big part of our life. It's just terrible. And we all accept it."

He said he once wrote a letter to a newspaper editor proposing that Middle East leaders be given LSD when they come together to talk about making peace. Newspaper readers may have thought it was a counter-culturalist rant. I saw it as a commentary on just how radically mankind would have to change to reject war. But Burkins said he wasn't ranting or playing with metaphors. He truly wonders why skeptics would reject the idea of using drugs to change our idea of one another when we so desperately need to change perceptions.

For all his counter-culture ideas, Burkins is accepted and respected in Montrose. In part that is because of his service.

Perhaps being at home means feeling whole again. Burkins has gotten to a place where all of his experiences can be unified and acknowledged.

"With the creation of WHM and the overwhelming support of the community to bring veterans to Montrose to live and to heal, I hope to give veterans insight into their own deeper personal strengths and help them with the support that Vietnam veterans never had," Burkins told me. "Veterans know the value of helping others. In battle, your life depended on everyone around you."

"In Hawaii, it was just a small group of us veterans helping one another. Here, it's the community. That's the amazing thing about Welcome Home Montrose: the community created it."

"All my life, you didn't know who veterans were. You didn't

talk about it. Now, here's a community that promotes it," he said. "Who knows where Welcome Home Montrose will go? "

Chapter 14

Jared's Challenge

Bolhuis detests the Fourth of July. He believes most combat veterans share his hatred of a holiday that can evoke battlefield horrors with its celebratory reenactments of war: rockets' red glare and bombs bursting in air.

A few days after the Fourth in 2014, Bolhuis was still feeling its influence. He holed up in his apartment after downing the cocktail of drugs prescribed to treat his PTSD and Traumatic Brain Injury. Suddenly, he heard a knocking. Bolhuis's medications can make him feel loopy, and he was unnerved. Like something out of Poe, the tapping on his door wouldn't stop. The more the insistent, unknown caller rapped, the less inclined Bolhuis was to answer. He hunted for his shotgun. He set it within easy reach, but did not put shells in the chamber.

"Even under the most high anxiety situation I've been in since I've been back, I fell into the military training on weapon safety."

Bolhuis called the police and gave them details as he might have briefed a fellow soldier supporting him on a battlefield. He told the dispatcher he had a gun, making it clear it was unloaded. He'd taken prescribed medication that was influencing perceptions already addled by brain injury, he added. He was a veteran, he summed up.

"I was keeping constant situational awareness to all parties involved. I wanted everybody to have as much information as possible."

He stayed on the line as two officers set out in a police car and neared his home. By the time they arrived, the visitor, whoever he or she was, had disappeared. Bolhuis told the dispatcher he was leaving his gun inside and going out to meet the police.

He made another military-style report to the cops. If they were impressed by his calm, they didn't show it with their reaction: they told Bolhuis they were arresting him on charges of handling a firearm while under the influence.

"We've got to take you downtown," they told him.

He would spend the rest of that night in jail. He had never been arrested before. He was mortified, an emotion that would linger long after he was released.

"I went with them. I was completely compliant. The police show up at a house, they see some random guy. They responded exactly as they should have. Should police treat a vet different from anyone else? No!"

His evening adventure made the police blotter section of the regional paper: "Jared Bolhuis, 26, was arrested Wednesday night in the 1200 block of North Second Street on suspicion of prohibited use of weapons."

Bolhuis hired a lawyer. He prepared for his court hearing, not knowing what to expect and fearing the worst.

"I was arrested because I did break the law. I didn't hide anything."

The case took three months to wend its way through the legal system. In the end, a judge weighed the facts. Yes, Bolhuis had violated statute. But he was the one who called the police and provided them with what evidence they had. The judge threw the case out, saying Bolhuis never should have been brought before him.

Vets, like anyone else, have to trust in the safety net provided by their communities. Bolhuis's story is a challenge to Americans. Can we rise to it, mustering the necessary patience and creative problem-solving to provide more and better care?

Bolhuis joked to me that the lesson of that night is Americans need to lay off the fireworks in deference to their vets.

Then, he got serious. Bolhuis knows that many people worry that veterans are unpredictable dangers to their communities. Even Kline, when she hears a report of a mass shooting somewhere in the United States, wonders whether the attacker had combat experience in Iraq or Afghanistan.

Vets from the Gulf wars were already in Montrose, Kline came to reason. Bringing in more might increase the risks. It could also increase awareness and that could save lives.

Chroniclers in the United States have noted a link between wartime violence and peacetime mayhem since at least as far back as the aftermath of the Civil War. Some of the men who took off blue or gray uniforms put on bandit's masks and helped give the 19th century American West its wild reputation.

Much of the mayhem that Gulf war vets are wreaking is against themselves. That, too, is likely no different from past wars, as is society's habit of looking away from the grim fact.

Another lesson Bolhuis drew from his troubled Fourth is that troubled vets are more likely to retreat into themselves than to lash out at relatives, friends, passersby. They hole up in their apartments while the sparklers flare and the scent of gunpowder wafts over suburban streets. Maybe the person knocking at the door was a neighbor who wanted to invite Bolhuis to a barbecue.

And Bolhuis stresses that he did not load his shotgun. He is confident that most of his fellow veterans would have done the same, falling back on the rules drilled into them aimed at protecting themselves and others.

Another former warrior told me he can almost hear civilians thinking when they hear that he is a vet: "This guy's gone to war. We don't know what he's going to do, what he's capable of."

Psychotherapist Tick has contemplated what must be done to heal the rift between civilians and veterans like those he has treated for decades. In his writings, he has urged civilians to emulate the commitment to service he has seen in veterans, and express it by listening without judgment to their stories and recognizing they have sacrificed for society. Most importantly, Tick has written, Americans must acknowledge veterans' need to continue to contribute.

Tick is concerned, though, that the divide between those who fought and those who stayed home has grown so wide that bringing the two sides together will be difficult. Healing will require empathy across racial, ethnic and economic lines. Tick laments that: "less than 1 percent of eligible people serve; the country has become dependent on a volunteer force in which poor, disadvantaged, disenfranchised and unemployed recruits crowd the ranks. All are one within the military but many are the hurting among them, and few are the Americans who join or serve them."

In Montrose, vets find a sympathetic ear in psychiatrist David Good. Good wonders if those who fear that a vet might explode at any moment aren't projecting their own unresolved volatility onto a stranger.

"It has nothing to do with who they are," Good said. "You don't even know them."

Good is an avid reader, attested to by the books I saw around his office and home. In conversation with me, he cited not a medical text, but, unexpectedly, a literary masterpiece about race in America, Ralph Ellison's *Invisible Man*.

Ellison opens his psychological novel with a description of whites who, instead of seeing blacks, see only their own potential for destruction as if in a distorted mirror. Good proposes that those who do not understand mental illness often are grappling with fear and prejudices that have nothing to do with the person they encounter who is suffering from PTSD or some other disorder. It is the unwillingness or inability to see clearly and to empathize that lead to tensions.

I had years ago read *Invisible Man* as an African-American story. Intrigued by Good's analysis, I re-read it as an American story, or one of the many possible stories we need to understand to understand our nation. Ellison's language is so vivid and beautiful that his book published in 1947 is still fresh. His protagonist is anguished, alienated and traumatized by a brutality into which society thrust him, then refused to acknowledge. After Good made the connection for me, I was able to hear the words of this fictional character coming from the mouths of very real veterans: "All things were indeed awash in my mind. I longed for home."

Ellison ends his book with a question from his main character: "Who knows but that, on the lower frequencies, I speak for you?"

Any one of us could find ourselves in a perilous fight for identity and sanity and in need of patient guidance. The namelessness of Ellison's Invisible Man symbolizes all that was stripped from Americans like him by some of the most brutal passages of American history: capture, the Middle Passage, slavery, the brutality that followed the Civil War and the era of Jim Crow segregation.

The Invisible Man is resilient, but also as angry and suspicious as some of the vets I have met in Montrose. Ellison's portrait reminds me, as did that early Montrose chronicler Galloway, that all narratives must be given their due if we are to make sense of the whole of our national story

Dr. Good has more than once heard people drop their voices to sotto to ask the same question in response to hearing what he does for a living: "How can you work with those people?" They're not just talking about vets. They're expressing a larger stigma about mental illness. That stigma is laced with an extra dose of fear when it comes to veterans.

"Those people," Good responds, come to him because they have the sense to acknowledge they have a problem.

"And they're doing something about it."

"You have an infection in your lungs, you can understand that. A heart attack, you can understand that. When it comes to psychiatric issues, people still have a lot of strange notions. When you don't understand something, you make things up. They don't realize these things are physical illnesses."

Good, who has offices in Montrose and the nearby town of Delta, has seen veterans withdraw into nightmares and memories, afraid to leave their homes. They're more likely to turn on themselves than on their neighbors.

It would be too easy to dismiss the suspicion surrounding struggling vets and mental illness in general as a product of small-town isolation. But urbanites have the same prejudices, the doctor is sure.

While misconceptions cross the line between urban and rural, a small town psychiatrist has challenges peers in the cities do not.

It's harder, for example, to stay on the cutting edge of research in Good's field.

Searching for a metaphor for the hodgepodge arsenal of advice, methods and drugs from which he can draw to offer succor to a PTSD sufferer, Good hits upon a story older doctors in town like to tell about practicing medicine here before well-equipped, well-staffed hospitals were built. Once, when doctors determined fluid was building up in a woman's skull, they used a power drill to relieve the pressure.

Small-town professionals use the tools and experience at hand.

"This is what we're doing today in psychiatry," said Good, adding the woman subjected to the hardware store drill is still alive and doing well.

From Montrose, Good travels to regional conferences on the use of treatment drugs. He scours journals and scrolls the Internet to keep himself abreast as best he can. He also talks with the few other psychiatrists in the region.

A few years ago, as he found himself increasingly interested in treating veterans, Good approached Veterans Affairs officials and became what was known as an accredited rural provider. That meant local vets could use their benefits to see him in Montrose instead of driving an hour to see a therapist at the nearest VA hospital, in Grand Junction, or half a day to see a specialist at the state's main VA center, in Denver.

Good found that few vets were being told of his availability. Those that did hear found a tangle of red tape between them and an appointment. They had to contact an insurance company handling the program, which would in turn contact the VA, which would eventually OK an appointment.

Good's secretary, a vet herself, called the VA to try to encourage officials in Grand Junction to advertise Good's services and to try to decrease the number of steps between a patient and the doctor. She said she got a man on the line who told her that directing a veteran to a contractor would mean lost fees for the VA.

"Then, he hung up on me," she told me. "I didn't get his name, or I would have reported him to someone."

Good turned to Welcome Home Montrose, whose drop-in center is a short distance from his office on the compact downtown grid. Welcome Home Montrose began directing vets to him. Many of the vets associated with the project have high praise for Good.

Good doesn't hang out at the Welcome Home Montrose drop-in center. He tells vets that when he sees them on the streets, he won't greet them first so they can maintain their privacy if they choose. Montrose is small enough that many people know Good is a psychiatrist, and not everyone wants to advertise a tie with him.

The 60-year-old Good, with only the faintest of accent betraying his Arkansas roots, first encountered vets early in his training. His studies included a stint at what he still refers to as Fort Roots, though the venerable Little Rock institution is now called the John L. McClellan Memorial Veterans Hospital.

Good remembers from his time there decades ago that "ward after ward after ward" of beds were filled by veterans. A few World War I survivors would argue with World War II vets about whose was the "big war." Not every veteran of those conflicts was an Elliott, the nonagenarian in Montrose who was able to jump right back into civilian life after Iwo Jima.

"I didn't talk to the World War I vets as much as I should have," Good said. "I didn't realize history was sitting right there."

Good had an uncle who served in the Pacific during World War II. Years later the uncle started to drink heavily, suffer nightmares and tell Good stories of watching other soldiers dig gold out of the mouths of Japanese dead. The uncle eventually checked into Fort Roots. He left a calmer man.

Good's stepfather, John Hart, fought in the Battle of the Bulge.

"My step-father would tell me about having nightmares of blood in the snow," Good said. Hart as an elderly man traveled to Europe with his daughter and retraced the geography of his wartime experience. After the do-it-yourself course of exposure therapy, he told Good he never had another nightmare about blood.

It was only as an adult that Good came to see that his uncle and stepfather suffered what we today call PTSD.

Hart "was a family doctor in a small town, Clinton, Arkansas. If a veteran walked in the door, there could be 50 people in the waiting room, and the veteran would go straight to the front. I feel the same way."

"I may not be supporting what the government is doing," said Good, who questions in particular the rationale for the war on Iraq. "But I'm supporting the soldiers. They went into the military for different reasons. For some of them, it's family tradition. It doesn't mean they were in favor of attacking Iraq. They were given orders and they followed them. The military is not a democracy.

"I'll always stand behind these guys."

As he saw his stepfather support the vets of another era.

"My personal experience with vets growing up was a wonderful experience," Good said. "Even though they had PTSD, they taught you values: responsibility, honesty. Those guys came back knowing what life is worth. I don't think today's vets are any different."

After earning an undergraduate degree in the South, Good traveled to the University of Colorado at Denver for a medical degree and to do his psychiatric internship. He got a chance to train at the state mental hospital in Pueblo, in southwestern Colorado, in the 1980s. A Pueblo clinic that had a government contract to treat PTSD asked Good to serve as its medical director, a job that gave him experience in using drug therapy for the condition.

Good's career took him to private practice in Longmont, near Denver. Then he returned to Arkansas to practice with his father, who also was a psychiatrist, in Little Rock. When he tired of the southern humidity, Good escaped to Colorado. He found the market saturated with psychiatrists in the more urban areas on the eastern steps of the Rocky Mountains where he had studied and practiced earlier. He turned to Montrose. He had come to know and love the region while on camping trips during his earlier stint in Colorado. He has practiced in Montrose for 20 years.

Veterans and other patients come to see Good in Montrose in a 1930s craftsman cottage off Main Street. Similar old homes nearby also are now commercial, occupied by a lawyer, a dentist, a locksmith. Good has added a cement wheelchair ramp and painted his façade a soft white. Visitors are ushered across gently squeaking wood floors through a sunny reception into a room that looks like it could have belonged to Good's stepfather. A plaid couch and two leather arm chairs form a niche for talking. An escritoire holds books. A watercolor print on one wall shows the campus of Good's alma mater, the University of Virginia. The image is more personal than a diploma, but makes the same point. You are in trained hands in this office.

The warriors often can, at least in the early psychotherapy sessions, stand less than a minute of talk about conflict. When the stress becomes too much, Good switches the topic to football or fishing. He comes back to the main matter, gently but persistently, as the vet builds stamina. Good prescribes drugs to blunt the rising blood pressure and heart rates that can result from re-experiencing trauma. Sometimes, a vet sits with his or her spouse in the office, the partners comforting one another.

One patient Good came to admire was never very specific about his military exploits, which occurred during a time when the United States was not officially at war. The patient liked to escape to the wilderness areas around Montrose. When he returned, he would tell Good: "I was turning off the switches. The Army is great about turning on the switches. But when they discharge you, they don't tell you how to switch them off."

The vet died of cancer at 56 in early 2014. At Good's request, even when the vet was sick, he stepped in to mentor an Iraq war vet in his 20s.

The older man would "do anything for another veteran. All I had to do was call him, and he was on it. He was a strong man. He was a good man. If he had lived longer, he could have taught me a whole lot more. I can see why veterans just hold onto one another. Everything else is fragmented, patchwork. The only cohesion is their group."

The younger vet who was mentored by Good's patient was a paratrooper. He had returned from war with a back injury and a paranoia that made it impossible to leave his home.

"The only time he felt safe was at night," Good said. "Nighttime was when he went on missions in Iraq. He knew the night. He understood the night."

"A lot of these guys, it's either with another veteran or alone that they feel safe," Good said.

Good probed the paratrooper repeatedly about what it would take to coax him from his home. It doesn't help, the paratrooper said, that everywhere he looked, he seemed to see American civilians carrying guns so blithely, as if they did not understand the violence they were capable of inflicting. While gun activists say their weapons make them feel safe, they made public spaces seem the opposite to the paratrooper.

Finally, the paratrooper said a bike might make him feel more secure outside. It would return to him some of the agility and speed he lost because of his back injury. Good loaned him an old bicycle. The recluse became a Little League coach, warning the other coaches they might have to cover for him if he ever suddenly felt overwhelmed and headed home in the middle of practice or a game.

"That's how, slowly, we worked him back into public," Good said.

Another man Good treats revisits his trauma by going through a collection of photographs he took of the bloody mayhem following a battle.

One of his vets was a proud housekeeper, but returned from war with a back injury that made it difficult for her to make beds according to her own exacting standards. Her frustration was a feature of her sessions with Good. Instead of trying to persuade her that it wasn't necessary to bounce a quarter off the spread, he challenged her to find a way around her disability. She bought knee pads so she could kneel alongside rather than bend over the bed and found a way to use a stick to pull the covers taught. She reported proudly to Good: "I found a way."

Good said veterans have shown him the rewards of perseverance, of finding new tools to reach goals that are important to them. Part of his therapy involves giving them a task, getting them thinking beyond bitterness and anger.

He tells them, "I don't want to hear, 'I can't do that.' Let's think about how we can skin the cat. Let's think about how else we can do it."

Sometimes, another way means asking for help, something Good's vets may struggle with most.

"You're still in charge," Good assures them. "You're not helpless. Think of the person you're asking to help you as a tool."

"You really have to work on this issue of feeling helpless. They're not helpless, if they will be clever, think of new ways," Good said. "Some people will take on anything. Some people just hate being disabled. Others turn their disability into their identity, and that's the trap."

Good takes the lesson home, where he finds that as he ages, he's gradually losing strength and energy to plough his garden or water his vegetables. He looks for ways to cope, and hopes he does so as gracefully as the men and women he has met who lost their vigor suddenly and in their prime.

Good was a military history buff and had considered applying to the Air Force Academy until he was told a football knee injury made him ineligible. He was never a soldier. But he can share his own war stories. His enemy was depression. He offers himself as proof that treatment can change a life. His openness is a model for fighting the stigma surrounding mental disease.

"I'm not a vet. I can't say I know what war's like," Good said. "But I certainly can understand depression."

The sharing and the camaraderie end when the session is over and the patient treads those squeaky floors out of Good's office. Sometimes, the vet leaves behind images of war that Good, the lifelong civilian, cannot shake. Among the most haunting was painted by a patient who had been passing through an Iraqi village and stopped to chat with a family. No more than a courtesy call. When the soldier and his comrades returned the next day, they found the entire family had been killed. The attackers, presumably, were insurgents who suspected someone had traitorously shared information. Everyone in the family, even the children, had been beheaded. The heads were displayed like trophies outside the home.

"Somehow, you've got to get out of that and get back here," Good had told the soldier after listening to the story. Then, the doctor told himself.

"This I have come to believe: If you can think of it, someone out there is doing it," Good said. "I've just heard too many things over the years, both from civilians and from vets. Evil exists. I've seen it. I've heard about it and I've talked about it. You don't have to live it, but you have to accept it."

"I have to work to see what is beautiful in the world, what is good about the world."

His home is outside town. A house and garden on 90 acres at the end of a dirt road in a rural area between Montrose and the next town, Olathe

"I half-jokingly say at the end of the week: 'Only if you walk on all fours can you come on my property.'"

Among the four-legged visitors Good welcomes are the neighbors' cattle he allows to graze in his meadow. He can pull on shorts, shove a baseball cap over his graying hair, grab a beer and climb a small rise to a pond. From there, he can see his neighbors' farms and ranches, beyond them the Uncompahgre Plateau, and beyond that the craggy, cloud-like outline of the San Juan Mountains. The view is both stirring and restful.

"If you want to come and get your head together, this is the place," Good said one late afternoon, sitting on a rough bench with his back to the pond. Later, he would dig potatoes he had planted himself and offer them to me alongside grilled hamburgers.

He could imagine inviting vets for a weekend of fly fishing or gardening in his retreat. But they have buddies for that.

"You've got just me to help you with your treatment," he tells them.

The warriors who come to Good seeking help have enriched him personally and professionally. The key, he said, is listening.

"That's where you learn what works."

Good said that when he asks a vet to do something to get better, the former soldier does it.

"If all my patients were like that," the good doctor said, "my job would be so much easier."

They have modeled dependability and reliability for their doctor. For all of us. Think of Bolhuis, carefully setting the ammunition to the side when he placed his gun nearby that tense July night.

Chapter 15

Not Alone

Bolhuis blames himself, not the police, for his night in jail and for the months on edge that followed. It is the cops' job to enforce the law, and they often put their lives on the line doing it, he says.

Why, though, does it so often falls to our first responders to cope with not criminal intent, but mental stress? Men and women like Bolhuis, wounded fighting for their country, might help point us to better solutions for themselves and for the rest of us.

The issue has been a quandary for national policy makers. The U.S. Justice Department has probed encounters between officers and the mentally ill during several investigations of police departments accused of violating the civil rights of Americans. The Associated Press reported in 2016 that departments in cities like Portland and Seattle have responded with new training in crisis intervention. But Vanita Gupta, head of the Justice Department's Civil Rights Division, told AP that for progress to be made, police need wider help.

"It's not about casting blame on specific actors. It's about making sure that there is adequate support for community-based mental health services in compliance with federal law," Gupta said.

In my hometown, police have experimented with sending mental health workers along with officers on some calls. During the 2016 test phase, *The Denver Post* reported, passersby were alarmed by a man screaming incoherently on a busy downtown street. The mental health worker who responded along with police was able to determine the man was a patient of the Mental Health Center of Denver who had not been taking his medication. An incident that could have escalated and ended in jail instead led to the man being taken from the street to the center under the care of his case worker. The pilot for the city of 650,000, which cost $500,000 and was funded by private grants and public money, involved six social workers and clinicians from the nonprofit Mental Health Center of Denver.

In another Colorado population center, state Judge David Shakes, who sits in Colorado Springs, knows bringing battlefield responses home is a hallmark of post-traumatic stress disorder, or PTSD. Bolhuis's hyper-alert impulse to reach for a gun when he felt threatened landed him in jail in Montrose, but might have saved his own or a buddy's life in Afghanistan.

Judge Shakes plays a key role in one attempt at the systemic change he believes is needed. Shakes, an Army vet, presides over a special civilian court to which veterans who have broken certain laws can be diverted. Instead of sending defendants in his Veterans' Trauma Court to prison, Shakes can sentence them to closely supervised probation and require them to seek treatment for alcoholism, drug dependency, PTSD or, as is often the case, some combination of any of the above. Successful graduates can have their cases dismissed.

I have watched the prosecutor, parole officer, public defender and vets who volunteer as peer mentors collaborate closely in Shake's courtroom. They clearly do not see themselves as adversaries, as they might be in a traditional court. They work as a team to keep vets from breaking the law again and from stumbling into more serious trouble. Such diversionary programs were first used for drug and youthful offenders. The experience with vets could help build a broader case for relieving taxpayers of the burden of keeping people in jail who could be productive.

The Colorado Springs court was established in 2009 and operates in an area that is home to the Army's Fort Carson, several Air Force bases and the Air Force Academy. The court was the first in Colorado and among the first to be established of some 300 that were active across the country by 2015. Shakes told me he laments that few such courts are in rural areas of the United States. The six in Colorado are all in the state's more populous east. Small towns might not produce enough vet offenders to make a special court viable. But perhaps one regional court could serve several small towns, or a judge in a city could preside by video over a defendant in a small town. Shakes told me he would be willing to hold TV court.

In Montrose or other towns in sparsely populated western Colorado it would be difficult to find enough of the mental health and other service providers on whom Denver police and Shakes can rely. And even bigger towns struggle to meet their needs.

Others looking at system-wide changes to help vets can be found working for the federal Department of Health and Human Services Substance Abuse and Mental Health Services Administration, or SAMHSA. SAMHSA has made outreach to veterans a priority. In response to a SAMHSA call, officials in states including Colorado are working to determine what gaps need to be filled and which players are already at work in the arena and how they might better coordinate.

Caring for vets is "everybody's job, not just the military's," Donna Aligata told me. She is the Denver-based project director of SAMHSA's Service Members, Veterans and Their Families Technical Assistance Center.

According to statistics compiled by SAMHSA, 18.5 percent of fighters returning from Iraq or Afghanistan have PTSD or depression. SAMHSA adds half of those returnees who need mental health treatment seek it and only slightly more than half who receive treatment receive adequate care.

At SAMHSA's urging, states have created task forces to study such questions as where veterans have settled, what their access is to VA services and whether civilian mental health care providers who often have to fill the gap are familiar enough with military culture to earn veterans' trust. Other issues to be researched are the rates of suicide and homelessness in the military community. The information gathered could help strengthen services for civilians as well as veterans.

"Veterans are helping us, again," Laura Williams of Colorado's state office of behavioral health told me.

According to SAMHSA estimates, a third of veterans live in rural areas, while overall a fifth of the U.S. population lives in rural areas.

"In rural towns, we do know there's a military culture. The degree of patriotism and commitment to the military is high," Aligata said.

While some vets may simply be going back to their small-town homes, others may be seeking isolation. Bolhuis has seen that "a lot of vets, when they come home, they just want to disappear."

Charlie Smith is SAMSHA's Denver-based director for Colorado, Montana, North Dakota, South Dakota, Utah and Wyoming. He noted during an interview that his region has bigger towns as well as rural communities that have a frontier mentality. Smith grew up in such a town. He recognizes the "we're tough as nails" attitude that keeps some from seeking help. That coupled with poor access to mental health care can lead to suffering alone.

It's not just mental health care that is lacking, Smith said. He told me about one small Colorado town he knows of that has no doctors of any kind. There, the pharmacist also serves as the dispenser of medical and mental health care advice.

If a judge can rule via the internet, why can't a doctor advise at a distance? Mental health therapists in population centers do use computer conferencing tools to lead group sessions in which each member may be in a different town. A smartphone app for recovering alcoholics that the Department of Veterans Affairs has used offers relaxation tips, alerts users when they're near bars and includes a button they can press to quickly connect with counselors.

Fixes beyond technology include pooling resources across regions and recognizing that some resources, like nurses and emergency medical technicians, may not be being fully tapped. Better coordination also requires improving communication so that a general practitioner in one town knows which mental health workers can take a referral in the next. Scattered communities who come together to recruit sorely needed health workers may find they can put together a more attractive package. SAMSHA's Smith said they should remember to include veterans among those they are trying to lure, noting they left the military with specialized skills they can put to work for civilians and will also have a special connection to fellow vets.

Vets "can be not just contributors, but leaders," Smith said. I have seen that in Montrose.

Aligata, of the SAMHSA veterans outreach program, said that if small towns can "gather support to improve services for vets, then it's going to help everyone."

Improving services includes raising awareness about conditions such as Post Traumatic Stress Syndrome, which many mistakenly see as affecting only or even primarily veterans. War is a trauma factory. But civilian life also offers plenty of ammunition for psychological damage.

I began to see the world differently because of what I learned in Montrose. As I cruise through Denver traffic these days, I find myself wondering whether an angry driver was honking because I was slow to turn, or was he a Vietnam vet who never got treatment for PTSD? When I interviewed inner city teens for an article about gangs, I asked myself how the trauma they were seeing on their neighborhood streets would affect them later in life. I sat on the couch watching the BBC miniseries adaptation of *Wolf Hall*, Hilary Mantel's brilliant novel about Thomas Cromwell. I wondered whether Damian Lewis as a hyper-vigilant, easily angered Henry VIII was drawing on research for a previous role as U.S. Marine Sergeant Nicholas Brody in Showtime's *Homeland*. My husband rolled his eyes. I turned to the Internet, and found similar speculation at the heart of a 2009 History Channel documentary, *Inside the Body of Henry VIII*. Lucy Worsley, chief curator of Britain's Historic Royal Palaces, took part in the program and told reporters that a jousting accident that almost killed the king, and that was portrayed in *Wolf Hall*, "provides the explanation for his personality change from a sporty, promising, generous young prince, to a cruel, paranoid and vicious tyrant." She added: "Damage to the frontal lobe of the brain can perfectly well result in personality change."

Kline had a similarly belated, but more profound, realization of the depth and breadth of the challenge presented by PTSD and traumatic brain injury. It was only after Kline started Welcome Home Montrose that, looking back, she realized her second husband, who was a Vietnam vet, was a sufferer.

"I thought it was just alcoholism," she said. "I didn't realize the rage, the pain and the drinking were symptoms."

She had followed the vet to Cape Cod, Massachusetts with her two young sons and blended her family with his three children. Their marriage collapsed after a few years. Kline at the time found support in Al-Anon, which offers a recovery program for the families and friends of alcoholics. Kline said the program helped her analyze her own choices and learn not to act out of fear. That gives her empathy with the vets and their families she meets through Welcome Home Montrose. She is quick to advise anyone who is troubled to seek counseling and to offer her own example as proof that progress is possible.

Such realizations are surely rippling across Montrose. It is an unexpected result that is hard to measure, and more significant than any of the more concrete benefits anyone might have imagined when the idea of Welcome Home Montrose first emerged from a discussion about economic development.

Call it an empathy dividend. It might spur some to seek support for themselves or loved one at a Welcome Home Montrose coffee. It might lead other to come up with innovative ways to get help to people beyond the veterans' circle.

The U.S. National Institute of Mental Health estimates that nearly 8 million Americans have been diagnosed as having Post

Traumatic Stress Syndrome. The institute, part of the government's National Institutes of Health, says that to give that diagnosis, a psychiatrist or psychologist must determine that a patient has suffered such symptoms as flashbacks of a terrifying event or feeling angry or tense for at least a month.

Symptoms can build until it is impossible to live a normal life or imagine a better future. But they may not appear for weeks or months after the trigger. Many people are reluctant to seek help, so their cases go unreported. It's unclear how far the official figure of nearly 8 million falls short. What is clear is that not all those who suffer are vets. A child who has been abused, a man who has witnessed a fatal car accident, a woman who has been raped can also develop PTSD. It is nonetheless the experience of those who have gone to war that has drawn attention to PTSD. Research aimed at helping our warriors could one day help civilians.

For now, though, experts can offer few answers. For a sense of how many unanswered questions scientists have, scan the multiple Web pages listing National Institutes of Health-funded clinical trials seeking subjects for PTSD studies. Researchers want to look into:

- What drugs work, and why?
- Can yoga help?
- Could a dose of hydrocortisone soon after trauma is experienced help prevent PTSD surfacing later?
- How does psychotherapy physically change the brain, and is it effective when delivered online?
- Can anesthesia drugs be used to control emotional reaction during treatment?
- What genes are at work?
- What are the factors that shield most people from experiencing PTSD after a shock?
- How does experiencing trauma early in life affect an adult's ability to recover from a shock?

- What are the consequences of repeated trauma?

That last question is particularly significant for veterans of Iraq and Afghanistan. Researchers already suspect repeated deployments increase the risk of PTSD. In the war on terror, America has turned again and again to the same small pool of volunteers and professional soldiers.

"Many more post-9/11 veterans (44 percent) than pre-9/11 veterans (25 percent) say that their readjustment to civilian life has been difficult," Pew Research Center interviewers found in 2011 when they surveyed 712 veterans of the war on terror.

"Also, a greater share of post-9/11 veterans than pre-9/11 veterans report that they are carrying psychological and emotional scars arising from their time in the military. Some 37 percent of all post-9/11 veterans (and 49 percent of post-9/11 veterans who served in a combat zone) say they have suffered from post-traumatic stress. Among pre-9/11 veterans, the comparable figures are 16 percent for all and 32 percent for those who saw combat."

A PTSD fact-finding committee appointed by Congress looked at the deployment records of nearly 850,000 active duty personnel and more than 200,000 National Guard members who were eligible for Department of Defense health care in 2012. More than 40 percent had been sent to war more than once. Army and Marine Corps members had the greatest average cumulative deployments, of 21 and 16 months respectively, since the beginning of the Iraq and Afghan conflicts.

"The frequency and duration of exposure to traumatic events during deployment has been associated with an increased risk of PTSD," the committee found, noting a dramatic increase in the proportion of service members with PTSD since the launch of the war on terror. In 2012, the committee found, more than half a million veterans visited a VA hospital at least twice for PTSD treatment, comprising 9 percent of all VA users. That percentage was up from 4 percent in 2002.

The committee members held hearings, visited hospitals and reviewed volumes of research before making a 2014 report to lawmakers that was prefaced with a quote from Goethe: "Knowing is not enough; we must apply. Willing is not enough; we must do."

The VA has been accused of not trying hard enough. The PTSD committee found that VA staffing increases were not keeping up with demand for PTSD treatment. The committee also found that it was difficult to even document whether the treatment being offered was reducing the problem. In 2013, only about half the Iraqi and Afghan vets who had a PTSD diagnosis and sought care at the VA received the recommended treatment of eight psychotherapy sessions over a 14-week period.

Don't look for a silver bullet in seeking outside help. The VA has been pressed to do that and has responded by purchasing services for former soldiers from civilian providers. The congressional researchers discovered that "the Reaching Rural Veterans Initiative in Pennsylvania found that primary care providers in the purchased care system frequently lacked knowledge and awareness of PTSD and were unaware of treatment resources available at VA that might help their veteran patients."

Those gaps are important. About one in five primary care providers reported that over a third of their veteran patients had mental health problems, but fewer than one in ten providers felt that they had adequate knowledge of current mental health treatments for these problems.

Psychotherapy is the standard PTSD treatment offered today. The old-fashioned talk therapy often is accompanied by doses of drugs that can, as patients build emotional strength, counter the anxiety, heightened heart rates and other debilitating responses so that the patient can get on with the work of facing and conquering horrific memories.

Experimental treatments such as regimens involving yoga, acupuncture and pet therapy have been tried. The sobering fact is, no single treatment has been shown to work for everyone. Perhaps a third of people in the general public are resistant to PTSD treatment, and the failure rate might be as high as 50 percent for cognitive therapy, aimed at helping a patient see that he or she need not feel guilt or shame because of a traumatic event.

In 2011, as the United States reached the 10th anniversary of the war on terror, the Pew Research Center released the results of a poll of veterans and other Americans. The social science think tank found nearly three-quarters of post-9/11 vets were experiencing flashbacks or finding it impossible to shake memories and dreams of wartime trauma. Nearly half reported feeling irritable or angry or that their family ties were strained. Combat vets who had experienced trauma were particularly hard hit, with half describing a sense of despondency or hopelessness. Veterans who have PTSD show up in large numbers among those in jail, on the streets, addicted to drugs or unemployed.

Tick, the psychotherapist and author, believes PTSD is a wound that has been known as long as humans have made war. It leaves the patient feeling he or she will never again truly be at home:

"What we call post-traumatic stress disorder was diagnosed as 'nostalgia' among Swiss soldiers in 1648. Early German and French doctors called it 'homesickness.'"

"Testimony of the wound runs throughout history, mythology, literature, sacred writings and survivors' tales. It has been treated with similar strategies to what we try today and call 'new': natural and synthetic drugs, food and rest out of danger and in nature, gentle talk and tending, expression through the arts, electroshock, isolation and confinement, intimidation and accusations of cowardice."

In 2006, Tick and his wife and fellow therapist Kate Dahlstedt founded the nonprofit Soldier's Heart in Troy, New York. Their organization offers therapeutic retreats and pilgrimages and guides meditation and other spiritual practices. It also connects community groups that reach out to veterans.

Welcome Home Montrose volunteers may lack Tick's training

and experience. But they have proven to be compassionate and close observers. They have come to conclusions similar to Tick's about the efficacy of creating a place where veterans feel safe to gather and talk. They have brought generations together for mentoring and mutual support. They have offered those who have served a chance to continue contributing.

Welcome Home Montrose has found partners in the professionals at the Center for Mental Health, a nonprofit that is part of a network stretching across Colorado. From a main office in the city of Montrose, the center serves a broad swath of western Colorado. Jon Gordon, whom I interviewed shortly before he retired as executive director of the Center for Mental Health, brought decades of experience to the job. He started at the organization in 1996.

Suicide rates among the general population are high in Colorado. Perhaps it is that guns are within easy reach in ranching and farming communities where hunting is a way of life. Perhaps the spirit of rugged individualism that they proudly claim prevents Westerners from seeking help when they need it.

Mental health professionals "have to take some of the responsibility, too," Gordon said. Do enough people "know we're here? Do they know they can get help?"

Attempts over the years to raise awareness about the center's suicide prevention programs had stalled, Gordon said. Veterans had proven to be a difficult subset of a difficult problem.

Gordon once launched a special vet-to-vet outreach program and trained a veteran to lead it. After a half year with little result, the effort was abandoned.

Soon after, Jeannie Ritter, now an outreach and education specialist with the Mental Health Center of Denver, began spearheading awareness campaigns with a special emphasis on veterans during her husband's 2007-2011 tenure as Colorado's governor. Gordon tried to piggy back on Ritter's statewide campaigns.

"We did some advertising. We had posters all over town. It just didn't succeed."

Gordon saw another opportunity in Welcome Home Montrose. He participated in the community meetings Kline held to plan the project. He contacted her after it had been launched to offer his center's services. But, again, he did not see more vets coming to his center.

"It's hard for them to come in and sit and talk to a therapist," he said. To establish trust and rapport, "you almost have to have lived through some of what they have lived through."

Then, in 2012, Gordon hired a new suicide prevention coordinator. Robin Berndt had been executive director for the local office of Habitat for Humanity. Her CV also includes volunteering at the Center for Mental Health before taking a staff position there, helping build a skate park for Montrose kids, working with children with special needs as a para-professional in the town's schools, starting an eating disorder support group and officiating at weddings as a Universal Church minister.

"I'm just kind of a driven person," Berndt said. I saw in her the fierce desire to serve I had seen in vets, and the habit that small town citizens have of taking on multiple tasks to ensure things get done.

Berndt brought a new approach to vets to the Center for Mental Health. Instead of inviting vets to her place, she went to them.

Part of Berndt's job at the center is leading a course called Mental Health First Aid. The program was developed in Australia in 2001 and brought to Montrose and other U.S. communities in 2008. After Berndt took on outreach at the Center for Mental Health, the First Aid program was offered at the Welcome Home Montrose drop-in center.

The eight people who showed up at that first encounter included vets, a spouse or two, a trainer who teaches disabled vets to ski, an observer from the local VA clinic. They gathered on a summer day in 2014. They took an all-day course designed to teach participants how to detect whether a friend or loved one is under mental stress and to whom they can turn to for help. Berndt hopes participants will emerge less fearful of mental illness.

The vets were at home in a room they knew well, where they had had shared intergenerational war stories over coffee. During breaks between electronic slide show presentations and short films, Berndt noticed how easily each person in the room picked up on what anyone else had to say. Little time was wasted on explanations or context-setting.

As she listened to the talk, Berndt, who admits she doesn't follow the headlines much herself, realized the vets were closely following news from the Middle East. Conflict far away had changed the lives of men and women from places like Montrose across the country. They returned home with an intimate knowledge of the costs of wielding American military might, and of the limits of that power.

Berndt met with vets on a Saturday in late August. The day before, militants in central Iraq raided a Sunni mosque. Friday is the Muslim day of worship, and dozens of worshippers were killed. That attack may have been in retaliation for the attempted assassination of a Shiite chief in the same region, an area that at the time was a battleground for Iraqi government forces fighting the Islamic State.

Berndt could tell the vets at her mental health training session were worried that others would be going to Iraq or Syria. The prospect left them questioning if their own sacrifices in the Middle East had resolved nothing.

"They're really struggling with that," Berndt said. That insight would inform her outreach and the work of the center's therapists.

Gordon and Berndt saw the training session at Welcome Home Montrose as an important first step. The center has also assigned a therapist to meet with vets at the center, though his schedule did not initially fill up quickly.

"Until Robin came along and started teaching mental health

first aid, we didn't have much momentum with Welcome Home Montrose," Gordon said.

Welcome Home Montrose serves "a critical, critical population. I hope we can be a resource for them."

While he does not shy from the responsibility, Gordon was worried about his capacity to fulfill it. Gordon oversaw a budget of $10 million and a staff of 120 responsible for six counties: Montrose, Delta, Gunnison, Hinsdale, Ouray and San Miguel. That embraces 10,000 square miles and some 85,000 people.

"If you break your arm, you go to the emergency room. If you're depressed for more than two weeks, go see a therapist. That's what we tell people, over and over," Berndt said.

You won't wait months for care in an emergency room. You could wait months, though, to get an appointment with a psychiatrist. Gordon has four on his staff, and none are full-time, either because they are in semi-retirement or divide their time between the center and private practices.

Gordon was struggling to recruit psychiatrists. Few wanted to live in the small towns where Gordon needed them. There were alternatives, including an online program called My Strength. Nurse practitioners and life coaches can provide mentoring and advice, even if they cannot prescribe medications. But those professionals also were in short supply.

Good, the Montrose psychiatrist who has reached out to vets, told me he would be retiring in five or six years. The local Yellow Pages lists two other psychiatrists. And the directory covers not just the city of Montrose but a region encompassing the counties of Montrose, Delta, Ouray and San Miguel. Some rural Colorado communities have no psychiatrists, *Denver Post* reporters discovered in researching a four-part series on mental health published in 2014.

"Each year in Colorado, about 260,000 adults and children need treatment for the most severe illnesses - schizophrenia, bipolar disorder, major depression and serious emotional disturbances. Yet tens of thousands go without care; nationally, only about a third of people who need treatment get it," the newspaper reported.

Montrose's Good had been talking with the region's other two psychiatrists about a strategy for recruiting new therapists. They were looking for people who can see what they see in Montrose. Perhaps the psychiatrists needed to organize a session with sticky notes and pens, as Montrose entrepreneurs had once done to brainstorm economic revival.

"I'm lucky to be here," Good said. "There are great doctors around here. They could be making more money elsewhere. But they're here. Because they want to be."

"Most psychiatrists don't practice in small towns," Good said. "They're in big cities, where the money's better. And most psychiatrists are the intellectual sort. They want the stimulation of museums, concerts, restaurants."

The best restaurant in Montrose is probably at the main hospital. That sounds like a punch line, but the well-regarded chef ensconced off the lobby at Montrose Memorial Hospital pioneered a trend in Colorado by bringing a sophisticated, locavore sensibility to a hospital kitchen. His menu items include a sausage and mussels stir fry with Andouille from a local farm, or chili lime crab and fish cakes garnished with baby greens from another area producer.

A citified doctor looking for entertainment in Montrose could check out the four-decade-old Valley Symphony Orchestra, which tours the region with classical and pop programs. The Magic Circle Players Community Theatre, with its own 300-seat Montrose house off the main thoroughfare into the mountains, has been entertaining audiences since 1959. I caught a production of "The Dresser" at the Magic Circle. One of the actors was trained at the American Academy of Dramatic Arts. During intermission at the Friday night show I saw during football season, I heard as many patrons chatting about missing the Montrose High School football game as about the action on stage. The lack of pretension was refreshing.

Perhaps it is Montrose's mix of small-town charm and big city aspirations that attracted Good. He wouldn't want Montrose to be a metropolis. Not because the literature-loving psychiatrist is an intellectual slouch. But he has sought a life akin to that lived by his father and step-father, both small-town doctors. He has worked at clinics where he felt administrators "were grading me on productivity, which means how much money I was bringing in.

"They were going a business direction that I just couldn't do."

In private practice in Montrose, Good feels he has the respect of his neighbors and a measure of independence from institutional medicine and insurance regimes.

"If you want to call your own shots, you've got to move to small-town America," he said. "A lot of doctors will start figuring that out."

Bolhuis may have felt alone that Fourth of July night when he was disturbed by a mysterious knocking. He was not.

Welcome Home Montrose is not alone in taking on the challenges of returning warriors. That Fourth of July night isolated in his apartment, Bolhuis fell back on Marine training and showed some of what it takes to navigate in unknown territory. He shared information with people who had his back. He did not let setbacks and missteps discourage him. He proceeded with caution, but he proceeded. He got home.

Chapter 16

Self Medicating

Wanderers. That's what white settlers called the Utes they encountered in the patch of the Americas that would become Colorado. The label implied that they had no attachment to or little understanding of the landscape. But it was the later arrivals, who called their own wandering "exploring," who did not know where they were.

The Utes were home. They prided themselves on having laid out the early highway that would come to be known as the Spanish Trail. They followed what was as much calendar as map, establishing routes as they hunted for deer and other game and gathering plants according to a schedule that allowed for nature to renew itself. Their harvests included berries and roots for food; yucca for soap and cord; sumac for baskets and shoes; ligusticum portieri, also known as osha, for antibacterial and antiviral medicines.

That history was on my mind when I visited a farm near Montrose. My nose picked up something minty and earthy in the air. I learned it was the scent of osha. I was breathing the past.

The farm sat at the end of a dirt road with its back to the San Juan Mountains. The spread facing a stretch of the Uncompaghre River once was Ute territory. In 1880, a year after the death of their leader, Ouray, the last Utes in the Montrose area were forced onto a reservation in neighboring Utah. The body of Chief Ouray, who died in 1880, was eventually brought to Montrose for burial on what are now the grounds of a state-run museum devoted to the tribe. He rests alongside his wife Chipeta, who died in poverty in 1924 on the Utah reservation, which was named for Ouray.

With the Indians out of the way, entrepreneurs moved in. Cabbages, carrots, onions and potatoes once were grown on the farm I visited. Those crops, no more exotic to me than yucca, sumac and osha were to the Ute, were sold to 19th century miners for their suppers. When the Gunnison Tunnel made farming more profitable elsewhere, farmers switched from growing cold crops to raising cattle and hay.

The farm's current owners, Sheila and Tim Manzagol, researched all of this as part of putting down roots in the county next door to Montrose. Their county was, like the Utah reservation, named for Ouray.

The Manzagols had left fast-paced lives in northern California two decades before I met them on a late summer day. They were growing medicinal plants on their 40 acres of ancient, storied land. The couple made a tool shed of a century-old barn clad in salvaged pressed tin. They added a greenhouse to the property for seedlings coddled by Sheila, who is a biologist.

Tim, a geologist, can tell you where the soil on his property is best and where it holds too much clay and salt. He said his water rights, crucial in the West, are "good," a world of satisfaction evident in his voice as he pronounced the unadorned adjective.

Sheila's seedlings grow to be used in balms for sinusitis, herbal insect repellent and other remedies. The Manzagols' crops include arnica, hawthorn and licorice. In a processing room, Sheila pulled out a blue plastic bag about half the size of a kitchen trash bin and opened it to reveal a tangle of roots. As I breathed in, she told me the Utes had observed bears emerging from hibernation digging up such roots. The Indians went on to discover osha has properties that include stimulating digestion.

Sheila told me of plans to add marijuana to their inventory of osha and arnica.

"I love being part of people's wellness. That's absolutely my motivation," she said.

She brought her training as a scientist to the marijuana question. She pored over studies that she said show marijuana can be a treatment for insomnia, nausea and epileptic seizures.

"There's a lot of evidence that it's beneficial for PTSD," Manzagol added. Medical experts are not so sure.

Sheila said she enjoys a glass of wine in the evenings.

"I don't think I'm in a position to tell someone who likes to relax with cannabis that they're better or worse than me."

Marijuana is part of what makes Colorado unique, though with every election it seems more and more states are embracing legalization. Colorado will nonetheless always be a marijuana pioneer, the state to which others looks for models to emulate or mistakes to avoid when it comes to drafting regulations, dealing with a skeptical federal government or addressing social, medical and other consequences of legislation. And when it comes to one small Colorado town and its vets, marijuana presents a complex geography shaped by politics, science, hope and fear.

In 2000, the vote across Colorado in favor of Amendment 20, which legalized marijuana for medical use, was 915,527 for, 786,983 against, according to the secretary of state's office. In Montrose County, 8,018 voters said no; 6,126 said yes. In the Manzagols' Ouray County, 1,258 voters said yes to 919 no's.

Under a program launched the year after the medical marijuana vote, Colorado's Department of Public Health and Environment issues medical marijuana "red cards" to Colorado residents who pay small fees. Doctors must confirm applicants suffer from one of eight conditions: cancer; glaucoma; HIV or AIDS; the weakness and wasting caused by chronic illness; persistent muscle spasms; seizures; severe nausea and severe pain. PTSD is not on the list.

In 2012, the year Welcome Home Montrose opened its doors, came Colorado's Amendment 64, which legalized the sale of marijuana for recreational use. That was approved statewide 1,383,140 votes to 1,116,894. Ouray County also said yes, by a vote of 1,947 to 1,215. Montrose rejected retail pot, 11,037 opposed, 8,553 in favor.

Colorado and California voters were the first in the United States to approve recreational marijuana, and Colorado regulators and retailers were the first to get sales off the ground. Recreational marijuana is more expensive than medical weed because it is taxed at a significantly higher rate. But you don't need a note from your doctor or to be a resident to get recreational marijuana.

Local governments across Colorado can choose to ban marijuana sales in their jurisdictions, just as some states have "dry" counties where liquor is not sold. The city of Montrose is among those that have said no to weed. According to the marijuana enforcement division of the Colorado's Department of Revenue, in 2014 the majority of Colorado local governments, 228 out of 312, prohibited medical and recreational sales.

Still, thousands of Montrose residents did vote yes on medical and recreational marijuana. The people in Montrose who want pot only have to drive outside town to get it. The first marijuana shop is 10 minutes beyond city limits, past Ouray's grave and the Walmart. The shop in a rustic shed of a building fits in well with nearby curio boutiques and roadside attractions. It is located opposite an RV park, convenient for seasonal visitors.

In Colorado, weed has libertarians in cowboy hats who are suspicious of any government regulation siding with people they probably think of as long-haired hippies. Among the thousands who voted "no" to liberalizing marijuana laws in Colorado were Republican social conservatives and suburban soccer moms who skew Democratic.

In Montrose, then Mayor Judy Anne Files told reporters when the city barred retails sales that two reasons swayed her City Council: "Voters in the city and county of Montrose voted sizably no on Amendment 64. Second, we are sworn to the federal constitution, and the federal constitution says marijuana is still illegal."

Marijuana is classified by the federal government along with LSD and heroin as among the most dangerous illicit drugs.

A 2015 *Montrose Daily Press* editorial praised city officials for protecting "citizens from the pitfalls of marijuana growing and distribution.

"The effects of the stuff on users' brains is a big enough concern," the newspaper continued. "Followed by public safety and hazardous conditions potentially affecting innocents."

The next year, Montrose Police Chief Tom Chinn linked an increase in heroin use in his community to a permissiveness he saw symbolized by the statewide votes to legalize medical and then recreational marijuana. "Some people believe any illegal drug is OK to use," Chinn told a *Montrose Mirror* reporter.

"I have been working in law enforcement here a long, long time. I can remember three cases or less of (heroin) possession over the past 40 years, maybe one confirmed overdose in the past 10 years. But in July of 2015, our Drug Task Force officers bought 2.8 grams of heroin - we had tried to buy before but had been unable. In August, we bought 3.5 grams ... even our patrol officers are running into it occasionally, which means it is out in the open."

In contrast in next-door Ouray County, commissioners adopted an ordinance allowing marijuana to be cultivated in their jurisdiction. The commissioners started slowly, allowing only five licenses in 2015. The Manzagols were among the first to get a license for their farm outside the town of Ridgway, home to fewer than 1,000 people.

Sheila Manzagol compared her hometown of Ridgway, which cultivates an artsy folksiness, to Sedona, the Arizona community with a New Age reputation. Ridgway has a True Grit Café, but little of the grittiness of the 1968 novel by Charles Portis or the 1969 movie based on the book that was filmed in this region. Book and movie (the latter brought John Wayne to Ridgway for filming) were produced in a period colored by the Vietnam War and take a mordant view of the post-Civil War Wild West. The fictional accounts are certainly full of all-American independence of spirit, but also violence and greed. Wayne's whiskey-swigging U.S. marshal character could well be self-medicating a case of PTSD.

One of the young vets who came for the Welcome Home

Montrose internship program told his hometown paper in Iowa that marijuana was among what he saw as the benefits when he was weighing the pros and cons of a move to Colorado. He did not mention that to me when I met him in Montrose. Perhaps it was because he did not believe it was a fit subject for the article I was writing *for Stars and Stripes,* a federal government publication.

In the interview with the Iowa paper, the retired Marine described how war had left him physically maimed and psychologically shaken. Marijuana relieved overwhelming anxiety. It was only after dosing himself with weed, he said, that "I could leave the house without fear."

Still, the Marine vet cautioned: "I'm not going to sit here and BS you and say marijuana is the perfect cure-all."

Welcome Home Montrose founder Kline has listened to vets and concluded marijuana can be a gentler alternative to prescription medication for vets who are hurting.

Medical experts though caution marijuana use could mask deeper problems or could fool users into thinking they don't need other help.

Veterans Affairs has expressed concern about marijuana use among veterans seen in its health centers suffering from PTSD and a substance abuse disorder, or SUD. The latter is a condition that occurs when using alcohol or drugs leads to problems such as distress or physical ailments. In a note to care-givers, the VA noted marijuana use disorder has been the most common SUD among PTSD sufferers since 2009, and increased from 13 percent in 2002 to 22.7 percent in 2014.

"Marijuana use by individuals with PTSD may result in short-term reduction of PTSD symptoms. However, data suggest that continued use of marijuana among individuals with PTSD may lead to a number of negative consequences," the VA continued. "People with PTSD have particular difficulty stopping their use of marijuana and responding to treatment for marijuana addiction."

Sally Schindel recalled that her 31-year-old Army veteran son started out medicating himself with marijuana. Then, he wanted to stop.

"He told me he found it much harder to quit than he thought it would be," the Arizona woman told *The Associated Press*. "He'd buy it and smoke it and then flush the rest of it. The next day he bought it again."

He committed suicide in 2014. He left a note that said "marijuana killed my soul and ruined my brain."

The VA had diagnosed Schindel's son Andy Zorn with PTSD after he served in Iraq. Later, diagnoses of marijuana dependence, depression and bipolar disorder were added.

Dr. Good, the psychiatrist who treats vets and other patients in Montrose, doesn't like the idea of a psychotic patient choosing to take marijuana, a hallucinogen, alongside prescribed drugs. But Good added he does not force the pot issue with his vet patients.

"Many of them find it calming," Good said. "It helps some of them with their pain. I'm more concerned with their alcohol abuse than their marijuana use."

Vets have questioned why PTSD is not included among the disorders that can be treated with medical marijuana under Colorado regulations. They argue their own experimentation has convinced them it alleviates some of their symptoms. They add conventional treatments have so often proven ineffective.

Other states, including Colorado's neighbors Arizona and New Mexico, do consider PTSD to be a qualifying condition for medical marijuana. But three times, Colorado's Board of Health has rejected proposals that PTSD be added to the medical marijuana list. The third time PTSD came before the board, in mid-2015, the chief Colorado medical officer had reversed his previous position to recommend PTSD be on the list. Not, Dr. Larry Wolk told reporters, because he had reason to believe marijuana could be an effective treatment for the disorder. But Wolk said he knew many vets were self-medicating by buying recreational pot. He thought it would be better if they at least consulted a doctor.

That wasn't good enough for the Board of Health.

"We can't have physicians counseling people in favor of it because we don't have data to show it's correct," one board member said when she and her colleagues gathered to vote.

Dr. Sue Sisley, an Arizona psychiatrist who has been given Federal Drug Administration approval to study whether marijuana is a safe and effective treatment for PTSD, was in Denver for the vote. She heard anguished testimony from veterans who wanted to be treated with marijuana. Veterans she has consulted have told Sisley marijuana helps. Chief medical officer Wolk's opinion had led Sisley and others to think momentum was moving in a direction that would lead to PTSD being added to the list of marijuana-treatable conditions. Vets who had come to the meeting room were angered when that did not happen. Sisley shared their frustration.

"I believe my patients when they say they're better," Sisley told me. But "I still don't believe anything until it's gone through the rigors of a randomized, controlled study. We need objective data."

Even with FDA approval, marijuana's federal status as illegal has slowed Sisley's own and others' research, in part by making it difficult to get samples of the drug. Almost a year after Sisley spoke to me about the Colorado Board of Health vote, she emailed me a note with the subject line: "Excellent news." The federal Drug Enforcement Agency had formally approved the first randomized and controlled study of marijuana to be ingested by smoking as a treatment for veterans suffering from PTSD. As a result, Sisley in Phoenix working with 38 veterans and a colleague at Johns Hopkins University in Baltimore with another 38 subjects gained access to marijuana for studies funded by Colorado's Department of Public Health and Environment. So state health officials did not close the conversation with their votes against adding PTSD to the medical marijuana list. Given evidence, they might change their minds.

The $2.156 million Phoenix and Baltimore studies are overseen by California-based Multidisciplinary Association for Psychedelic Studies, known as MAPS.

"We are thrilled to see this study overcome the hurdles of approval so we can begin gathering the data," Amy Emerson, executive director and director of clinical research for the MAPS Public Benefit Corporation, said in a statement that Sisley shared with me. "This study is a critical step in moving our botanical drug development program forward at the federal level to gather information on the dosing, risks and benefits of smoked marijuana for PTSD symptoms."

Sisley wants to answer such questions as which strains of marijuana are helpful, which strains are to be avoided, and what amounts are safest to take. Her study called for testing four marijuana strains and a placebo. Neither she, her subjects nor independent vetters will know who is getting which dose, making it a triple blind study. It will take two years to gather data. Then, Sisley estimated, it will then take her six months to analyze that data and perhaps another year to review whatever findings emerge.

Months after Sisley got FDA approval for her marijuana study, another arm of the federal government, the Drug Enforcement Agency, rejected formal petitions that marijuana be removed from the federal list of illegal drugs considered most dangerous. That category is known as Schedule I.

"A substance is placed in Schedule I if it has no currently accepted medical use in treatment in the United States, a lack of accepted safety for use under medical supervision, and a high potential for abuse," DEA Acting Administrator Chuck Rosenberg said in a letter informing the petitioners of the rejection.

The petitioners were the governors of Washington and Rhode Island and a psychiatric nurse in New Mexico who had argued in part that removing marijuana from the Schedule I list would make it easier for researchers like Sisley to investigate marijuana's possible medical uses. The DEA's Rosenberg offered some hope in that regard, saying in his letter that the DEA would allow more laboratories to grow marijuana for research beyond the single University of Mississippi lab now doing so. New labs will have to meet tough DEA standards. Rosenberg said marijuana's scheduling could be changed, but only if data supports such a shift. He said he would rely on the Food and Drug Administration for the science.

"The FDA drug approval process for evaluating potential medicines has worked effectively in this country for more than 50 years," Rosenberg said. "It is a thorough, deliberate and exacting process grounded in science, and properly so, because the safety of our citizens relies on it."

Science cannot be hurried. Sisley, the Arizona psychiatrist and researcher, knows veterans are impatient.

"You've got people suffering now," said Sisley, who did her residency at the VA hospital in Phoenix and continued to care for vets later in private practice.

Meanwhile, the Manzagols continue farming on their historic plot, mindful of old traditions.

"Marijuana is more than medicinal or recreational," Tim told me. "This is not something that just sprung up in the last 100 years. It's been used spiritually."

Sheila said her own research has convinced her cannabinoids, part of the chemical makeup of marijuana, can be a safe and effective alternative to more powerful drugs that have been used to treat insomnia, nausea, inflammation and other ailments. She also believes "it's pretty beneficial to help mitigate the symptoms of PTSD."

"We've been making herbal-infused products for 16 years," Sheila told me. "For us, marijuana is another botanical. It's a very powerful botanical, but it's another botanical."

On her farm, with its evocative fragrances and verdant vistas, it can be tempting to look for simple answers. Rural America, though, has never been an easy place. Its idyllic landscapes are silent witnesses to complex histories and to the generations that have been steadfast in the face challenges.

Chapter 17

Getting to the VA

It's over an hour's drive from Montrose to the nearest Veterans Affairs hospital in the regional population hub of Grand Junction. Many start the journey even further away than Montrose in the rural areas of the county of the same name or surrounding counties.

Once you pass through the neighboring towns of Olathe and Delta, the only signs of fellow humans are the two-lane highway itself, mile after mile of post-and-wire cattle fencing and the occasional farm house.

When I made the drive, I found myself contemplating how much bleaker the road would feel if I had been going for a lab test to diagnose an ache or to find out how I've been healing since surgery. When I got to the VA hospital, its Customer Relations Officer Dawn Schadegg sympathized.

"It's a significant drive. It's stressful in the wintertime. It's not pleasant," she said. "Here, you have people who've worked hard, they're not living below the poverty line, but they're struggling. So, say they make four trips from Montrose a month. When gas is $3 a gallon, that's a lot of money that they don't have."

Then, she told me a story that rivaled anything I had been imagining.

Schadegg, seated in her cubby hole of an office on the hospital's ground floor, described working with a Vietnam-era vet from Montrose who needed specialty cancer care that was available only at the VA hospital in San Francisco. To get him there, she found a donor to pay for his air fare, but only from Denver.

The government covers travel expenses for care for vets who meet certain criteria. Becoming travel eligible involves filling in paperwork with details of service and health. Schadegg's vet had never established that he qualified.

"He really didn't feel that he wanted to dredge everything up," said Schadegg.

She did get the process started, but it could take months. Doctors believed the patient could not wait to start treatment. A friend agreed to drive him the five hours from Montrose to Denver, where he could collect his donated plane ticket and head to California.

"Everything was good until the car broke down," Schadegg continued.

She fielded calls from her patient from the road and her Good Samaritan waiting with the ticket in Denver. In the end, the car was repaired and the vet made his plane and headed to San Francisco for the first of what was expected to be a long series of treatments.

"Hopefully, for the next visit, he'll be travel eligible," Schadegg said.

"In the rural areas, we just don't have the kind of care that a lot of the vets need. In fact, that a lot of Americans need," she said. "We have the same sicknesses here that they have everywhere else in the world. We just don't have the same doctors."

Paul Sweeney, the spokesman for the hospital, told me that over several years starting in 2009 the VA increased the number of mental health care-givers at its Grand Junction facility from nine to 58.

"When we started hiring people, we stripped the Western Slope of a lot of their providers," Sweeney said, referring to the largely rural swath of Colorado across the Rockies from the state's eastern population hubs.

Sometimes, it goes the other way. When I visited the VA medical center in Grand Junction, its chief of staff was preparing to step down from that position so he could work as a cardiologist, part-time for veterans at his hospital and part-time for civilians in nearby Steamboat Springs, a town of 12,000 with no heart specialist. A VA staffer who can build and fit prosthetics sometimes performs those services for civilian as well as veteran patients because "that is one of those medically underserved areas in the Western Slope," Sweeney told me.

"Partnering is something we've done a lot of here," Sweeney said. "With rural facilities, it comes down to being creative and using what you have. Many times, we realize we have the ability, but have to figure out how to put it to use."

Telehealth, which means dispensing counseling or advice via video conferencing, helps staff reach far-flung patients. Drugs can be mailed from the Grand Junction VA hospital's pharmacy.

The Grand Junction facility oversees four smaller clinics and serves 15 counties in Colorado, two in Utah and half of Wyoming's Carbon County. Its doctors have to be responsive to the region's unique challenges. That can mean consulting a respiratory therapist when it comes time to discharge a patient with lung problems who is going home to a cabin at 7,000 feet, from Grand Junction's elevation of about 5,000. If the patient has only a wood-burning stove for heat, does it make sense to send along a potentially dangerous tank? Might it be better to keep him or her at the hospital a few more days until extra oxygen is no longer necessary?

The 64-bed facility at Grand Junction has a staff of 700. The beds include a 30-bed hospice and rehabilitation facility known as the Community Living Center, which can feel like a retirement home with its calendar of bowling, bingo, and visits from barber school attendants offering free haircuts. The hospital also has a five-bed Intensive Care Unit, a dental clinic and a recreational therapy program that offers kayaking and hunting trips.

As I walked along gleaming linoleum floors past walls painted in calming shades of gray, green and blue, VA staff kept pointing out what was lacking. No ophthalmologist. No dermatologist. No audiologist. No equipment for dialysis or mammograms. Grand Junction, a town of 60,000, had no liver specialist, civilian or VA. No wonder vets seeking care at Grand Junction and similar hospitals across the country have to get in line. Schadegg, a note of exasperation in her voice, spoke to me in June about a patient who needed an adjustment in her hearing aide, and would have to go to Denver to get it.

"We can't get her an appointment until August 21. That's ridiculous."

A vet who had driven 100 miles or more with a broken leg has shown up more than once at the Grand Junction VA. When such patients are asked why they did not go to the nearest emergency room, the answer might be that the VA, with an emergency room that can provide only limited care, *was* the closest medical facility. Other vets might worry about getting a hefty emergency room bill from a civilian hospital. More than likely, the VA will cover the costs of care at a civilian hospital's emergency room, but that is not necessarily guaranteed.

And in some cases, Sweeney said, vets trust the VA. If that sounds like public relations spin, consider the results of a survey of vets by the Pew Research Center. It found that half those who had served since 9/11 rated the VA excellent or good in terms of the job it was doing to meet their needs of military veterans. The think tank's researchers added that "among post-9/11 veterans who say they've received benefits from the VA, 60 percent give the agency excellent or good marks for meeting the needs of today's veterans. The VA receives lower ratings from those who have not received benefits (only 39 percent rated the agency excellent or good)."

A key reason for that is likely that most VA hospitals are like the one in Grand Junction in that many of the staff of members are vets themselves. Schadegg and Sweeney are among the 37 percent of the Grand Junction VA staff with military backgrounds.

Veterans standing up for themselves and for each other is a long tradition, one into which Welcome Home Montrose tapped. During the Depression, veterans demanding help marched from across the country to Washington, where they camped in a shanty town. The protest was broken up by federal troops but, according to a Veterans Affairs history, helped draw attention to the suffering of those who had served their country. In 1930 the VA was created to consolidate a range of pension and medical efforts that began to emerge with the Civil War, pushed by veterans of that conflict. The new entity took as its motto a line from Civil War President Abraham Lincoln's second inaugural address, when he called on Congress to "care for him who shall have borne the battle, and for his widow, and for his orphan."

A team of investigators lauded the sense of purpose they found within the Veterans Health Administration, which is the main branch of the VA and the one that oversees its hospitals. The independent assessors from RAND, McKinsey & Company, the Centers for Medicare and Medicaid Services Alliance to Modernize Health Care and other think tanks who compiled a 2015 report found that the VA hospital division's mission of honoring "America's veterans by providing exceptional health care that improves their health and well-being - is inspirational and widely accepted by ... staff."

Congress ordered that assessment at the same time it voted to create the Veterans Choice Program. The program was designed to address a specific problem, the time veterans had to await VA medical care, by allowing them access to non-VA care under certain circumstances. The assessors, meanwhile, were asked to look more broadly at what ailed the VA. What they found after visits to 87 sites, including 38 medical centers, encouraged them to look beyond the metric of how long a veteran has to wait for care.

On average, a veteran in 2014 spent 43 days awaiting an initial primary care appointment, with a range of between two days to four months. "Comparison from a review of Massachusetts physicians in the civilian sector showed average wait times of 50 days for internal medicine and 39 days for family medicine appointments," according to the report to Congress. "This suggests that on average the (Veterans Health Administration) is not that different from the civilian sector."

But the VA has promised vets exceptional care, not merely

average. In part, the researchers blamed Congress for the agency's inability to make good on that promise, citing the 1996 Veterans' Health Care Eligibility Act, which was meant to keep the VA within budget and created a confusing tangle of categories to ration care.

"When demand exceeds capacity to deliver care within the budget, the inevitable result is a decrease in access to care and unmet demand for some veterans," Congress was told.

Turning a ship as enormous as the VA won't be easy. In 2014, it oversaw 1,600 health care sites, among them 167 medical centers, employed about 300,000 staffers and cared for nearly 6 million vets. The vets the VA serves tend, compared to vets who get care elsewhere, to live on lower incomes and in rural areas, to be in poorer health and to lack access to other health insurance.

The Grand Junction VA hospital sits on land donated by the city, a gift from a grateful country at the end of World War II. While the original structure has had a few extensions since it was completed in 1949, it still has the look of a simpler era. The biblical scenes depicted by stained glass windows in its chapel date from before the ranks of U.S. soldiers included Sikhs and Wiccans.

The VA system of which Grand Junction is a part was built for another time. In the 1990s, it was looking back, at the Vietnam vets and at what their aging would mean for the kinds of care it needed to provide. The VA was no more expecting 9/11 and the wars that followed than was the country as a whole.

In the era of the war on terror, the soldiers who come back have survived a more dangerous and deadlier conflict. Pew researchers who spoke to returnees found 60 percent served in a combat zone, compared with 54 percent of their Vietnam era comrades and 53 percent of surviving veterans of the Korean War and World War II. Overall, 16 percent of post-9/11 veterans reported they were seriously injured while serving in the military, compared to 10 percent of veterans of previous wars. Pew researchers, citing Department of Defense statistics, wrote that thanks to advances in medical treatment, troops wounded on the battlegrounds of the war on terror are surviving trauma that would have killed them in an earlier era. Pew cited what is known as the "wounded-to-killed ratio," or the number of service members wounded in action compared to the number who died. It was 7.4 to 1 for Iraq and Afghanistan; 2.6 to 1 for Vietnam; and 1.7 to 1 for World War II.

Todd Love, the Marine who helped inspire Welcome Home Montrose when he was shown on TV learning to kayak, has been the subject of numerous newspaper and broadcast articles because of both the severity of the injuries he survived and the flare with which he survived them. In addition to kayaking, he has sky-dived, completed endurance races and even wrestled alligators despite having lost both legs and part of an arm.

An extraordinary series of medical interventions saved his life after Love triggered an improvised explosive device while on foot patrol in Afghanistan in 2010. His comrades were able to stabilize him and he underwent an initial operation at an Afghan air base. That was followed by more surgery at a larger U.S. military installation in Afghanistan before being flown to Germany and then on to the United States, where he spent two years at Walter Reed.

Thanks to similar care after a roadside bomb exploded under his vehicle in Iraq in 2009, Army infantryman Brendan Marrocco became the first American fighter in Iraq or Afghanistan to survive a quadruple amputation.

Robert Gates, an Air Force veteran who served as U.S. Secretary of Defense for Republican President George W. Bush and Democratic President Barack Obama, saw the faces behind the numbers during a 2009 trip to Afghanistan. Before his visit he had ordered the addition of 10 medevac helicopters and three forward surgical hospitals to support troops in the southern and eastern parts of that country.

"One of the surgeons there told me they often could not save the life of a soldier or Marine who had lost both legs; now they did so routinely," Gates wrote in his memoirs.

Back in Washington, Gates saw the ramifications.

"I believe that at the outset of the Afghan and Iraq wars, neither Defense nor VA ever conceived of, much less planned for, the huge number of wounded young men and women (overwhelmingly men) who would come pouring into the system in the years ahead. Many of our troops would not have survived their wounds in previous wars, but extraordinary medical advances and the skills of those treating the wounded meant that a large number of complex injuries (including traumatic brain injuries and multiple amputations) faced prolonged treatment, years of rehabilitation, or a lifetime of disability."

Gates went on to describe his struggle to get the VA and his own department to reorder priorities and cut the red tape that stood between a wounded combat vet and care.

The drafters of the report on the VA for Congress said the agency needed to improve its forecasting in order to better prepare to serve vets in the future. But they added the newest population of vets might make that difficult.

"Iraq and Afghanistan veterans are more likely to have service connected disabilities than other veterans," their report said, adding that while in the past veterans have relied less on the VA as they aged, gained access to employer health plans or for other reasons, those who fought in the war on terror may have a different trajectory.

The assessors echoed some of the points Gates made about the kind of transformation the VA hospital system needed. They called on Congress and the VA to make hard choices about which vets to serve and on which medical conditions to focus. Some of the shift might be physical, they said, noting states like Colorado are not "currently well-served by VA facilities" while veteran populations in the Ohio Valley and the Midwest were expected to dwindle.

Because of my time in Montrose, a particular passage in the report to Congress resonated: "Although the broader VHA culture includes a deep commitment to mission at all levels of the organization, it is also characterized by risk aversion and distrust, resulting in an inability to improve performance consistently and fully across the system."

In Montrose, Kline established trust by talking, at first one-to-one and in small groups with leading citizens in her town, then at bigger meetings pulling in more and more voices. Welcome Home Montrose was, in a way, built word by word. Its central component, the Warrior Resource Center is a space to exchange ideas and create momentum for action.

VA officials were welcomed to the early brainstorming sessions at which Welcome Home Montrose was mapped out. The project's Warrior Resource center has hosted town hall meetings at which VA leaders can count on the honest assessments they need if they want to improve. VA health and outreach workers make the drive from Grand Junction to offer counseling and other services at offices Welcome Home Montrose provides them at the resource center. VA counselors in Grand Junction tell vets they meet from Montrose about support groups and other services offered by Welcome Home Montrose.

Tom Ziemann, a social worker at the VA hospital in Grand Junction told me he had seen many grassroots initiatives to help vets find jobs or financial assistance or opportunities to relax. But he had never seen anything quite like the way Welcome Home Montrose has rallied a community to embrace its vets and look for ways to move forward together and comprehensively.

Ziemann remembered the planning meetings held before Welcome Home Montrose had a name. He was struck by seeing people "from every walk of life" determined to help vets.

"I don't think many communities think in these terms," he said. "I think any community can do this. But they'll have to have a champion that's willing to spend the time and energy to get people together."

Welcome Home Montrose sees the VA as a key partner in an enterprise that demands broad and deep collaboration. As part of that collaboration, Kline seeks ways beyond the VA to get vets the help they need.

On a morning at a café on Montrose's Main Street, the sweet smell of bread baking mixed with the bitter scent of coffee brewing. The combination was as welcoming as the smile with which the owner ushered Kline to the communal table at the back. Kline needed the big table because friends were as likely to drop in on her here, and sit for an extended chat, as at the Welcome Home Montrose drop-in center.

That day, Kline had an appointment with Dr. Carol Giffin-Jeansonne, a psychologist from the nearby town of Delta who illustrates the expertise that can be rallied in rural America. Kline wanted to talk about classes for relatives of vets and health care professionals who might come into contact with men and women who have suffered brain injuries.

Giffin-Jeansonne warned Kline she would have to get past a certain arrogant ignorance on the part of doctors. The psychologist recounted a story she'd heard from a woman vet who was told her symptoms after surviving an explosion were caused by premenstrual tension.

"Most physicians, you can sit there and describe your signs and symptoms of a brain injury, and it will go right over their head," Giffin-Jeansonne said, no irony intended. "Most don't think they see many, if any, head injuries."

She recommended making it as easy as possible for the doctors by holding classes at convenient times and places for them. A list of possible trainers came quickly to the mind of Giffin-Jeansonne, the western Colorado executive director of Area Health Education Center, or AHEC, a national network devoted to improving access to health care in underserved parts of the United States. A year before Giffin-Jeansonne settled at the bakery table with Kline, AHEC, created by federal legislation in 1971 to address how to improve health care in rural areas, got a grant to train mental health workers in recognizing and treating traumatic brain injury and post-traumatic stress disorder.

Giffin-Jeansonne brought more to the table than professional expertise and contacts. She brought commitment inspired by personal experience.

Eighteen years earlier, Giffin-Jeansonne got word that her son, Christopher had had an accident while on duty as a National Guardsman based in Colorado. He had been driving a military vehicle along a highway when a collision in an oncoming lane sent debris flying toward him. He was struck in the head and has been in a nursing home since, severely disabled.

Christopher Giffin-Jeansonne's relatives moved from Louisiana to Colorado to be near him. His sister, a nurse, found a job in Montrose. His parents moved to nearby Delta.

Giffin-Jeansonne thinks not only of her son, but of all victims of head injuries.

"Having a son who sustained a head injury in the military and coming from a military family, it's a passion for me," she said. Her husband is Navy, her brother Marines.

Giffin-Jeansonne and Kline had an easy rapport. One a mother whose "career Guard" son was grievously injured without even going to war; the other a mother who is thankful her sons stayed safe and close to home. Their conversation ranged from the plans for head injury workshops to the need for suicide prevention programs not just for vets, but for anyone struggling in small town America where mental and other health resources are scarce.

Welcome Home Montrose "is something big that has started here that can awaken communities across the country to our returning warriors. Our national history is that we forget, and we forget quickly," Giffin-Jeansonne said. "Historically, we've ignored our returning warriors."

She and Kline looked like sisters, one head of curls, the other sporting a no-nonsense short cut, each bowed over her respective smart phone. They checked their electronic calendars to find a date for their next meeting.

Chapter 18

A Measure of Success

Kline turned a book shelf at the Welcome Home Montrose drop-in center into a shrine to small-town can-doism. On it, she displayed mugs and post cards she bought in North Platte, Nebraska on a road trip. The pilgrimage was inspired by a documentary about volunteers offering sandwiches and coffee to servicemen on troop trains passing through North Platte's station on their way to World War II battlefields.

North Platte was a community with a mission on the main line of the Union Pacific Railroad.

Soldiers were being transported by train east to west before being shipped to the Pacific theater or west to east on the way to Europe. The troop trains, sometimes a dozen or more a day, stopped for only 10 minutes in North Platte, home to about 12,000 people at the time. Rae Wilson, whose brother was an Army captain, proposed in a letter to the editor of a now-defunct newspaper that townspeople make the most of those 10 minutes. She envisioned a canteen where volunteers could ply the young men headed to war with food, drink and kindness. It started the Christmas of 1944. Nearby towns pitched in with supplies for feasts of fried chicken, egg salad sandwiches, coffee, cookies, milk, chewing gum. Magazines and Bibles also were donated.

"This was not something orchestrated by the government; this was not paid for with public money. All the food, all the services, all the hours of work were volunteered by private citizens and local businesses," journalist Bob Greene wrote.

By the time Greene arrived to do his reporting for a 2003 book, the station had been torn down decades ago. The last passenger train passed through North Platte in 1971. But Greene was able to track down women in their 70s who had been canteen volunteers.

They told him of scrimping on sugar for their own coffee and tea so as to have plenty of sweetener for treats for the soldiers. Greene also found veterans like 75-year-old Russ Fay, who was an 18-year-old on the way from his induction into the Army at Fort Sheridan near Chicago to basic training in California. Fay told Greene he still remembered the taste of North Platte's pheasant sandwiches with mayonnaise.

"We were there for such a short time. The rest of the way, we kept thinking that maybe there would be other places like that. We wanted it to happen again. But it never did," Fay told Greene. "Utah, Nevada, it got pretty desolate and we'd stop to take on water and coal, but no one ever met us. We never ran into anything like that before, or after."

Greene called the book he wrote about the North Platte canteen *Once Upon a Town*. But what happened once in North Platte was built on a spirit that was surely alive elsewhere. Perhaps all that other towns needed were women like letter writer Wilson to propose an idea around which people could rally. Perhaps all today's North Plattes need are women like Kline.

We think of World War II era America, especially small-town America, as a place where neighbors depended on one another. Today, perhaps we are too quick to imagine finding hatred and danger not only beyond our borders, but right next door.

"It looks like the whole world's falling apart and there's all this stuff to be afraid of and you should just hide in your house," Kline told me. She ventured out of her house, spoke to her neighbors, and discovered you can "meet wonderful people in your community. You meet people who are strong and committed."

Kline looked to North Platte for inspiration. And she hopes communities across the country will look to Montrose as a model for how to create cohesion in America as the war on terror drags on. Montrose cannot help every veteran. But every American town can, Kline believes.

"The goal is for the idea to spread and be successful."

When someone who has read about Welcome Home Montrose in a newspaper or heard about it from a veteran tracks Kline down, she is happy to engage. She will exchange ideas or offer advice by phone or email. Or she will invite visitors for a tour or travel to them for a face-to-face talk.

In 2014, I tagged along with Kline to Fort Collins, a Colorado university town on the northeastern plains that is 350 miles from Montrose. We entered a sunny conference room provided by a regional community development group. Kline was greeted by a half dozen men and women from a variety of backgrounds who shared an interest in the welfare of veterans.

Among Kline's hosts was Donna Chapel, a financial planner whose son had served in Afghanistan. She described herself as a "Marine mom" who had seen first-hand how some young men and women struggle to make the transition from battlefield to home.

Chapel told Kline that the group wanted to start something similar to Welcome Home Montrose to serve veterans across Northern Colorado. Her team included David Broccoli, a Vietnam veteran and businessman from nearby Loveland who a few years before had helped establish a group to raise funds for fellow vets who were homeless or otherwise in need of support. Also in the room was Jenny Pickett, an Air Force retiree and director of a Colorado State University office that supports student veterans. And there was Lonnie Berett, the veterans service officer for Larimer County and convener of an umbrella Veterans Advisory Group that holds monthly meetings open to anyone who wants to reach out to veterans.

"Seems like every month, we find another organization we didn't know about," Berett told Kline.

For VA services, veterans in Fort Collins typically go to a clinic in town or to bigger facilities in Denver or across the Wyoming border in Cheyenne.

In other words, northern Colorado had no shortage of help for veterans, both public and private. But supporters are scattered, making it difficult for vets to know what is there for them. Chapel, Broccoli, Pickett and Berett told Kline they believed they could have a role improving coordination and communications and increasing outreach to those with no ties to the military who wanted to be involved.

Broccoli had traveled west to volunteer during a Welcome Home Montrose outdoors festival for vets. On that visit, he noticed banners listing sponsors of the event. He counted more than 100 names.

"It was incredible," he remembered.

Kline told Broccoli and the others in Fort Collins that building that kind of community support took patience and persistence. It started years before the first kayaks hit the water at the festival. She described the meetings convened to determine what was already being done for vets, what needed to be done and who could fill the gap.

"The first thing you need to do is engage your community," Kline counseled. "All the rest will follow."

Welcome Home Montrose "was supposed to happen," Kline told her audience in Fort Collins. "Everything has fallen into place for us and I am convinced it will for you. Because it has to happen."

Kline went home to Montrose. The Fort Collins group continued talking among themselves and with others. The collaborators were able to identity and move to fill gaps in support for veterans in northern Colorado. For example, before the group was formally established in August of 2015 as the independent, non-profit Veterans' Compass of Northern Colorado, members reached out to the Fort Collins Municipal Court. The court in 2014 launched a program that offers alternative sentencing for some people who run afoul of certain city laws. The project would have been unlikely in Montrose, where attitudes toward law and order are more rigid. What happened in Fort Collins shows the flexibility of the Montrose model.

Like the Veterans Trauma Court in Colorado Springs, the Fort

Collins program tries to address underlying problems. Instead of fining or jailing a homeless person who violates the city's no camping or trespassing laws, the special court might order him or her to seek counseling or sign up for social services.

Unlike the Colorado Springs court, the Fort Collins program did not focus on vets. Until approached by volunteers for what would become Compass, the court program's staff did not even ask violators if they were vets. Now, court staff members ask, and have the option of pairing a vet in trouble with a mentor supplied by Compass.

I heard about the court partnership in 2016 from Pickett. In the two years since I first met Pickett, she had left her Colorado State University post to devote herself full-time to the unpaid job of president of the board of Compass, a name chosen to indicate a desire to help veterans who have lost their sense of direction. Pickett was able to volunteer full-time because she had military retirement benefits to fall back on.

"It seemed like the gap here (at Compass) was bigger than the gap at CSU," said Pickett, who had been at the university long enough to see the campus vet center, which had been started by a psychologist, bring in a psychiatrist as well. The CSU vet center serves veterans enrolled as students there, at the University of Northern Colorado in nearby Greeley and at a community college that has several campuses in the region.

Pickett, a Texan, first came to Fort Collins in 2009 when the Air Force sent her to CSU to direct training for the Reserve Officers' Training Corps, which prepares students for futures as military leaders. Pickett stayed in Fort Collins because she liked the mountain views and physically active culture of the small city known for its avid runners and cyclists.

Pickett faced me across a desk that along with two chairs and a filing cabinet were the only pieces of furniture in Compass's small office. It had opened only the month before I visited. The space in a bank building had been provided by a Compass supporter.

It was too early, Pickett said, to say whether Compass would evolve into the community hub that Welcome Home Montrose's drop-in center had become. Compass was relying on word of mouth for advertising. Pickett's office didn't even have a sign. But it was a place to meet veterans who come to her with questions about benefits and support services. From her window, Pickett can see the courthouse where the county veterans services specialist has his office.

Pickett struck me as a taller, grayer version of Welcome Home Montrose's Kline. Pickett is too modest to accept a comparison to the woman behind Welcome Home Montrose.

Pickett's board includes several of the men and women I had met back in 2014. The other board members help, but it often falls to Pickett to meet with potential donors and partners, or accompany a nervous veteran to a meeting with a benefits adviser. She expects to keep shouldering most of the load until Compass has the budget for an executive director.

Ensuring Welcome Home Montrose was embraced by so many in a community of 20,000 was a challenge, one Kline has shown can be met. The population of Fort Collins is more than seven times that of Montrose, making outreach even more daunting. Pickett said that Compass had so far been too busy responding to veterans' needs to organize the kind of community meetings held in the early days of Welcome Home Montrose, but that that step remains one of her goals.

Grassroots projects like Compass and Welcome Home Montrose are an important part of a larger solution to the challenge of helping the returning warriors feel at home again. It is an issue engaging policy makers at the highest levels of government, business and philanthropy. Under what's known as the post-9/11 GI Bill, service members with at least three months active duty since September 10, 2001, are among those eligible for help paying tuition. The U.S. Chamber of Commerce has sponsored job fairs for vets across the country. Companies like Walmart have stepped up, with the national retail chain promising a job to any honorably discharged vet who meets the company's standard requirements and applies within a month of ending his or her service.

In circles where social change is on the agenda, a good idea is one that can be applied to many communities and situations. Welcome Home Montrose may be a good idea, but copies have yet to pop up across the United States. Its very success may be one reason why: the range of programs likely make Welcome Home Montrose intimidating to those trying to decide how to start to address the needs of veterans.

Kline works to explain Welcome Home Montrose. But people she meets still see a fait accompli, not a series of steps, layers of ideas, multiple meetings of like minds. Explaining the project is further complicated by its breadth. It's difficult to copy what you can't label. Still, Welcome Home Montrose has deep meaning for many people.

Welcome Home Montrose is not the drop-in center; it's the opportunities the center creates for vets to find themselves and for people who want to help to find them. It is not the coffee mornings; it's the conversations had over the warm cups and cold donuts. It is not the answers jotted on sticky notes at community meetings; it's the questions and the courage it took to pose them. If you understand Welcome Home Montrose as a process and not any one outcome, it's possible to see that what is happening in western Colorado is already part of a larger movement.

In Caldwell, a north-central Idaho town with about twice the population of Montrose, veterans and their allies have been working since 2012 to transform a library into a facility similar to the Welcome Home Montrose drop-in center. As in Montrose, the project started as an effort to solve a problem that was unrelated to veterans: saving a library building that was among hundreds erected across the United States in the late 1800s and early 1900s thanks to donations from steel magnate Andrew Carnegie.

The school district, which had housed administrative offices in the library for years, was moving to larger quarters. While it was unlikely the historic building would be razed, it could have faded away without an owner and a use.

Mayor Garret Nancolas told me about community meetings to workshop ideas about the building's future. They sounded similar to the meetings that laid the foundation for Welcome Home Montrose. In Caldwell, some townspeople wanted the building to return to its original library use, though it had last loaned books in the 1970s. Others proposed a computer center.

"Conversations change. They are dynamic. You go from one idea to another," Nancolas said.

A group of veterans who had been discussing the need for a one-stop center where they could seek services took part in those conversations. Proposals from them resonated in a town known for its patriotism, Nancolas said, as the Welcome Home Montrose vets got the stalled river park project moving again in western Colorado.

In Idaho, Mayor Nancolas said, the proposal to turn the old library into a center for vets was seen as "a way to say to our veterans, 'Thank you for your service.' In a concrete way."

"It kind of hit everybody in the heart.

"This was truly born out of a desire to help all vets. This was just to honor every person who's ever donned a uniform."

The city paid the school district $200,000 for the red-brick Carnegie library and handed it over to the Caldwell Veterans Council on a 100-year lease at $1 a year. The council, formed specifically for the library project, was backed by a coalition of veterans' organizations that echoed the support Welcome Home Montrose received from such groups: the American Legion, the Veterans of Foreign Wars and Disabled American Veterans.

The Caldwell Veterans Council organized an all-volunteer, all-donor construction project. It planned to provide services to veterans in the building once renovations were complete and pay expenses going forward by renting event and office space in what will be known as Veterans Memorial Hall. Its spaces will be grand, with nine-foot windows and a main room that is to be restored to 1913 condition with period lighting and varnished floors. Officials expected the project to be completed in time for Veteran's Day in 2017.

"It's something this community will be proud of for a hundred years to come," Mayor Nancolas said.

Like Montrose, Caldwell had placed faith in men and women who had served and who wanted to continue serving. In both towns, veterans found reason to trust their communities. Stitch by stitch together, they are mending a tear in the fabric of America.

Tick, the psychotherapist who has treated and observed traumatized veterans around the world since the 1970s, has called on communities to listen without judging to warriors returned from battle. It is a way to take part in and share responsibility for the violence done on society's behalf.

"What are warriors asking from their communities and society?" Tick has written. "To be seen as they are, for who they are, for what they gave, for their struggles now, and to be loved and honored for their unchanging essence of devotion and sacrifice."

As Tick and Pew researchers have noted, few of us are fighting the current wars. As a result, many Americans may not know a veteran of the war on terror. In Montrose, Kline had thought she would be bringing vets from other towns to the welcome she believed they deserved. She would discover many veterans were already in town, but keeping their experiences to themselves. Ellison's Invisible Man was a metaphor. Invisibility is all too real for many veterans.

Caldwell's Mayor Nancolas did not follow his Korea veteran father into the military. Vietnam was ending as the younger Nancolas was graduating from high school.

"I had my draft card. I was ready to go if needed," he said. "I've always felt this deep sense of patriotism. I just have the highest regard for veterans."

John Muirhead, who served on a U.S. Navy submarine in Vietnam and now chairs the Caldwell Veterans Council, said the mayor's dedication to the library renovation and to veterans in general helped inspire others.

Nancolas always has a hug for veterans when they appear at city council meetings to discuss the library renovation or other issues, and "he never passes up an opportunity to talk about the (library) project," Muirhead told me.

Those words brought to my mind images of Kline showing her wounded warriors video to everyone she could in Montrose. The mayor told me his campaign included tucking updates on the project in water bills sent to citizens.

"It takes a little while to build momentum," Mayor Nancolas added. If his own energy ever flagged, he, like Kline, had a reservoir of faith from which to draw.

"I believe prayers are being answered," Nancolas said. "I believe there's a much bigger hand than any of us has that is helping us get it done."

The mayor, for his part, said it is veterans like Muirhead and Terry L. Harrell, a retired Army lieutenant colonel, who have made the library project a success. Nancolas said he has heard time and again from his constituents that veterans have inspired them to help out with the library renovation.

"You need champions like John and Terry who are actual veterans," the mayor said.

Whether it was the vets or the mayor that moved them, Boy Scouts and construction union members have contributed labor to the library renovation. The local Home Depot store, part of a chain that is a national supporter of veterans causes, has donated supplies and organized employee work crews who have put in many hours installing, to give one example, insulation.

"Even though it's a small town, it's still connected to the bigger world through these corporations," Muirhead said.

The library was still a construction site on Veteran's Day in 2015.

Organizers nonetheless decided to hold their annual ceremony on its steps.

School children sang and dignitaries spoke on a cold, brisk morning, as was the case in previous years when the ceremony was held outside city hall. In the past, a crowd of 75-100 was seen as successful.

In 2015, "We had 375 people show up and stand outside in the cold for over an hour to honor the vets," Nancolas said.

Nancolas believed the crowd was larger because of the enthusiasm and visibility that has been built around the renovation project.

"Any day, you can go by that building and you can find volunteers down there," the mayor said. Part of what has worked, he said, is that people who don't have money to give can still feel included, again reminding me of the Montrose initiative.

For all the echoes to Montrose, Kline only heard about Caldwell once the library renovation was already underway. Nancolas, Muirhead and Harrell weren't following a blueprint. They were simply doing what small towns do when they have a mission to complete.

Kline is not sure who shared with her one of the regular email updates Muirhead sends out about Caldwell's veterans hall. When she saw it, she called him. The two have had several conversations since. Muirhead said the exchanges have helped people in Caldwell refine what the center will be once it is opened. At first, he and other veterans saw the Veterans Memorial Hall as a place where volunteers and professionals could meet with veterans to guide them through the process of applying for benefits or old warriors could gather for PTSD group therapy. After talking to Kline, plans were added for weekly coffees and classes like the tai chi, job readiness and suicide prevention sessions that have been held at Montrose's Warrior Resource Center.

Muirhead, like the Vietnam era veterans I met in Montrose, feels a connection to younger men and women who have served.

"I remember what it was like coming back to the United States from overseas deployment. All the protesters. It was horrible. No one would have brought us a coffee or lunch. They spat on us," he said. "Veterans have now achieved some level of respect that wasn't there before. For us, that's just incredible. But it could swing the other way. There are people out there who don't like vets. There are young people who don't understand what veterans have done."

After Vietnam, Muirhead studied project management and for 30 years worked around the United States and around the world for an engineering company that built nuclear power plants. Where ever he went, he preferred small town life. One of his last jobs for the company was managing a project at the Idaho National Laboratory, a federal nuclear energy research and development center. He ended up working at the lab in Boise but living 30 miles west in Caldwell. He is now retired and can put his background in engineering and construction to good use on the library project. He spoke to me by phone from the site, apologizing at one point when he had to break off to consult with an electrician.

"This building became that thing that all of us do for a living," he said of himself and other veterans who are dedicated to the project.

Curious about his background before settling in Idaho, I asked Muirhead where he was from. I started when he answered: North Platte, Nebraska. Even over a phone line, I could tell he was surprised I knew about its wartime canteen. It was a legend where he grew up, he said, but he didn't think outsiders were aware of his small town's outsize contribution.

I realized Murihead had never visited Montrose to see Kline's shrine. After I got off the phone with Muirhead, I called her to relate the coincidence. She wanted to know whether growing up in North Platte had shaped his desire to serve. A fair question. I got back in touch with Muirhead.

"The stories and the accounts of women who worked at the

canteen helped to fortify and bolster my patriotism, which ultimately led me to an enlistment in the Navy," he told me. "I volunteered for sub duty because my father served on a submarine in World War II."

Now in Idaho, he is dedicated to the library project "because I want to do something meaningful to help vets who maybe didn't leave the military in as good a condition as I did."

I was fortunate to have asked the right question to the right person. Sometimes that is all it takes to give meaning to our nation's legacies.

A prayer I first read at a bat mitzvah counsels "humility that we may be more aware of our own faults and ... wisdom to be more forgiving of others. Give us the courage to be true to our highest selves and the kindness of heart to see the best in those around us."

The people I met as I worked on this book are mindful of and humbled by their faults, but have courage enough to reach beyond them. Because Welcome Home Montrose was created despite differences and disappointments, irritations and irritability, what the citizens of Montrose have been able to make is all the more instructive to other places with problems of their own.

Or, as Kline has put it: "We're not that unique."

"We're awesome," she continued, and laughed. "But there are awesome people everywhere."

Epilogue

Here we were, almost three years to the day after the airing of that 2011 Sunday morning news show on wounded vets that inspired Kline to start Welcome Home Montrose. Kline looks to the community spirit epitomized by North Platte, Nebraska during World War II, and it was her idea to party like it was 1945 for what was both a celebration and a report back to her town.

At the event a singer evoked a USO dance with renditions of "Ain't Misbehavin'," "All of Me" and "Summertime" in front of a jazz trio. Kline tamed her dark curls with a fascinator and pulled on polka dot gloves. Bolhuis, the Marine and wounded Afghan veteran Kline brought to Montrose after seeing him in that Sunday morning show, wore a fedora, vest and tie. Other guests turned bandana head scarves, cuffed jeans and work shirts into Rosie the Riveter costumes

Emily and Sheldon Smith went all out. Emily was in a candy apple red dress with a swingy skirt, red and cream spectator pumps and a hairdo that was all curls and swoops, as shiny and exuberantly voluminous as a Frank Gehry building.

Sheldon ordered a uniform from a war re-enactment supplier he found online. His trousers were khaki and relaxed, his jacket jauntily short, his tie tucked into his placket. He was especially proud of the period gleam of his brown boots, claiming he'd spent as much time shining them as Emily had spent having her hair constructed.

Who can begrudge them a bit of false nostalgia? The inspiration and energy they drew from a story of the past are real enough.

The evening included a speech from a visitor from Denver, the head of the state chapter of the Employee Support of the Guard and Reserve. The dignitary, Dick Young, explained that he had come to bestow an award he had created when he heard about what was happening in Montrose to honor "the most veteran friendly city in

Colorado."

"I hold you out as the perfect example of what a community can do, and I'm doing everything I can to make sure you don't win it every year," said Young, whose organization is the lead Department of Defense agency that reaches out to employers on behalf of members of the National Guard and Reserve.

In a way, my journey to this award-winning town in the heart of America began offshore.

After 18 years as a foreign correspondent, when I returned to the United States in 2012 I was baffled at what struck me as an absence of discussion in my homeland about U.S. military involvement in the Middle East. Abroad, the conflicts were so often the focus of talk, whether around dinner tables or the proverbial water cooler. Coming to Montrose was a chance for me to question my own assumptions. Was I expecting a solidarity reminiscent of World War II? Vietnam-era protests? Was it simply that I had returned at a time when Americans were weary of contemplating war?

I found not so much weariness as wariness in Montrose. Discussion of the war, like so many issues in 21st century America, tends to quickly degenerate into us-against-them arguments. It was happening at the very top, as Robert Gates, America's secretary of defense from 2006 to 2011, described in his wartime memoirs. Gates wrote of senior government and military officials' unwillingness or inability to listen to one another. Their disagreements gave unintended weight to perceived snubs and fueled rivalries and suspicions, hardening positions and keeping leaders from recognizing they had common ground and certainly shared goals. For those with no decision-making power, remaining silent seemed a rational course, especially when there were worries and divisions closer to home to contemplate.

The compassion that drives Welcome Home Montrose, though, was something anyone could share.

In 2002, I was the Cairo-based news editor for The Associated Press. The day the U.S. bombing began in Iraq, I ran into our

Egyptian landlord in the lobby of the AP Middle East bureau's office building. He was agitated. He asked me, the words coming in stops in starts past his anxiety and anger: "I guess you are happy, aren't you?" I was too overcome with emotion myself to say anything other than, "No, no."

I also had been in Cairo on September 11, 2001 when al-Qaida leader Osama bin Laden's followers flew to their deaths and took with them some 3,000 people from the United States and dozens of other countries.

The Egyptian capital is hours ahead of the United States. My work day was winding down when the first plane struck the North Tower. I had a telephone interview for a story whose subject I no longer recall, so had retreated to the quiet of my office off the main newsroom. As I scribbled notes with the receiver pressed to an ear, a colleague came to my door, looking grave. I mimed an "I'm on the phone" dismissal and continued with my interview. My colleague went away, but she came back almost immediately, probably as the second tower was struck. I was annoyed as I disengaged from my call, wondering what could be so important. I walked out of my office, and saw on the newsroom televisions the scenes that Emily Smith was watching in her Colorado apartment. The TV monitors were positioned over windows that looked out on the Nile, a view I'd always found calming. It was difficult to hold onto calm that day.

I worked with Associated Press colleagues from around the world, many of them Egyptian, Lebanese, Iraqi and other Arab nationalities. Many of them Muslim. We were united as we watched the TV reports from New York in assuming that the investigation into the attacks would lead to the Middle East. We were as certain of that as Sheldon Smith was, far away in the Colorado mountains, that the United States was on the brink of war.

From my base in Egypt, I had traveled throughout the region to report on the Arab and Muslim world at a time when it was easy to be cynical. I saw brutal, short-sighted autocrats, some of whom were long and closely allied with Washington. I saw little hope for democracy. Bin Laden, who admired fundamentalist Egyptian thinkers and made one his top lieutenant, saw tinder for a conflagration he had determined was necessary to burn away what he defined as the rot of secularism and Westernization in the Muslim world.

Bin Laden had laid down a challenge to Westerners with the oft-quoted declaration that his followers desired "death more than you desire life." He built his arguments on citations from ancient texts, including the Quran, as well as the latest headlines. He appealed to nostalgia and a sense of wounded pride among some Muslims. He offered an explanation for political and economic uncertainty in countries that share, along with faith, poverty, inequality and a sense of helplessness against their own governments and global forces. Bin Laden was perhaps no different from so many other such figures over the ages. But his influence was magnified in our era of instant, dramatic and wide-reaching communication.

I and many of my media colleagues would, for years to come, be preoccupied with learning about the 19 men who were the September 11 attackers: their personalities, their families, their influences. We would all come to know more about the man who had inspired them, bin Laden, who shared Saudi roots with many of his operatives. The Middle East is a big place. An Egyptian can understand a Moroccan, but they speak different forms of Arabic. It was and is a region of anti-American passions and militant Islam, but also of American allies and fierce secularists. My reporting often focused on perceptions of America's intentions and leadership in the world.

Upon returning home, I approached another aspect of this huge story. In a way, I had to go to Montrose to understand the fear and uncertainty my Egyptian landlord had expressed. I had not taken the time the morning that the Iraq war started to try to make a connection across fraught divides. In a small Colorado town, I saw people trying to make connections every day that they gathered in a nondescript Main Street shopping center.

They brought imagination to the task. That led to a measure of understanding, and from there to empathy and compassion.

As a journalist in the Mideast, I had been guilty of being too busy covering conflict to contemplate it much. My journey to Montrose became a meditation on war, which runs through history like a river. At times, it roars with implacable force. Even when the surface is calm, the depths can be treacherous.

I would have to have the audacity of a veteran like Burkins, a Welcome Home Montrose volunteer who has seen war, to imagine a world without war.

Wars are, we are told, a tool of diplomacy. They arise from issues so large that few of us can hope to influence their sweep. That is the clear-eyed view. Why not also be clear-eyed about the consequences on the small stages of everyday lives? I hope young fighters of the future find neighbors as imaginative as the people of Montrose to welcome them home.

Afterword

Kline and I were headed to lunch on an autumn afternoon in 2014. She paused at the reception desk of the Warrior Resource Center to ask the volunteer on welcome duty if she would take over the duty of ensuring each donation to Welcome Home Montrose was recorded. Kline had been doing it herself since founding the veterans' support project in 2012. She was falling behind in her logging of gifts and cash. That was delaying what she saw as the crucial task of getting thank you notes to supporters.

By the time I returned with Kline from lunch, the eager volunteer had made her way through a file folder of checks.

With that, Kline made progress on what she saw as another crucial task: disentangling herself. She firmly believed that if her grassroots effort to help vets and her town was to live on, it could not be dependent on any one person.

"This has already been a success. I'm proud of all we have accomplished." Kline told me. But she was not content to speak only of the past. She was looking to the future.

"If this is short-lived, it will be my fault."

Kline retired in early 2016. When I made plans to see her a few months after she made that announcement, I let her choose where we would meet. She confirmed when we sat down together that it was no accident we were having coffee and bagels at a deli on the south side of town, a few miles from any downtown restaurant or café where she might run into Welcome Home Montrose staff or volunteers.

She had shown before that she knows how to disengage. When she retired from her jewelry business in 2012 and handed her two shops completely over to her sons, she truly gave them up. She looked on as her sons abandoned business practices she had developed.

"You don't have to do things the way I did them," she said.

After leaving Welcome Home Montrose, Kline busied herself making jewelry and teaching others the craft at a bench installed in a home on the east side of town into which she and her husband had recently moved, abandoning a house that was closer to the Welcome Home Montrose drop-in center. The new home came with a large and established garden that demanded her attention, as did her family.

Kline had by no means cut all ties to Welcome Home Montrose. She made herself available for consultations and enjoyed the occasional video and junk food fueled girls' night out with Smith and other former colleagues who were now close friends. But she said she restrained herself from giving advice too freely. She had trusted in her town's sense of itself. As a result, Welcome Home Montrose was born. Now, Kline had to have confidence that her community would shepherd the project forward, whatever future was ahead.

Afghanistan veteran Kenney has missed seeing Kline at the Welcome Home Montrose drop-in center or at the jewelry store she once ran across Main Street from his fly fishing and hunting guide and supply business.

While he remained active with Welcome Home Montrose, other demands on Kenney's time were growing.

When we caught up by phone as the summer of 2016 was ending, Kenney called me from the road after dropping a daughter off at college in southern California. Once he got home, he and his wife would resume planning another daughter's wedding, which would be held on the rural plot where Kenney had built the family home.

The bride was "going to get married on the exact spot where she shot her first elk," the proud father informed me.

Kenney's son, meanwhile, was playing soccer, despising piano lessons and starting third grade.

Kenney was back in school himself. He had been studying taxidermy, a pursuit he said he found soothing. And his Toads

Guide Shop was thriving.

"So far, I'm still making payments on my building, which is good," Kenney told me, sardonic as always.

He had hired a clerk and guide for Toads, freeing him from interactions with customers he sometimes found stressful. Taxidermy was something he could do largely on his own from a home studio. Clients looking to have a hunting or fishing trophy stuffed and mounted can find their way to him through his shop.

Kenney was setting up the Purple Heart Taxidermy Studio with the help of a grant from Semper Fi, a support group for veterans of all services founded by military spouses in California.

Kenney sees part of his role at Welcome Home Montrose as making sure his hometown kept in touch with national groups like Semper Fi. At the same time, he said, he wants to ensure Kline's commitment to veterans closer to home remains central to the local mission.

He's still not above raising his voice to make a point, Kenney told me. But he also expressed confidence in the neighbors now shepherding Welcome Home Montrose.

"There's enough people that are doing good things," he said.

Goals Kline had set were priorities for a board brought together shortly before she retired. The new board members moved to stop using the name Welcome Home Montrose in favor of Welcome Home Alliance For Veterans, making clear they had ambitions beyond their corner of Colorado.

Smith remained executive director after Kline's retirement. Smith told me that now that Kline has stepped down, it has become clearer how much of Welcome Home Montrose's institutional memory was in her mentor's brain.

"She did all of the finances for this whole organization and she carried it all in her head," Smith told me. "You try to show someone else what she was doing and they say, 'That takes four people!'"

In the past year, Welcome Home Montrose hired a part-time

assistant for Smith. New board chairwoman Terri Wilcox, who spoke with me alongside Smith in the Warrior Resource Center, said part of the goal was to free Smith to do more strategic thinking about the project's future. The board, meanwhile, would focus on raising funds. Smith said she had grown because of Welcome Home Montrose, and now saw a chance to grow more.

"A thousand lives impacted later," Smith began.

"More than a thousand," Wilcox interjected.

"I think the biggest impact has been on me," Smith concluded.

Half a continent away, Smith's old co-executive director also was contemplating the impact Welcome Home Montrose had had on him. Bolhuis, the Marine with brain injuries, had encouraged other wounded warriors to come to Montrose and helped the town build a water park. Now he looked back on the park's ribbon-cutting festivities. Sitting around a campfire during that event, he recalled another veteran saying: "Someone should really make a movie about stuff like this."

"It just kind of hit me: 'You know what, that's not a bad idea.'"

He spoke to me by phone from Florida, where he had been enrolled in film school for more than a year. The school emphasized hands-on training and Bolhuis had already worked as a crewmember in both off-campus productions and on fellow students' projects. He often found himself in the role of first assistant director. The job, which he had not known existed before he started school, put him in charge of logistics and organizing the rest of the behind-the-camera crew. Bolhuis compared it to leading a squad on the battlefield.

"I feel bound to a life of service. From the Marine Corps to helping get Welcome Home Montrose started to going to film school. It's just the next tool in my personal crusade."

Bolhuis added that he often wears a T-shirt with the Welcome Home Montrose logo around campus. The conversations the shirt helps him start have shown him many people want to help vets. One day he might even make a movie about the Colorado town with the big heart.

I recall that Kline once fleetingly considered whether her town could boost its own name recognition by exploiting its connection to the late Academy Award-winning scriptwriter Dalton Trumbo, who was born in Montrose in 1905 and is known as much for his work on the movies *Roman Holiday* and *Spartacus* as for refusing to testify before the House Un-American Activities Committee in the 1940s. Imagine the townspeople of Montrose starring in their own movie.

I learned working on this book about vets' fierce desire to keep serving. Bolhuis exemplifies that spirit, and Welcome Home Montrose has shown civilians share it. I trust together they will keep finding creative ways to express it.

Personal Interviews

Abbas, Izzy
Alfred, Harry
Aligata, Donna
Anderson, Frank
Angell, Susan
Badoud, Pat
Bain, Brian
Baldwin, Julie
Barlow, Davida
Baskis, Steve
Becker, Gary
Bell, Bill
Berndt, Robin
Bish, John
Bolhuis, Dave
Bolhuis, Jackie
Bolhuis, Jared
Boyce, Judi
Blackwelder, Pat
Bronner, Mike
Brown, John
Burkins, Lee
Chinn, Tom
Deutsch, Chris
Elliott, Cleo
Elliot, Stan
Ellis, Gary
Ellis, Kathy
Everhart, Chloe
Files, Judy Ann
Giffin-Jeansonne, Carol

Glasscock, Bill
Good, David
Gordon, Jon
Gratton, Gary
Haley, Travis
Hall, Melanie
Havens, Randy
Head, Sandy
Heck, Joshua
Hollabaugh, Craig
Jensen, Hyrum
Johnson, Sally
Jukes, Chad
Kenney, Tim
Kidd, Steven
Kline, Melanie
Kuboske, Merry Lee
Lawrence, George
Lease, Carol
Love, Gary
Lyons, Ed
Manzagol, Sheila
Manzagol, Tim
Martinez, Leo
May, Dan
McAteer, Sheilagh
McDermott, Carol
Mercado, Jim
Michaels, R. Lance
Mitchell, Lisa
Mitchell, Myrisa

Muirhead, John

Murphy, Scott

Nancolas, Garret

Otto, Katy

Parr, Rich

Pickett, Jenny

Power, Kathryn

Rizzo, Scott

Roberts, Val

Rosen, Jeremy

Ryan, Stacey

Sisley, Sue

Scroggins, Marc

Shakes, David

Slattery, Michelle

Sawyer-Smith, Rebecca

Sayles, Laura

Schadegg, Dawn

Schultz, Pamela

Seaborn, Cindy

Smith, Charlie

Smith, Emily

Smith, Sheldon

Sweeney, Paul

Taus, Alexander

Tupa, Elizabeth

Venrick, Fred

Warvi, Dan

Wilcox, Terri

Williams, Laura

Wirkus, Kathryn

Witte, Sharan

Ziemann, Tom

References

Adichie, C. (2009) "The danger of a single story", *TED,* July [Online]. Available at http://www.ted.com/talks/chimamanda_ adichie_the_danger_of_a_single_story (Accessed Feb. 12, 2017).

Alvarez, L. (2010) "Spirit Intact, Soldier Reclaims His Life", *The New York Times,* July 2 [Online]. Available at http:// www.nytimes.com/2010/07/04/nyregion/04soldier.html?_ r=3&pagewanted=all& (Accessed Nov. 30, 2016).

Beck, G. (2014) "This town wants to be the friendliest vet town in America," *The Glenn Beck Program,* July 12 [Online]. Available at http://www.glennbeck.com/2014/06/12/this-town-wants-to-be-the-friendliest-vet-town-in-america/ (Accessed Aug. 28, 2016).

Bennett, M. (2010) "Robin Berndt: Serving with spirit". *The Monitor Magazine,* Fall [Online]. Available at https://issuu. com/monitormagazine/docs/the_monitor_magazine_fall_ issue_2010 (Accessed Feb. 20, 2017).

Bonn-Miller, M. and Rousseau, G. (2016) "Marijuana Use and PTSD among Veterans", *Department of Veterans Affairs,* Feb. 23 [Online]. Available at http://www.ptsd.va.gov/professional/co-occurring/marijuana_use_ptsd_veterans.asp (Accessed Nov. 29, 2016).

Brohl, B., Kammerzell, R. and Koski, W. (2015) "Annual Report", *Colorado Department of Revenue* [Online]. Available at https:// www.colorado.gov/pacific/sites/default/files/2014%20 MED%20Annual%20Report_1.pdf (Accessed Nov. 29, 2016).

Brown, J. (2016) "Mental health workers join cops on streets", *The Denver Post,* Sep. 3. pps. 2A, 8A.

Brundin, J. (2015) "A Colorado Teacher Shortage Puts Rural Schools On The Brink Of Crisis," *Colorado Public Radio,* Sep. 29 [Online]. Available at http://www.cpr.org/news/story/colorado-teacher-shortage-puts-rural-schools-brink-crisis#sthash.rlHddT7I.dpuf (Accessed Apr. 17, 2016).

Burkins, L. (2003) *Soldier's Heart: An Inspirational Memoir and Inquiry of War*, Bloomington, AuthorHouse.

Centers for Medicare & Medicaid Services Alliance to Modernize Health Care (2015) *Independent Assessment of the Health Care Delivery Systems and Management Processes of the Department of Veterans Affairs*, Washington, Department of Veterans Affairs [Online]. Available at http://www.va.gov/opa/choiceact/documents/assessments/Integrated_Report.pdf (Accessed Dec. 1, 2015).

Chandrasekaren, R. (2014) "A legacy of pain and pride," *The Washington Post*, March 24 [Online]. Available at http://www.washingtonpost.com/sf/national/2014/03/29/a-legacy-of-pride-and-pain/ (Accessed Nov. 16, 2016).

Committee on the Assessment of Ongoing Efforts in the Treatment of Posttraumatic Stress Disorder (2014) *Treatment for Posttraumatic Stress Disorder in Military and Veteran Populations*, Washington, The National Academies Press [Online] Available at https://www.nap.edu/read/18724/chapter/1

Cortes, A., Henry, M., de la Cruz, R. and Brown, S. (2012) *The 2012 Point-in-Time Estimates of Homelessness* [Online]. Available at https://www.hudexchange.info/resources/documents/2012AHAR_PITestimates.pdf (Accessed April 16, 2016).

Department of Veterans Affairs (2016) *America's Wars* September [Online]. Available at http://www.va.gov/opa/publications/factsheets/fs_americas_wars.pdf (Accessed Nov. 29, 2016).

Department of Veterans Affairs (Undated) *VA History* [Online]. Available at http://www.va.gov/about_va/vahistory.asp (Accessed July 2, 2016).

Gates, R. (2014) *Duty: Memoirs of a secretary at war*, New York, Alfred A. Knopf. Ebook.

Gordon, M. and Trainor, B. (2006) *Cobra II: The Inside Story of the Invasion and Occupation of Iraq*, New York: Pantheon Books.

Greene, B. (2002) *Once Upon a Town: The Miracle of the North Platte Canteen*, New York: William Morrow.

Ellison, R. (1994) *Invisible Man,* New York, The Modern Library.

Filkins, D. (2008) *The Forever War,* New York, Alfred A. Knopf.

Filkins, D. (2014) "Wider war," *The New Yorker* June 23.

Filkins, D. (2014) "Choices at the top," *The New Yorker* June 30.

Filkins, D. (2014) "The fight of their Lives," *The New Yorker* Sept. 29.

Filkins, D. (2014) "What we left behind," *The New Yorker* April 28.

Finley, B. (2014) "Petraeus praises Obama's approach," *The Denver Post* Sept. 12 p. 20A.

Finley, B. (2016) "Veterans are using pot to ease PTSD, despite scant research," *The Associated Press* March 22. Available at http://bigstory.ap.org/article/2493e0c4cbad4188a8539cccaf896ba6/veterans-are-using-pot-ease-ptsd-despite-scant-research (Accessed Nov. 29, 2016).

Fischer, H. (2015) "A Guide to U.S. Military Casualty Statistics: Operation Freedom's Sentinel, Operation Inherent Resolve, Operation New Dawn, Operation Iraqi Freedom, and Operation Enduring Freedom," *Congressional Research Service,* Aug. 7 [Online]. Available at https://www.fas.org/sgp/crs/natsec/RS22452.pdf (Accessed Nov. 29, 2016).

Frey, W.H. (2014) *A Population Slowdown for Small Town America* [Online]. Available at http://www.brookings.edu/research/opinions/2014/03/31-population-slowdown-small-town-america-frey (Accessed Dec. 1, 2015).

Galloway, A. (1940) *Passing of the Two-Gun Era: Memoirs of the late Alva W. Galloway, Cowboy, Rancher, County Official and Businessman.* Montrose, unpublished manuscript archived at Montrose Regional Library District.

Garner, E. (July 2014) *Region 10 _ Why do Demographics and the Economy Matter?* Denver, Colorado Department of Local Affairs.

Goldberg, R. (1981) *Hooded Empire: The Ku Klux Klan in Colorado,* Urbana: University of Illinois Press.

Hildner, M. (2006) "Remembering a son, a brother, a hero," *Montrose Daily Press* Sept. 3 [Online]. Available at http://www.montrosepress.com/news/remembering-a-son-a-brother-a-hero/article_ebf3dd27-54ed-53bd-bfdd-dbe780d4a15e.html (Accessed Jan. 10, 2017).

History.com [Online] Available at http://www.history.com/ Accessed Jan. 12, 2017).

Hughes, J. (1991) *American Indians in Colorado*, Boulder, Pruett Publishing Company.

Jones, E. (1995) *Many Faces, Many Visions: The Story of Montrose, Colorado*, Ridgway, Country Graphics.

Kean, T. et al (2004) *The 9/11 Commission Report*, New York, WW Norton & Company.

Kovic, R. (2012) *Born on the Fourth of July*, New York, Akashic Books. Ebook.

Kusmin, L. (2016) Rural America at a Glance [Online]. Available at https://www.ers.usda.gov/webdocs/publications/eib162/eib-162.pdf (Accessed Nov. 29, 2016).

Landler, M. and Peters, J. (2014) "U.S. General Open to Ground Forces in Fight Against ISIS in Iraq," *The New York Times* Sept. 16 [Online] Available at http://nyti.ms/1qUG5kk (Accessed Sept. 16, 2014).

Lemmon, G. (2016) "When Women Lead Soldiers Into Battle", The Atlantic Sep. 9 [Online] Available at https://www. theatlantic.com/international/archive/2016/09/women-combat-leaders/498800/ (Accessed Feb. 20, 2017).

Mathews, Z. (2013) "Should the Washington Redskins Change Their Name?" *KOOL* May 1 [Online]. Available at http:// kool1079.com/should-the-washington-redskins-change-their-name/ (Accessed Feb. 11, 2017).

Obama, B. (2009) *Remarks by the President at the Veterans of Foreign Wars convention* Aug. 17 [Online]. Available at https://www. whitehouse.gov/the-press-office/remarks-president-veterans-foreign-wars-convention (Accessed Jan. 12, 2017).

Obama, B. (2014) *Remarks by the President at MacDill Air Force Base* Sept. 17 [Online]. Available at https://www.whitehouse.gov/ the-press-office/2014/09/17/remarks-president-macdill-air-force-base (Accessed Jan. 12, 2017).

Office of the Press Secretary (2011) *Fact Sheet: President Obama's Commitment to Employing America's Veterans.* [Online]. Available at https://www.whitehouse.gov/the-press-office/2011/08/05/fact-sheet-president-obama-s-commitment-employing-america-s-veterans Accessed Nov. 16, 2016).

National Institute of Mental Health (2016) *Post-Traumatic Stress Disorder,* February. [Online}. Available at https://www.nimh.nih.gov/health/topics/post-traumatic-stress-disorder-ptsd/index.shtml (Accessed Nov. 29, 2016).

Reid, C. (2011) "Freeing disabled vets with kayaks," *CBS News,* Nov. 1 [Online video]. Available at http://www.cbsnews.com/news/freeing-disabled-vets-with-kayaks/ (Accessed Nov. 29, 2016).

Romero, D. (2015) "Message from the Mayor," *City Beat Newsletter,* Fall [Online]. Available at http://cityofmontrose.org/documentcenter/view/31546 (Accessed Jan. 10, 2017).

Rosenberg, C. (2016) Letter, *Drug Enforcement Agency* [Online]. Available at https://www.dea.gov/divisions/hq/2016/Letter081116.pdf (Accessed Nov. 29, 2016).

Sitton family (2006) "Corporal Christopher Franklin Sitton" *Montrose Daily Press,* Aug. 29 [Online]. Available at http://www.montrosepress.com/obituaries/corporal-christopher-franklin-sitton/article_1eca8cca-e9a7-5a1e-9e56-88d67e4b6ffd.html (Accessed Jan. 10, 2017).

Smith, D. (1986) *Ouray: Chief of the Utes,* Ridgway, Wayfinder Press.

Southern Ute Indian Tribe (2017) *History of the Southern Ute* [Online]. Available at https://www.southernute-nsn.gov/history/ (Accessed Jan. 9, 2017).

Substance Abuse and Mental Health Services Administration (2014) *Veterans and Military Families* Sep. 29 [Online]. Available at http://www.samhsa.gov/militaryFamilies (Accessed Nov. 29, 2016).

Switzer, C. (2016) "Heroin use explodes in city of Montrose," *The*

Montrose Mirror, March 21 pps. 1, 9.

Taylor, P. (2011) *The Military-Civilian Gap: War and Sacrifice in the Post-9/11 Era*. Available at http://www.pewsocialtrends.org/files/2011/10/veterans-report.pdf [Online]. (Accessed Nov. 29, 2016).

Thorpe, H. (2014) *Soldier Girls: The Battles of Three Women at Home and at War*, New York, Scribner.

Tick, E. (2014) *Warrior's Return: Restoring the Soul After War*, Boulder, Sounds True. Ebook.

Tucker, E. (2016) "Justice Dept. focuses on police treatment of mentally ill," *The Associated Press* Aug. 29 [Online]. Available at http://bigstory.ap.org/article/9d88ceb5e01541e59f23f5d27b5cce26/justice-dept-focuses-police-treatment-mentally-ill (Accessed Nov. 29, 2016).

Unsigned editorial (2015) "Pot expedition right move," *Montrose Daily Press*, Jan. 30 [Online]. Available at http://www.montrosepress.com/opinion/pot-expedition-right-move/article_71fdc220-a83d-11e4-99b9-0fdec1d0bcfd.html (Accessed Nov. 29, 2016).

Washington Post Staff (2014) "Transcript: Hagel testifies to the Senate Armed Services Committee on the Islamic State," *The Washington Post*, Sept. 16 [Online]. Available at https://www.washingtonpost.com/world/national-security/transcript-hagel-testifies-to-the-senate-armed-services-committee-on-the-islamic-state/2014/09/16/a4909e26-3dab-11e4-b0ea-8141703bbf6f_story.html?utm_term=.dfdecd60a4a9 (Accessed Sept. 16, 2014).

Wax, J. (2013) "Marijuana: Greeley and Montrose ban pot businesses," *Westword* June 5 [Online]. Available at http://www.westword.com/news/marijuana-greeley-and-montrose-ban-pot-businesses-5876594 (Accessed Nov. 29, 2016).

Wellner, B. (2013) "Edward Lyons: For once I could leave the house without fear," *Quad-City Times* Dec. 15 [Online}. Available at http://qctimes.com/news/local/edward-lyons-for-once-i-could-leave-the-house-without/article_70ed5b32-ffa8-573b-84bc-946e01977985.html (Accessed Nov. 29, 2016).

White, J. (2015) *The Warrior Within* [Online video]. Available at https://vimeo.com/122663858 (Accessed Jan. 10, 2017).

Woodward, B. (2209) "McChrystal: More Forces or 'Mission Failure'," *The Washington Post* Sept. 21 [Online]. Available at http://www.washingtonpost.com/wp-dyn/content/article/2 009/09/20/AR2009092002920.html (Accessed Jan. 12, 2017).

Wyatt, K. (2015) "Colorado rejects PTSD as ailment eligible for medical pot," *The Associated Press* July 15. [Online]. Available at http://bigstory.ap.org/article/8b547c58229c439bac2395852044 a64c/colorado-eyes-ptsd-ailment-eligible-medical-pot (Accessed Nov. 29, 2016).

Young, R. (1997) *The Ute Indians of Colorado in the 20th Century,* Norman, University of Oklahoma Press.

Chronos Books
HISTORY

Chronos Books is an historical non-fiction imprint. Chronos
publishes real history for real people; bringing to life
people, places and events in an imaginative, easy-to-digest and
accessible way - histories that pass on their stories to a generation
of new readers.
If you have enjoyed this book, why not tell other readers by post-
ing a review on your preferred book site.

Recent bestsellers from
Chronos Books are:

Lady Katherine Knollys
The Unacknowledged Daughter of King Henry VIII

Sarah-Beth Watkins
A comprehensive account of Katherine Knollys' questionable paternity, her previously unexplored life in the Tudor court and her intriguing relationship with Elizabeth I.
Paperback: 978-1-78279-585-8 ebook: 978-1-78279-584-1

Cromwell was Framed
Ireland 1649

Tom Reilly
Revealed: The definitive research that proves the Irish nation owes Oliver Cromwell a huge posthumous apology for wrongly convicting him of civilian atrocities in 1649.
Paperback: 978-1-78279-516-2 ebook: 978-1-78279-515-5

Why The CIA Killed JFK and Malcolm X
The Secret Drug Trade in Laos

John Koerner
A new groundbreaking work presenting evidence that the CIA silenced JFK to protect its secret drug trade in Laos.
Paperback: 978-1-78279-701-2 ebook: 978-1-78279-700-5

The Disappearing Ninth Legion
A Popular History

Mark Olly

The Disappearing Ninth Legion examines hard evidence for the foundation, development, mysterious disappearance, or possible continuation of Rome's lost Legion.
Paperback: 978-1-84694-559-5 ebook: 978-1-84694-931-9

Beaten But Not Defeated
Siegfried Moos - A German anti-Nazi who settled in Britain

Merilyn Moos

Siegi Moos, an anti-Nazi and active member of the German Communist Party, escaped Germany in 1933 and, exiled in Britain, sought another route to the transformation of capitalism.
Paperback: 978-1-78279-677-0 ebook: 978-1-78279-676-3

A Schoolboy's Wartime Letters
An evacuee's life in WWII — A Personal Memoir

Geoffrey Iley

A boy writes home during WWII, revealing his own fascinating story, full of zest for life, information and humour.
Paperback: 978-1-78279-504-9 ebook: 978-1-78279-503-2

The Life & Times of the Real Robyn Hoode
Mark Olly

A journey of discovery. The chronicles of the genuine historical character, Robyn Hoode, and how he became one of England's greatest legends.
Paperback: 978-1-78535-059-7 ebook: 978-1-78535-060-3

Readers of ebooks can buy or view any of these bestsellers by clicking on the live link in the title. Most titles are published in paperback and as an ebook. Paperbacks are available in traditional bookshops. Both print and ebook formats are available online.

Find more titles and sign up to our readers' newsletter at http://www.johnhuntpublishing.com/history-home

Follow us on Facebook at https://www.facebook.com/Chronos-Books

and Twitter at https://twitter.com/ChronosBooks